I0088170

History
of

𝖉𝖔𝖛𝖊𝖗
𝕭𝖆𝖕𝖙𝖎𝖘𝖙 𝕮𝖍𝖚𝖗𝖈𝖍

Dover, New Hampshire

1840-1945

By William Edgar Wentworth

History
of
Dover Baptist Church

1840-1945

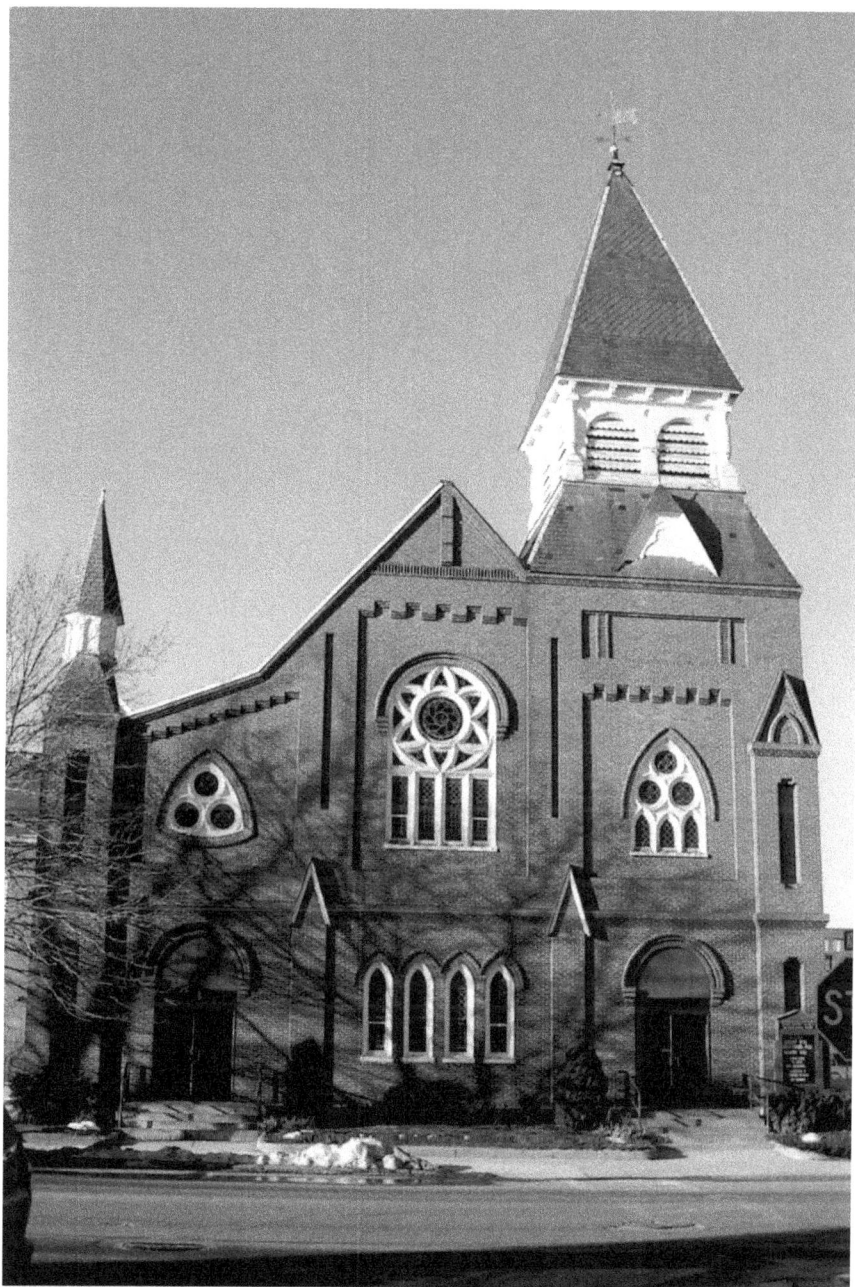

Dover Baptist Church in 2004

History
of

𝔇𝔬𝔳𝔢𝔯
𝔅𝔞𝔭𝔱𝔦𝔰𝔱 ℭ𝔥𝔲𝔯𝔠𝔥

The First Century
1840-1945

Including its connection with
The Morning Star newspaper
and the anti-slavery movement

By William Edgar Wentworth

2016

Copyright © 2016
William E. Wentworth
All rights reserved
978-1-940609-63-8

This book is available from

William E. Wentworth
PO Box 1605
Dover, NH 03821-1605

Printed by
FWB Publications

Preface

Writing the history of a church can be a tricky business. Some histories are "authorized," and those authors tend to write mostly about the good memories concerning the congregation and its leaders. That's fine.

But with an authorized history we often miss the complete story. After all, churches are made up of human beings with all their shortcomings and eccentricities. There are good times and bad. There are good people and bad.

So this is not an authorized history of Dover Baptist Church. I have attempted to put together the whole story, the good and the bad, so we can see the "humanness" of those who have been a part of it throughout the years. That is in no way to infer that present members and leaders have not been enthusiastic and quite helpful in providing assistance and suggestions in my attempt to show a complete history of Dover Baptist's first 100 years. I owe them a great debt.

For most of its first century, Dover Baptist was actively involved in the Freewill Baptist denomination.

The Freewill Baptist movement in the northern states began with a congregation organized by Benjamin Randall in 1780 in New Durham, N.H. Randall and his followers believed that Christ died for all, not just the elect, thus differing with Baptists of the Calvinist tradition. By 1792, evangelistic tours by Randall resulted in the establishment of additional Freewill Baptist churches. Congregations continued to join the movement.

The churches eventually were organized into Quarterly Meetings, each one made up of churches in generally local areas; and then Yearly Meetings were formed covering wider areas. The New Hampshire Yearly Meeting included all nine of the state's Quarterly Meetings and met in a more or less supervisory capacity. Some of the larger states had several Yearly Meetings. An example would be Maine, which had three for its 18 Quarterly Meetings.

With rapid growth in the denomination, it was deemed advisable in October 1827 to form the General Conference of Freewill Baptists, composed of delegates from the Yearly Meetings. It had moral authority to discipline Yearly and Quarterly meetings, associations and churches, but had no authority to alter or change decisions by individual churches or any Quarterly or Yearly meetings.

We will see the importance of some of the decisions made by the General Conference and the Quarterly Meetings as we record the first 100 years of Dover Baptist Church's history.

Much of that history is taken from the extensive early records of the church, as well as the records of the Central Avenue Baptist Church before it merged with what was then the Washington Street Freewill Baptist Church, to become Dover Baptist. Additional material is from records kept by the Quarterly Meeting and from various newspaper and other publications.

Necessarily intertwined in this history is the story of the *Morning Star* newspaper and the Freewill Baptist Printing Establishment in Dover, since they were closely associated with the church for many years. That connection brought sustained opposition from some sources, especially concerning the church's opposition to slavery in its early years.

This is not just a timeline of events in the life of the church, but an attempt to explain its history in the context of events occurring in Dover and in the nation during a very eventful century. Dover changed dramatically, and so did the United States of America.

Included in numerous appendices are newspaper and other published accounts of major events in the life of the church. They give more complete accounts of some events, and give a better understanding of much of what happened, especially in the formative years prior to the Civil War.

This church was a great influence in the life of Dover and the Freewill Baptist denomination during the 19th century and on into the 20th. Church leaders also were community leaders. Although little is mentioned in the records about church members who served both the town and city in various capacities, or even in the state Legislature, there were those who did so from time to time.

The church has had its ups and downs, to be sure, but the imposing brick building, and its auditorium with its beautiful gothic arches, stands as a monument to its past and a living reminder of what it can be as it nears the end of its second century in downtown Dover.

Introduction

A knowledge of the past can make the present more interesting. That is certainly true of what is currently represented by the brick building at the corner of Washington and Fayette streets in Dover, New Hampshire.

The history of Dover Baptist Church is of particular interest to me because of my family's connection with the church. My paternal grandparents were members of the Washington Street Freewill Baptist Church. My father recalled that his parents always sat in the pew numbered ninety-seven. My father was baptized and became a member of the church on May 1, 1904. In 1918, he was one of the 10 incorporators when the Baptist church on Central Avenue joined with the Baptist church on Washington Street to form Dover Baptist Church.

The history of Dover Baptist Church recorded in the present volume takes us to the pastorate of Rev. Buell Maxfield (1932-1945). I was six months old when Rev. Maxfield came to Dover, so he is the first pastor I remember.

For as far back as I can recall, going to Dover Baptist Church on Sundays was a regular family activity. When I became a member of the church in 1947, I had little knowledge of the church's history. Information about those earlier years is now available in the present volume written by William Edgar Wentworth. ('Edgar' was one of my friends at the church; he was also a high school classmate.)

Dover Baptist Church has always been an important part of my life. It was there, as a teenager, that I was challenged to serve the Lord as a missionary. It was there, in 1958, that I was ordained to the Christian ministry (Former pastor Buell Maxfield had a part in the service). It was also at Dover Baptist Church, in September 1988, that a memorial service was held for my first wife, Julie, who had passed away suddenly in Brazil. Since returning from Brazil in 1998, my wife Margaret and I have had the privilege of working with the senior citizen group at the church.

What Dover Baptist Church is now is due, in large measure, to what the church had been during its first hundred years of existence. Early viii

church leaders realized the importance of applying Biblical principles to current social issues.

The present volume reports that the sending of a couple to India in 1843 "was the beginning of a long history of missionary endeavor by the church which continues today both at home and abroad" (p. 46). We are indebted to Mr. Wentworth for bringing so much information together in one volume.

Rev. Robert H. Bennett
Gonic, New Hampshire

1.
Preparing the way

W hat one day would become Dover Baptist Church was organized on Feb. 4, 1840, by a small band of Freewill Baptists—eight men and five women. They met at what now is 392 Central Ave., Dover, N.H., within sound of the busy looms of the giant Cocheco Mfg. Co. mills.

All those who met that night in an upstairs room just south of the Cochecho River were dissident members of the only Freewill Baptist church in town. Their grievances noted that the church was "neglecting necessary discipline" and "laboring to uphold an impure ministry."

That may have been the official reason for organizing the new church, but Freewill Baptists of the 1840s, even though detesting slavery, were mired in controversy over whether the church should get involved in the anti-slavery movement. Those leading the dissidents already were involved in the movement, despite much criticism from fellow Freewill Baptists, and when they drew up their new church covenant they included a statement that they would endeavor to promote the abolition of slavery.

It wasn't that the slavery issue struck very close to home. Dover's 1840 census showed that out of a population of 6,458 there were only four blacks, two men and two women. But it was the very idea of slavery that fueled the campaign to abolish it.

At least four of the future pastors of the church were involved in the Freewill Baptist Anti-Slavery Society. So were some of its prominent members and founders. So the question of emancipation seems to have been at least a secondary, if not primary, reason for dissension among Dover's Freewill Baptists.

The Freewill Baptist Printing Establishment in Dover, which printed a denominational newspaper as well as books and hymnals, never had an official connection with Dover Baptist Church, but the histories of both were closely aligned for many years, with church leaders and pastors involved with the newspaper. The church and newspaper even occupied the same building for nearly 25 years.

But the real story of Dover Baptist Church would not be complete without a journey back in time to the organization of the First Freewill Baptist Church in Dover in 1826, and even further back to the birth on June 22, 1806, of a son, William, to Theophilis and Sarah (Waters) Burr. They were parents of 10 children in a farming family of faithful Unitarians in the part of Hingham, Mass., known as the lower plains or West Hingham.

At the age of 33, William Burr—by then a newspaper editor, conservative in character and faith, and strongly anti-slavery—would be the moving force behind the Dover dissidents who at first simply declared in 1840 that "we do recognize ourselves" as the only legitimate First Freewill Baptist Church in Dover, despite the fact that they numbered only 13 of the old church's more than 220 members.

The move didn't work, of course, and on May 15 it was voted that the new church be called the Central Street Freewill Baptist Church, Dover, N.H.[1]

BEING SEVENTH of 10 children in the Burr family, William learned early the meaning of hard work and self-reliance. Farming tends to do that. He was a descendant of the Rev. Jonathan Burr of Dorchester, Mass., a Puritan.

The *Free Baptist Cyclopædia* says William was deeply impressed by the death of a brother when about 11 years old, and decided to give himself to the Lord, helped in that decision by a relative, a Freewill Baptist minister who was visiting with the family.[2]

Realizing in his early teens that because of family circumstances he would be unable to attend college, where he would have liked to study for the ministry, Burr determined that God would be able to use him as a printer, according to his biographer, Rev. J. M. Brewster.[3]

Brewster says Burr's parents taught their children "the great principles of Christian morality; but they claimed to have little sympathy with 'evangelical religion.' "

Young William attended a catechism school taught by his pastor, the Rev. Joseph Richardson, in what was then the First Parish (Unitarian) Church. Rev. Richardson was himself a controversial figure, some

---

[1] Dover Baptist Church Record Book (DBC), 1:40.
[2] *Free Baptist Cyclopædia* (FBC), 88.
[3] *Life of William Burr* (Burr), 19.

members departing when he arrived in town in 1806 because of differences over liberal or more conservative philosophies.[4] When only 15 years old, Burr went to Boston to search for an apprentice position in a printing shop. The trip proved futile. A few months later, he returned to Boston to make the rounds of printing establishments, still to no avail. Finally, persistence, which acquaintances saw as one of his great strengths throughout life, paid off when he was hired at the Boston printing office of a Mr. George Clark.[5]

After two years with Clark, during which Burr received only room and board and a pair of shoes, plus what little money he could make working extra hours, he quit his job. But by then proficient in the printing business, he was hired by one of the largest printing offices in Boston and remained there until July 1825, when again he quit his job because of the way his employer treated him.

He was unable to get another job in Boston, having been black-listed by his most recent boss. So Burr searched for work in Providence, R.I., finally obtaining a job at the *Patriot*. He worked there until invited back to Boston to work at a new newspaper, the *Traveller*, where he remained until early 1826, when an event occurred that would change the direction of his life forever.

Elders Henry Hobbs and Samuel Burbank arrived at the *Traveller* as part of a trip to Boston for Hobbs, Woodman & Co. of Limerick, Maine. The firm had been created for the purpose of publishing a religious newspaper. The men were searching for equipment for the project, but they also sought someone to take charge of the printing establishment. When the man they selected declined, William Burr was recommended, and the next month he received a letter as follows:

> Newfield, March 27th 1826.
> Mr. BURR,
> Sir you being recommended as capable of managing a Printing Press for us, and through the medium of Mr. Parmenter engaging to serve us for the sum we offered Mr. ---------. confiding in Mr. P. you being a stranger to us, we wish you to come on, and enter into the business as soon as may be. You will not now be enabled to arrive by the time we set in our letter to Mr. P. but you will arrive perhaps by the 10th, of April, perhaps before . . .
> Please to call on Mr. Elias Libby, trader at the village in Limerick, and put up with him until further directions.

---

[4] *Not all is changed: A life history of Hingham*, 68.
[5] Burr, 25.

We shall expect you without fail and shall look for a workman, as foreman, no further. A disappointment will greatly injure us . . .
Yours very respectfully
SAMUEL BURBANK[6]

Since Burr still feared possible persecution by his old employer, he decided to go to Limerick for a year until he became of age, when he could return to Boston without fearing interference from anyone.

So William Burr, who in his early days had faithfully attended Unitarian services with his family in Hingham, but who since going to Boston had almost completely neglected religious services, accepted a job at a fledgling religious newspaper which he knew nothing about, located in the small Maine town of Limerick. His life never would be the same.

Describing his trip to Maine, one writer says: "April 6, 1826, he took passage for Portland on board a packet. Safe in Portland, he found a seat in a mail wagon, and later he rode in a sleigh" to get to Limerick.[7]

What Burr was getting into was the result of a decision at the Freewill Baptist Quarterly Meeting in Parsonsfield, Maine, in 1825. Elders Burbank and Elias Libby convinced those attending the meeting that it would be good to publish a weekly religious paper, describing it thus: "The first two pages of the paper will be devoted to religious intelligence and Christian correspondence. The other two pages to news in general, and whatever may be attractive to the candid reader."[8] The Quarterly Meeting, which represented the Freewill Baptist churches in that area of York County, promised non-financial support, but nothing more.

Hobbs, Woodman & Co. would publish the journal. When Burr was hired to take charge of the printing, he never dreamed that his life would be dominated for the next 40 years by the Freewill Baptist denomination and the publication of its newspaper.

When he arrived in Limerick, Burr found the office of the as-yet-unpublished newspaper in complete chaos. But he set to work making it a printing establishment, and on May 11, 1826, the first number of *The Morning Star* was issued. Because of support by the Quarterly Meeting, there were initially 500 subscribers, but subscriptions grew rapidly and by the end of its first year the enterprise was meeting all its costs of publication.[9]

---

[6] Burr, 35
[7] FBC, 89.
[8] Burr, 46
[9] *Ibid.*, 53.

So Burr, raised and trained as a Unitarian, whom his biographer says now was attending the Congregational church in Limerick, was working daily with the Freewill Baptists and even sometimes attended their meetings.

Burr's conversion came during a religious awakening in Limerick in 1828. He had heard preaching by Elder John Buzzell. But when he heard revivalist Elder Clement Phinney preach, one of Burr's closest friends, Samuel Julian, accepted Jesus as his Savior and shortly thereafter Burr "was one of the early converts in the revival."[10] In October, he was baptized by Elder Abiezer Bridges and joined the Freewill Baptist congregation there in Limerick.

Although he had intended to return to Boston after a year or so in Limerick, and in fact already had made plans to leave the place, Burr now had reason to stay at his job. He had a new-found faith and a clearer sense of mission in his work. But another event in his life also worked to keep him in Limerick. In June of that same year, he was married to Miss Frances McDonald, young daughter of John McDonald of Limerick.

When Burr was just 23 years old, he was offered higher positions at the *Star*, but hesitated. Says his biographer:

> In the spring of 1829, at the commencement of the fourth volume of the *Star*, the position of both Office Editor and of Publishing Agent were tendered him; but while he accepted the latter, he declined the former. As a reason for this, he urged his youth and want of acquaintance with the denomination; and in this he exhibited his characteristic modesty. He performed, however, the duties of both positions . . . In fact, Mr. Burr had, during the previous three years, performed much of the labor which usually devolved upon an Editor, such as proof-reading, making selections, and the like.[11]

It was not long before Burr bought shares in the newspaper, and by 1832 the paper was sold to a new firm called Hobbs, Burr & Co. But the new partnership lasted only until October of that year, when the paper was "sold" to the denomination itself.

In reality, the denomination agreed to take over the venture but assumed no liability, opting to take over the operation only if the Book Agent and Publishing Committee assumed entire responsibility for the $3,700 cost of the property and its management. They agreed.[12] The agent

---

[10] Burr, 58.
[11] *Ibid.*, 62.
[12] *The Centennial Record of Freewill Baptists 1780-1880* (CRFB*)*, 206.

of the Book Concern that had been formed the previous year, at Burr's urging, was Elder David Marks of Portsmouth, N.H., and the Publishing Committee consisted of William Burr, Henry Hobbs, Samuel Beede, Hosea Quinby, Silas Curtis and Daniel P. Cilley.

By August 1832, Elder Marks was writing to Samuel Beede: "We have almost endless perplexities in publishing books in the country . . . Bro. Burr and myself are about discouraged. We think the removal of the office the only remedy; the sooner the better . . ."

By 1833, in a report to the General Conference, it was stated:

> Several disadvantages have been experienced by our Book Establish-ment on account of its unfavorable location. Being situated in an interior country town, those facilities for publishing, printing and distributing books and papers have not been possessed, that a place of more business and of more central situation would have afforded. Some particular inconveniences that have been suffered, we would state for the consideration of the Conference.

After studying the possibilities of moving the operation to Portland, Dover, Boston, Providence and other places, the Conference agreed "that the Printing Establishment be removed to Dover, N.H., as soon as convenient." Dover's central location was critical to the decision.

So William Burr and the whole operation of *The Morning Star* and Book Concern moved to Dover, setting up shop above a store at the corner of Main and Chapel streets, and Burr and his wife, Frances, joined the First Freewill Baptist Church of Dover.

FIRST MENTION of the old Dover church seems to be in Elder Enoch Place's Journal of Sept. 29, 1825, when he wrote, "I went to Dover and held a M. this evening at Br. Davises house and found more hard hearts than penitent ones."[13]   Elder Place was a Freewill Baptist pastor from Strafford, N.H., and often traveled by carriage or horseback to area towns to hold services. He was instrumental in the organization of several churches in the area, at the same time leading his own flock and eking out a living on the family farm.

The next day, Place wrote, "I preached three sermons at the Landing schoolhouse in Dover to full assemblies. I was treated with respect, but hope they will respect the truth and all Christ's commandments. Oh my heavenly father, do grant that this my first labours in this village may be blessed."

---

[13] Enoch Place's Journal (Place), No. 17.

By Nov. 27, he was more upbeat when he wrote in his journal, "I preached three times at Dover to an attentive audience in the evening, several hundred came together, many stood at the door and round the house. God helped me to preach the truth with solemnity, opposition gave way and the power of God was present to heal."

By May of 1826, Elder Place was writing, "I was enabled to preach three sermons in Dover at the Landing, there is some revival in this place."[14]

The church was fully organized by the end of that year. In a short listing in 1854 of historical items concerning the church, the clerk wrote in the records that Elder Place actually was the organizer and that the church at its inception had 25 members.

Members met for several years at various locations around town, including the Landing (Dover's waterfront area), at a school, at Garrison Hill and at Upper Factory on the river two miles west of town. Elder Place often was the preacher, and by the time the Burrs arrived the church probably had about 200 members. Records of the church are missing before 1843. The Burrs joined members worshiping in a new building that had been dedicated May 20, 1832,[15] at what is now the corner of Chestnut and Lincoln streets, although Lincoln Street was not there at the time. The church parsonage stood where Lincoln Street now intersects Chestnut. Both buildings still stand, the old parsonage having been moved to the rear of the church when Lincoln Street was laid out.

What the Burrs apparently found in Dover was a church struggling to maintain its unity. Unlike the folks who made up the church in Limerick, the Dover church struggled with factions that on one side were content with elders—godly men but often with little training—preaching and leading the flock; those more educated were not content with what they considered to be untrained clergy.

The church admitted as much in 1840 when it published a statement following the loss of the 13 dissidents in which it lamented an "aristocratic spirit which has ever more or less infested the church, and which we as an order, did in our first organization, set steadfastly our faces against, where an ambitious few perhaps possessed of more talents or learning wish to rule, direct, or coerce the many."[16]

One other controversy of the time was whether the General

---

[14] Place, No. 18.
[15] *Ibid.*, No. 27.
[16] *Dover Gazette and Strafford Advertiser (Gazette)*, March 17, 1840.

Conference should encourage the use of notes in preaching. But there is no mention of that controversy at the Dover church.

There is a curious mention of William Burr in the surviving records of the First Freewill Baptist clerk. After listing all the pastors of the church up until 1854, the clerk wrote the following: "Names of ministers besides the above who are and have been members of this church. H. H. Brock, Andrew Rollins, Wm. Burr, Daniel Littlefield." Burr was licensed to preach only in 1839 and 1840 during the time of the dissention in the old church which led to formation of the Central Street church. He gave up any preaching because of the press of business at the Printing Establishment. That one entry is the only mention of Burr in the surviving records of the old church, which now are at the New Hampshire Historical Society in Concord.

Burr and the newspaper were coming under increasing criticism not only by members of his own church but by others in the denomination who disliked what they considered the political direction in which some of the Freewill Baptists were headed in their opposition to slavery. Many blamed Burr and *The Morning Star* for stirring up the controversy.

2.

𝕿orn asunder

reewill Baptist church leaders, along with an increasing number of state and national political leaders of the late 1830s, were attempting to come to grips with what they considered a great national evil—slavery. Freewill Baptists had been early to join the fight against continued enslavement of their fellow human beings.

William Burr, who by 1835 had been made both editor and publisher of *The Morning Star* as well as agent for the trustees of what ultimately would become known as the Freewill Baptist Printing Establishment, began more and more in the columns of the newspaper to rail against the evils of slavery. It was a reversal of an earlier policy by editor Samuel Beede of not getting involved. But Beede had died suddenly in Dover early on March 28, 1834, after having been editor of the *Star* less than a year. Burr replaced him and would remain in control of the *Star*'s operation for the next 32 years.

According to Burr's biographer, "Among the last articles which Mr. Beede wrote was one entitled 'Slavery and Abolition,' in which he took the ground that, though slavery was an evil, it was one for which the North was equally responsible with the South, denounced the course of emancipationists and counseled the exercise of moderation and charity."[17]

It was the last time such "counsel" would appear in *The Morning Star.*

No one in the denomination openly disputed the fact that slavery was an evil. But many felt the subject was a political rather than a church issue and therefore should not be addressed by the clergy or church organs such as *The Morning Star.* Taking a stand on slavery was tantamount to taking a political party position.

The anti-slavery stance was a bold decision by Burr, as both a trustee of the Printing Establishment and editor of the paper, since one of the jobs

---

[17] Burr, 88.

of the trustees was to pay off a $6,000 debt that the operation had accrued.[18] The decision to pursue the abolitionist course nearly brought financial ruin to *The Star*. Subscriptions plummeted as those against getting involved in the movement dropped the paper. For at least two years, the shrinkage continued.

In relating the situation in which *The Star* found itself, it was written in 1881:

> To present more definitely the triumph of principle over policy, please consider a few specific facts. In 1836 the Printing Establishment had been twice refused an act of incorporation, because the *Star* was an abolition paper; $15,000 were due for our publications, and many persons refused payment unless a different policy was adopted; every mail brought letters, some of them vile and abusive, ordering the discontinuance of the *Star*, because of its abolitionism, and for two years the list of subscribers was constantly decreasing. The Trustees were then personally responsible for debts amounting to $6,000, and it was a time of very great pecuniary embarrassment. Some of our people were fearful of an utter failure of the Printing Establishment, and more were anxious to modify the utterances of the *Star*, so as to avert from the denomination the public odium heaped upon abolitionists, and to reconcile the disaffected members.[19]

The board of trustees that had been appointed in 1835 met to decide whether the abolitionist sentiment should be continued in the columns of *The Star*. The decision was a resounding yes.

Members of the board then included William Burr, Silas Curtis, Daniel P. Cilley, Jacob Davis, Enoch Place, Joseph M. Harper, Samuel Burbank, Truman Carey, Elias Hutchins, Seth C. Parker and Charles Morse. Elias Hutchins would in a few years become one of the early pastors of Dover Baptist Church.

When the national General Conference of Freewill Baptists was held in Greenville, R.I., in 1837, not a few of those present fought for a watering-down of the newspaper's stance in an attempt to keep the publication afloat. The delegates refused.

But some Freewill ministers went from church to church across Maine and New Hampshire demanding that the anti-slavery policy be changed. Burr's biographer writes that ". . . there continued both in and out of the denomination a deep-seated opposition to the anti-slavery

---

[18] *Star*, Jan. 20, 1836.
[19] CRFB, 196.

positions of the *Star*, and there were those, ministers and laymen, who were untiring in their efforts to effect a change."[20]

Rev. I. D. Stewart, who would one day be pastor of Dover Baptist Church (by then called Washington Street Freewill Baptist), and who in 1851 was secretary of the Freewill Baptist Anti-Slavery Society, wrote a history of the anti-slavery movement among Freewill Baptists. In it, he declared: "As our patriotic fathers, in their struggle for liberty, stood undismayed through the darkest gloom of our country's adversity, so the body of the denomination at this time proved themselves worthy of their noble ancestry, in opposing a system of oppression, with which British aggression bore no comparison."

What he was talking about was a resolution adopted at that General Conference which supported *The Star* in its position on slavery and then another resolution which in part declared:

> *Resolved,* That American Slavery is a sin of such exceeding enormity and magnitude, that every minister of the gospel should loudly testify against it, and every Christian should decidedly rebuke it.—That it is an outrage upon the rights and happiness of fellow countrymen, so cruel, so flagrant, and prevailing to so great an extent, that it becomes the duty of every friend of liberty, patriotism, and humanity, to bear decided testimony against it.[21]

The opposition continued, but did not come only from church members. Even the New Hampshire Legislature opposed the newspaper's position. As already mentioned, in 1836 it refused to give the Printing Establishment incorporation papers, according to the *New Hampshire Patriot* of Concord, after it was pointed out by the chairman of the House Committee on Incorporations that *The Star* ". . . was an advocate of abolition, and he felt no disposition that the Legislature should lend its aid to publications, which the Legislatures of our sister States were entreating us to *suppress.*" The vote was 188 to 34 against incorporation. It wasn't until the late 1840s, when the Legislature's complexion had changed dramatically on the question of slavery, that the act of incorporation was granted.

The *Dover Gazette and Strafford Advertiser* got into the fray when it advised the *Star* in 1838 to stick to the business for which it was designed instead of being "intermingled with Politics, Abolition, and the Lord

---

[20] Burr, 124.
[21] *Fifth Annual Report, Freewill Baptist Antislavery Soc.*, 10. (See Appendix B)

knows what, until some of the most respectable members, Elders and others of their own persuasion, have become disgusted . . ."[22]

It then appended a story which it said ran in the *N. H. Patriot* in Concord because the *Star* refused to print it, in which 11 Freewill Baptists, including apparently one deacon from Burr's own church, urged the *Star* to stop its anti-slavery campaign, which they called meddling in the "political contentions of the day . . ."

The Printing Establishment and the newspaper struggled for several years, but stuck with the decision and eventually prospered as more people began to see what a great evil slavery was in a nation that had declared that all men were created equal.

WHETHER INVOLVEMENT in the anti-slavery movement was a major issue in the dissension which plagued the First Freewill Baptist Church in Dover is not certain. Records for those years have not survived. It is certain that the church as a body opposed slavery, at least later.[23]

In a listing of significant events in the life of the church, the clerk of the First Freewill Baptists wrote in the records in 1854:

> In 1838 & 39 it was [a] time of severe trials which resulted in a secession of several members & the formation of the Central Street Ch., but to comfort bleeding Zion in her affliction the Lord sent Eld. A. Ayer in the latter part of 1839 & to the praise of God we record that his labours were blest in the conversion of scores of souls that were added to the church.[24]

The slavery issue was not listed as a reason for the minority leaving the fellowship of the Chestnut Street church; the actual reason never is spelled out in the records of Dover Baptist Church.

But it is certain that the leaders of the new church all were deeply involved in the emancipation movement and several also were involved in the operation of the *Morning Star* and its strong anti-slavery stand.

In fact, when a newspaper article was written when the church approached its 51st anniversary in 1891, it was stated: "During the anti-slavery conflict the church was almost the home of anti-slavery men and women of the city."[25]

---

[22] *Gazette*, May 15, 1838.
[23] FFBC, Vol. 2.
[24] *Ibid.*
[25] Foster's Daily Democrat (*Foster's*), Jan. 24, 1891.

In his journal, Elder Enoch Place mentioned a resolution submitted but not adopted at the Freewill Baptist yearly meeting in June 1837 in which delegates were urged to approve the "means, measures and objects" of the American Anti-Slavery Society. Elder Place thought the resolution went too far and that "it would not in general be approved of by the churches whose delegates we were and that the sentiments of our constituents would not be represented by us," and that "it was locking arms and amalgamating with the American Anti-Slavery Society which we had no right to do without the approbation of our churches in this thing."[26]

One of the delegates who urged adoption of the resolution, according to Place, was Enoch Mack, who until a month earlier was pastor of the old Dover church[27] and still was a member there. He was one of the 13 dissidents who left in 1840 to form the new church.

A report of the October 1839 Rockingham Quarterly Meeting shows that the same resolution was brought up again and passed by a small majority.[28]

WHATEVER PART the anti-slavery movement actually played in the parting of the brethren at the First Freewill Baptist Church in Dover probably never will be known for sure. But what the old church called an excuse for the schism came in 1838 and 1839, the result of what the church deemed "improprieties" by its pastor, Elder Alpheus Dexter Smith.

We might never have known the details of what precipitated the split if there had not come a time in 1840, after the dissidents had formed their own fellowship, when the First Freewill Baptist Church felt compelled to make its case public. From that we get a picture of events (from the perspective of the old church) which led to the formation of what eventually became Dover Baptist Church. There is no record of the dissidents disputing the old church's version of events.

Elder Smith, according to the long explanation sent to the *Dover Gazette and Strafford Advertiser* and published March 17, 1840, had made imprudent remarks to some children.

A council formed to look into the matter had reported that Smith had been "in a certain instance, guilty of rudely or improperly talking to sundry poor children; and in unguardedly using some loose and lascivious expressions; equivocating in some degree when questioned by sundry

---

[26] Place, No. 40, June 10, 1837.
[27] FFBC, Vol. 2.
[28] *Star*, Nov. 29, 1839.

individuals in regard to his conduct; and some other equivocal 'appearances of evil' which were improper in a minister of Christ . . ." But the council also decided they were "imprudences resulting more from constitutional frailties and inadvertencies of speech and manners than from any evil propensities of the heart." The phrase "constitutional frailties" probably alluded to the fact that Elder Smith had been in poor health at the time. In 1838, one report said, ". . . while engaged in extra meetings at New Market, he was taken with severe bleedings of the lungs."[29]

Elder Smith properly asked forgiveness of the children, the church and the town, as suggested by the council. The council met and determined the confession was adequate, but then voted "that we are decidedly of the opinion that under existing circumstances Elder Smith should for the present entirely desist from public labors as a preacher of the Gospel."

According to the church's statement, the minority that eventually left the church seemed to be satisfied with the outcome of the proceeding. That changed when Smith was allowed to resume his ministry three months later. The minority didn't think that was sufficient time for him to be banished from the pulpit and the dissension ensued.

Elder Place, who was instrumental in formation of the original Dover church, seems to have had no animosity against Smith, who was at Place's church in Strafford to preach in September 1839. In his journal, he mentioned Smith's visit and said it "has done good, although so much has been said against him recently at Dover . . ."[30] Five days later, the Strafford church raised money to help Smith pay for his trip to the Vermont church he was to serve[31] after leaving the Dover church.

But Place also had nothing against the new church, offering after talking with William Burr to preach to the Central Street congregation. Later that evening he did preach to about 500 people, he said.[32] The attendance probably is somewhat exaggerated, a habit Place never seemed able to overcome.

The old Dover church charged that William Burr and his followers, fearing they could not get a hearing before the majority of church members, went to the Rockingham Quarterly Meeting in January 1840,

---

[29] FBC, 603.

[30] Place, No. 49, Sept. 3, 1839.

[31] *Ibid.*, Sept. 8, 1839.

[32] *Ibid.*, No. 51, March 17, 1840.

where a council was formed and, without consulting the majority of the church members, it was, "agreed that the majority should confess to the minority of the church, that they have taken an unadvisable and improper course in dismissing A. D. Smith from the church, and in countenancing him in preaching and laboring with them after he had been suspended from the ministry, and for having fellowship with him after such incontestable evidences of his wickedness." The church had given him a letter of dismissal—or recommendation—to the Vermont church mentioned earlier.

The Morning Star, in reporting the Quarterly Meeting's action in its edition of Feb. 19, 1840, related the situation as follows:

> The subject of the difficulties that have existed for a long time in the church at Dover (on which several councils from the Q. M. had previously set, with whose decisions the majority of the church had refused to comply) came up by postponement from the preceding session. After a protracted sitting and a patient hearing of the whole case, Conference came to a decision similar to the decisions of the councils which had previously set upon it—and decided further, that if either division of the church refused to comply with it, such division should be disfellowshiped by the Q. M.
>
> The Conference then met the church and presented their decision. The minority agreed to comply with it; but after much time had been spent, the majority refused to comply, and consequently was disfellowshiped.

The above action by the Quarterly Meeting seems to be the reason that when the dissidents met on Feb. 4, 1840, they declared they considered themselves the only legitimate First Freewill Baptist Church in Dover.[33] Their declaration was meaningless, though, since the Quarterly Meeting could disfellowship a church but it had no power over the local church that would have allowed it to designate that minority of 13 members as the only legitimate church of that name.

In response to the disfellowshipping action and the claim by the dissidents that they were the only legitimate First Freewill Baptist Church in Dover, the old church in its public airing of the matter, which also claimed 16 persons were involved, scoffed at the action as follows:

> . . . We do not know, nor do the best judges of ecclesiastical powers and duties, of any right or power by which a Q. M. can sever a church,

---

[33] DBC, 1:1.

or cut off a part without cutting off the whole; or of any power by which they can transfer the name, rights, act of incorporation and immunities both civil and ecclesiastical from a church to a minority of the same church or to any other persons whomsoever; the Church of Rome in her proudest days hardly would have assumed such power.

That 16 individuals under the protection of sundry Q. M. resolves, should, from a church of 220 members, take their name, assume all the powers of said church, and claim to be the 'regular Freewill Baptist Church in Dover, and the *only* Freewill Baptist church in fellowship and standing in the place,' is a most curious anomaly among the transactions of the world, an attempt truly ridiculous and absurd, an act of audacious ambition; over sight and consummate folly, especially reserved to be recorded in the annals of church history for 1840.[34]

RATHER THAN continue to push their claim, the dissidents, after several months of standing firm on their assertion that they were entitled to use the old meeting house, voted May 15, 1840, that the group be designated the Central Street Freewill Baptist Church, Dover, N.H. Three days earlier it had voted to seek admission to the Rockingham Quarterly Meeting.[35]

The action seems to have ended the acrimonious dispute between the factions, and the two congregations went their separate ways. But the debate continued at the Quarterly Meeting.

Enoch Place noted in his journal on May 18, 1840, the following occurrence at the Quarterly Meeting held in Candia:

> The reports from several of the churches was refreshing. But when the Dover trouble came up all seemed to feel the spirit of debate. Sharp pointed and able speeches were made on both sides. The old church has received an addition of nearly 100 members since they were rejected on the last of the month of January 1839. A new church of 38 members requested to be received. This was opposed by Elders Dyer, Kimball, and others on account of some trials with several of the members &c. The debate was continued until a late hour in the night.

Then in his entry for May 20, Elder Place, with some dismay at the Quarterly Meeting's action, noted:

> The conference sat at seven this morning and debated much of the time until ten. They then obtained a vote to receive the Central Street

---

[34] See Appendix A.
[35] DBC, 1:40.

Church of 28 members and also passed a resolution that the First F. B. Church in Dover (of 300 members) are to all intents rejected from their Q. M. All this may be right, but I very much doubt it . . . I think that several preachers and churches will leave the Rockingham Q. M. and unite with other Q. M. or form a new Q. M. so that the Dover trouble first started with a labor with Elder A. D. Smith will be, as it already has been attended, with serious consequences. Oh, I do hope that this will be a warning to preachers to live holy and not only shun evil but every appearance of it . . .

Place's journal entries concerning the number of members in the new Central Street church, 38 and 28, both are in error. According to official church records, when the church was accepted by the Quarterly Meeting there were 11 men and 16 women members, a total of 27.[36]

Again in June, at the Yearly Meeting which included Freewill Baptists from all Quarterly Meetings in the state, the subject of the manner in which the old Dover church was rejected by the Rockingham Quarterly Meeting was brought up by Elders Dyer and Kimball, but according to Place's journal, ". . . the Yearly Meeting sustained the Q. M. by a very small vote, three or four only voting and none to the contrary," perhaps an indication that the other churches didn't want further involvement in the Dover dispute.

Place's fear that the controversy would result in some churches leaving the Rockingham Quarterly Meeting was confirmed when five churches left there and the New Durham Quarterly Meeting and formed the Deerfield & Nottingham Quarterly Meeting on May 23, 1841. They included churches from Deerfield, Nottingham, Raymond, Barrington and Poplin (now Fremont). Leaders in that movement apparently were the same Elders John Kimball and Samuel B. Dyer who had protested the admission of the new Dover church into the Rockingham Q. M.

When they asked to be dismissed from the Rockingham Quarterly Meeting to form their own, the move was refused. The churches then quit and the meeting voted that "the churches had gone out in disorder."[37] In New Hampton on June 10, 1842, the Deerfield and Nottingham Q. M. asked admission to the denomination's state Yearly Meeting. A committee was formed to look into the matter,[38] but the only other indication of its existence was when it was reported the group made no

---

[36] DBC, 1:12, 18.

[37] *Star*, Feb. 23, 1842.

[38] *Ibid.*, June 29, 1842.

report to the Yearly Meeting in 1847 after several years of decreasing membership.[39] The churches involved were later listed in either the Rockingham or New Durham quarterly meetings and they never seem to have been listed in the records as a separate quarterly meeting.

The Central Street Freewill Baptists remained in the Rockingham Quarterly Meeting until it was disbanded. The First Freewill Baptists later rejoined the New Durham Quarterly Meeting, of which it had been a member until switching to the Rockingham Q. M. in 1834 or 1835, and it stayed there until the church disbanded just after the turn of the century.

Although the two Dover churches never had a close relationship, the animosity felt at the time of the split must have faded in the ensuing years. By 1868, an entry in the records of the old church, by then called the Charles Street church after moving to a new building, reads as follows: "Voted to extend an invitation to Washington St. Church to hold their Sabbath evening meetings with us."[40] The invitation came at a time when the Washington Street church was preparing to build the present church at Washington and Fayette streets. Dover Baptist Church records indicate the Washington Street church did indeed meet with the old church on Sunday evenings, an entry in August 1868 reading, ". . . for more than two months we worshiped with the First Congregational Church on the Sabbath, holding our prayer meetings Sabbath eve with the Charles St. F. B. church . . ." Later that same year the old church asked the pastor of the Washington Street church to participate in the installation of its new pastor, John Malvern.[41] The examination of Bro. Malvern actually took place at the *Star* office before the installation was carried out.[42]

It should be noted that the question of emancipation was no longer a divisive issue since the Civil War was over and the slaves had been freed. Both Freewill Baptist churches in Dover now were helping mission projects formed to educate and help former slaves.

By 1877, the two churches had held a joint baptismal service. Although both churches note the baptismal service in their records, only the old church noted that it was a joint service.

Members sometimes switched from one Freewill Baptist church to the other for various reasons, sometimes even switching back. Contacts between the two churches were increasing by the end of the 19th century

---

[39] FBC, 462.
[40] FFBC, 2:36.
[41] *Ibid.,* 2:39.
[42] *Ibid.,* 2:40.

when the old church, then on the site of what is now Dover's Central Fire Station on Broadway, was nearing the end of its days.

THOSE WHO had formed the new Central Street Freewill Baptist congregation included many who continued to be in the thick of the fight for emancipation. William Burr certainly never wavered in his opposition to slavery. Elias Hutchins, one of the church's early pastors, was deeply involved in the fight, as was Isaac D. Stewart, already mentioned, who was pastor after the national struggle had successfully brought freedom to the slaves. The church's second pastor, Rev. A. K. Moulton, also was in the fight and in 1848 wrote a ringing defense of the anti-slavery movement.

It would not be the last time the church involved itself in the social issues of the day. For that matter, it would not be the last time it felt the sting of opposition. But as the move toward emancipation gained momentum, this little Dover church that had been formed as that struggle intensified went through some intense struggles of its own, weathering a period of refinement and growth.

3.
𝔄 new beginning

T he little group of 13 Freewill Baptists climbed the long stairway on
that cold night in 1840 to meet on the second floor in what came to
be known as the Central Street Vestry. They came together
convinced they no longer could fellowship with the majority of members
then comprising the First Freewill Baptist Church in Dover.

It was the 4th of February.

The purpose of the meeting was not specifically to form a new
church. Though themselves a minority in the old church, they pointed out
that the majority had been kicked out of the Rockingham Quarterly
Meeting, and the minority led by William Burr had been accepted by the
Quarterly Meeting.

The first entry in the record book spelled out, though without
specifics, the reason for the action of the minority:

> Whereas a portion of the church which had denominated itself the
> First Freewill Baptist Church in Dover, having become aggrieved by the
> course pursued by another portion of said church, represented as the
> majority, in neglecting necessary discipline, and in countenancing and
> laboring to uphold an impure ministry—And, whereas the aggrieved
> portion represented as the minority of the said church, appealing to the
> Rockingham Quarterly Meeting for assistance, which was answered by
> the appointment of a council or committee, before which their cause has
> had a hearing and a trial, and which subject has received further
> attention from the Quarterly Meeting by appointment of other councils
> or committees, and by giving the cause a final hearing and trial before
> the Quarterly Meeting conference; And, whereas the Q. M. conference
> at its late session, Jan. 28 and 29, 1840, reported terms on which said
> church should be considered in fellowship of the Quarterly Meeting;
> And whereas the conditions proposed by the Quarterly Meeting were
> accepted and fulfilled by that portion of the church denominated the
> minority, and rejected by that portion denominated the majority, the said

majority becoming by such rejection disfellowshipped by the Quarterly Meeting, and the minority by accepting the proposed terms being in fellowship of the Quarterly Meeting; And whereas the said minority is the regular Freewill Baptist church in Dover, and the only Freewill Baptist church in fellowship and standing in the connection, in this place — therefore

Resolved, by the persons constituting the aforesaid minority as assembled in notified meeting this evening, 4th of Feb. 1840, that we do recognize ourselves as the First Freewill Baptist Church in Dover . . . [43]

There follows in the clerk's records a re-written church covenant which, true to the beliefs of those who met that night, included a declaration that the church members would promote the abolition of slavery.[44]

William Burr, a leader of the dissidents, chief cog in the anti-slavery movement among Freewill Baptists and editor of the anti-slavery *Morning Star*, was named moderator at this first and many subsequent meetings. The remainder of his life was spent involved in the life of the church, where he served in other offices at various times, including church clerk. Interestingly, Burr resided in 1840 in a house on Fayette Street next to the present church building, having moved there from 2 School Street, where he had lived earlier just a block from the offices of *The Star*. By 1846, Burr had bought land and built his own home on the western corner of Washington and Hamilton (now Belknap) streets, a block from the present church. He lived there for the rest of his life.

The dissidents, besides Burr, included Enoch Mack, Tobias Scruton, Edward B. Chamberlin, Jonathan C. Gilman, Asa H. Littlefield, Marquis D. L. Stevens, Alfred Scruton, Lucy Y. Foss, Eunice Colbath, Elana Fuller, Chloe Holt and Mary Willard.

Who, exactly, were the charter members, besides Burr, of what would become Dover Baptist Church? Little is known about some of them, but brief sketches from that time show the following:

● Elder Enoch Mack had been pastor at First Freewill Baptist from October 1835 until he resigned in May 1837 to serve as agent of the Foreign Mission Board.[45] He still was a member there when the troubles came. He was listed in *The Morning Star* as an assistant editor and was on the paper's editorial council until suddenly dropped from both positions in the issue of Nov. 24, 1841. For several years his voice had already been

---

[43] DBC, 1:1
[44] *Ibid.*, 1:6.
[45] FFBC, No. 2.

heard in the anti-slavery movement and in 1841 he was listed as president of the Strafford County Anti-Slavery Society.

Elder Mack himself ran into trouble two years after the new church was formed. Although no specifications are listed in the records, he was asked to retract statements he had made and refused, so was excluded from membership. Five years later, he was welcomed back into fellowship, though a year after that he moved to New York. The Dover village directories beginning in 1846 listed him as a physician. All indications are that his problem with the church was opposition to a growing tendency in the denomination to require some sort of formal religious education for pastors. He had opposed a proposal on the matter and is quoted in the *Star* of Jan. 12, 1842, as telling the denomination: "Pass this vote and you have passed the Rubicon, and ruin will follow." Too much education, he felt, led people away from Bible truths.

● Tobias Scruton in 1840 was a carder at Cocheco Mfg. Co. and lived on Waldron Street. He was never very active in church affairs and moved to Sanford, Maine, three years later.

● Edward B. Chamberlin was a pressman at *The Morning Star* and lived for many years at 7 Nelson St. He was an active and involved member for the next 61 years and was mentioned in the clerk's records as one of only three charter members present when the 53rd anniversary of the church was celebrated in 1893. He died Feb. 17, 1901.

● Jonathan C. Gilman, who never became real active in church affairs, was dropped from the rolls in 1858 after having not reported himself for a number of years. He is not listed as even being a resident of Dover in years following the founding of the church.

● Asa Hayes Littlefield, for many years an active and involved member of the church, was a shoemaker most of his life. He lived at several locations in the city but eventually settled in a home on Washington Street for many years. He died Sept. 12, 1903, the last of the charter members of Dover Baptist Church.

● Marquis D. L. Stevens was listed in the 1843 Dover Village Directory as a journeyman printer at the *Star*, but he did not remain long in the church. By 1847, the leaders were dealing with him concerning his relationship to the church and, finding his position less than favorable, on June 7, 1851, they excluded him from membership because he had been absent for an extended time.

● Alfred Scruton was seldom mentioned in the records of the church, but each time he was mentioned it was because of problems with him. Just a month after the church was organized, the church took up the "difficulty" with Brother Scruton—the subject never made public—and he made his confession the next Sunday and the matter was dropped. The membership roll never had another entry following the original entry at the formation of the church. When the church was organized, he was listed in the city directory as a carder at Cocheco Mfg. Co. and as a resident of Williams Street. The last entry for him in the records concerns the fact that he had not answered a letter written to find out his status in relation to the church.

• Lucy Y. Foss, who married a Thompson and eventually moved to Barnstead, died Sept. 29, 1886.

• Eunice Colbath's name is found in the records only as a charter member in 1840 and in the membership list showing that she transferred her letter to a Sanford, Maine, church in 1843.

• Elana Fuller, a charter member who was on the rolls for the shortest period of time, moved to Canada in December 1840 just 10 months after the church was organized.

• Chloe Holt, also a short-time member, was dismissed Dec. 28, 1842, to a church in Lowell, Mass.

• Mary Willard's involvement in church activities is unknown. Besides the fact that she was a charter member, the only other mention of her is when it was indicated on the membership list that she had been dismissed to a church in Sutton. No date was given and no mention of the action is found in the church clerk's records.

THE GROUP'S second meeting, on Feb. 13, resulted in Burr being chosen as the church's first deacon, a post which he held until his death in 1866. Those present also welcomed six new members, but it is not indicated whether they came from the old church.[46]

The church records indicate that although the dissidents still called themselves the only legitimate First Freewill Baptist Church in Dover, they may not have felt they would win their argument in the long run. In the records of the Feb. 13 meeting, it was again voted "that we consider ourselves entitled to the F. W. meeting house, our proportion of the time, and that we take measures to secure it that time." But then those present immediately voted to continue holding their meetings in the Central Street Vestry ". . .'till some other more convenient place can be had."

It should be pointed out that in the beginning two separate organizations ran church affairs. The church itself ran the ecclesiastical or spiritual and benevolent part of the activities. What was called the Central

---

[46] DBC, 1:38.

Street Freewill Baptist Society was in charge of the fiscal and real estate matters of the church. Although members of the society usually were members of the church, there was no requirement that they be members.

No records have been found for the Central Street Freewill Baptist Society. It has been claimed that the society was formed April 8, 1840.[47] That it existed is certain, since deeds in the Strafford County Courthouse show that the society bought the lot on which the church built its first meeting house. Also, when the Washington Street Freewill Baptist Society was formed in 1855, to replace the Central Street society, all assets of the old society subsequently were transferred to the new society.[48]

TROUBLE QUICKLY arrived to plague the new fellowship. Apparently determined to avoid the moral problems that had plagued and were still plaguing the old church, the leaders of the Central Street Freewill Baptist Church quickly pounced on any and all reports of unchristian conduct by the members.

So even as Elder Joseph Bennett Davis, the first pastor, was arriving in town, the church was preparing to hold its first "trial" of a member who was the subject of scandalous reports about town.

On a Monday evening in November of 1840, a special meeting was called to ascertain the truth of reports that Thomas Young, who with his wife had joined by letter from a Tuftonboro church in April, had attempted to seduce a young woman whom he had promised to help settle a dispute with a local retailer. The clerk's records show more than eight pages of testimony before the church voted to expel Mr. Young more than a week later.[49]

Little more than a year later, as already mentioned, another major problem developed when the esteemed Elder Enoch Mack, once a pastor of the old church and a charter member of the Central Street church, apparently took it upon himself to declare certain positions that were not accepted by the church, including an attempt to rename the denomination. After several attempts to work out the problem, he was excluded from membership March 1, 1842.[50]

Elder Mack the next year was listed as the editor of a small newsletter called *The Disciple*, which was described as "Established in Dover, Dec.

---

[47] *New Hampshire Churches*, 324.
[48] Strafford County Deeds, Bk. 217:172.
[49] DBC, 1:42-51.
[50] *Ibid.*, 1:54-57.

20, 1842—a small sheet edited by Enoch Mack, devoted to the promulgation of primitive Christian faith in its application to the present times—acknowledging no sect or party but Christ's. It is distributed gratuitously and sent free to anyone wishing to receive it—supported by voluntary contribution—issued as often as the means contributed will warrant."[51] Mack later was listed in town directories as a physician. Five years after his exclusion he was welcomed back into membership when he "made a full & satisfactory acknowledgement to the church of the errors that led to his exclusion . . ."[52]

By 1850, he had moved to New York City and was dropped from membership. In New York, he became a city missionary for the northern part of the city and remained in that work for 19 years. He died in Catskill Station, N.Y., Feb. 20, 1881, at the age of 75.

Lesser infractions also brought exclusion.

Nancy McDaniels was excluded after it was reported that she had attended a party and taken part in "recreations improper for a Christian."[53] She refused to confess.

Mary Rolls and Deborah Reynolds were excluded for unchristian conduct, charges not specified. The same for Vienna Horne.[54]

There would be many more exclusions in the years to come, often for infractions which would seem inconsequential today. But it should be remembered that times were different and no one was excluded before the church tried to work with the persons involved.

THE FIRST FEW years were a struggle for the church. Meetings were held at several locations, including the original vestry, then as the fellowship increased in numbers it met at the old Belknap School building located to the rear of the First Parish Church at Tuttle Square. Later, meetings were held at the county courthouse across the street from First Parish, a fact mentioned in the records Feb. 15, 1842. Business meetings also were held occasionally at the old vestry on Central Street.

Elder Davis, the church's first pastor, who was born Sept. 24, 1812, in Walkill, N.Y., gained only a small amount of formal schooling in his early years, and when he decided to go into the ministry after his conversion in 1829 had to borrow books to study for full-time work. He began preaching even before he reached 21 years of age and it's said he even

---

[51] *Norris' Dover Village Directory, 1843.*
[52] DBC, 1:80.
[53] *Ibid.*, 1:60.
[54] *Ibid.*, 1: 64-65.

labored in revivals on his way west to study at Oberlin College in Ohio. He remained there only one year, but was ordained as a Freewill Baptist minister in 1836.

He remained only one year in Dover, although during that time about 40 new members were added. A church manual printed in 1885 says "a large and permanent congregation was gathered under his eloquent and effective preaching."

Davis went from Dover to a pastorate in Portsmouth.

Then came Albanus Kimball Moulton, who also remained just one year. But it was a year during which there was almost continuous revival, not only in Dover but across the nation. The result was that 102 new members were added during his pastorate.

Rev. Moulton is the only Canadian-born pastor to have served Dover Baptist, having been born just northwest of the northern tip of New Hampshire in Hatley, Quebec, Canada, Sept. 27, 1810. His education was for the teaching profession, and he also went to Ohio in his late 20s before deciding to enter the ministry.

The church manual says the revival in Dover was so great that meetings were held "more than half of the evenings of his pastorate." But he left the Dover church for a new work in Portland, Me.

Rev. Moulton died in an accident in Ohio in 1873. Returning from a Sunday school festival one dark evening, he fell from a high bridge and was instantly killed.

Although the next pastor, Ransom Dunn, also remained only one year, it was a time when the church, in conjunction with the Printing Establishment, completed its first permanent place of worship and the work became more settled and organized.

Dunn was a Vermont native, having been born in Bakersfield July 17, 1818. He was licensed to preach in 1836 and ordained the next year. Before accepting the Dover pastorate, he had spent some time preaching in Ohio, where the Dover church's manual says he preached an average of 300 meetings a year.

He was said to have contributed significantly to the strengthening of the young Dover church, although only one member was added by baptism during his year in Dover.

He later preached at the church in Somersworth.

Rev. Dunn in 1850, at the request of the Boston Quarterly Meeting, wrote a pamphlet on the freedom of the will, a 15-page explanation of one of the denomination's core beliefs. It was printed in Dover by William Burr. The discourse was taken from a sermon Dunn had preached March

1, 1850, when he was pastor of the Boston church.[55]

Church records indicate that after Dunn left the Dover church, Rev. Barlow Dyer acted as interim pastor until May 1845.[56]

Following these years of struggle, and of being able to retain a pastor only a year or so, things changed. The next pastor, Elder Elias Hutchins, a former evangelist and controversial anti-slavery advocate, remained 13 years. Although the church prospered during his ministry, it also was the center of controversy and opposition because of its stand on slavery and connection with *The Morning Star.*

---

[55] *Discourse on the Freedom of the Will*, 3.
[56] DBC, 2:3.

4.

𝔄 place of their own

When the news reached Dover in December 1841, it must have sent a shudder through members of the Central Street Freewill Baptist Church. The subject had been brought up of moving *The Morning Star* and the whole Printing Establishment to Boston or New York.

Although there never was any official connection between the Freewill Baptist Printing Establishment and the new church, removal of the concern would have meant departure of many of the church's leaders, including the moving force in its organization, William Burr.

The subject of moving the newspaper came up at a Freewill Baptist General Conference meeting in Varysburg, N.Y., Dec. 15, 1841, during a discussion about whether the Printing Establishment should erect its own building.

The trustees had recommended that since the *Star* and the rest of the printing operation was showing more robust growth, though still financially strapped, it needed its own place. They reported:

> The establishment needs a building of its own in which to prosecute its own business, and the business of our religious societies and such a building, in the opinion of the board, should be erected as soon as requisite means can be obtained from the sale of its publications and the collection of its debts to defray its expenses.[57]

A proposal that the operation might be moved to Boston, New York City or western New York State was discussed. But William Burr and Elder David Marks, who once had operated the Book Concern, quickly pointed out the advantages of Dover. Said Marks:

> I am aware that Boston and New York cities possess several advantages in a commercial point above Dover, but it is equally true that

---

[57] *Star*, Nov. 3, 1841.

in the present state of our connection the removal of our book establishment to either place, would cost more than the value of any additional advantages that would be secured . . . The fact that twenty-four thousand of our members, or more than half the denomination, are situated either east or north of Dover, in my opinion, gives preference to the present location.[58]

Those attending the general conference concurred and in the end, says a report of the meeting, agreed "on [a] motion that trustees be instructed (as soon as the funds of the Book Establishment will admit) to erect at Dover, N.H., a suitable building for its use."[59]

There was only one stipulation. Burr had to agree that the book concern wouldn't think of erecting a building before the state of New Hampshire, which had so far refused to do so, gave the Printing Establishment permission to incorporate.[60] It wouldn't have been good business.

But it was a fact that the business needed a building of its own and would be adversely affected if it didn't have one. So while *The Morning Star* continued its strident opposition to slavery, and the New Hampshire Legislature refused to grant incorporation because of that stand, another method was devised to help the establishment get its own place.

William Burr was still a driving force in all three organizations involved—the church, society and publishing concern—although if one looks at the clerk's records he seems to have kept in the background most of the time. But probably because of that connection, an agreement was worked out that allowed the society, which was in charge of all church property and financial matters, and the trustees of the Book Concern—rather than the Book Concern itself—to go ahead with a building program. The society was to buy the land, the trustees personally would take on the debt and agree to build the ground floor and entrance from the sidewalk to a wide stairway to the second floor where the society agreed it would construct its meeting house.[61]

The society clerk's records apparently have been lost, but a deed filed at the Strafford County Courthouse shows that for $500 the Central Street Freewill Baptist Society on Feb. 13, 1843, bought from Winthrop A. Marston of Dover a plot of land on Washington Street that measured

---

[58] *Star,* Nov. 3, 1841.
[59] *Ibid.,* Jan. 12, 1842.
[60] *Ibid.*
[61] Strafford County Deeds, Bk. 191:503.

approximately 68 feet in width and 85 feet in depth. It was located on the north side of the street and on the westerly corner of a public way no longer existing (Myrtle Street) that was directly opposite the junction of Washington and Locust streets.

The agreement between the trustees of the Printing Establishment, officially known as "Trustees of the Freewill Baptist Connexion," and the Central Street Freewill Baptist Society, also filed at the courthouse in Dover, spells out the conditions under which the building would be erected.[62]

So the Central Street Freewill Baptist Church, still a young and struggling congregation that had been without a pastor for many months until Elder Ransom Dunn had arrived just a short time earlier, and its unofficial, but financially struggling Printing Establishment partner, were able to move into their own facilities for the first time. The dedication took place Sept. 21, 1843.

OFFICIAL CHURCH records make only one reference to the new building, showing only that the dedication would be Sept. 21 and that Elder Elias Hutchins of Newmarket would be asked to take part in the dedication. The missing society records normally would have contained all information concerning the building and its construction.

There are no drawings of the inside of the building, although photographs of the outside of the building do exist, both before and after alterations were made to the original structure. The ground floor and basement were of stone and brick, with the upper floor of wood frame construction. There were three windows across the front of the second floor and photographs indicate the possibility that there may have been a cathedral ceiling in the auditorium.

Elder Enoch Place gives some idea of what the building was like and describes the date of the dedication in his journal:

> On this day Sept. 21, 1843, the new and most beautiful Chappell over our printing office of 72 pews or more was opened and dedicated to the worship of Almighty God. Sermon by Elder Elias Hutchins of Newmarket, dedicating prayer by E. Place, a large number of ministers and an overflowing congregation attended. The sermon was good and full of pith and feeling. The Central St. Freewill Baptist Church will worship in this house.
>
> The annual meeting of the Home Mission Society was attended and the officers chosen &c. I was chosen president and one of the executive

---

[62] Strafford County Deeds, Bk. 191:533.

committee, on this account I had to tarry another day.

In the evening, Elder Dunn gave viz. (in the new chappell where he is to preach) one of the most useful and able abolition addresses I ever heard by any man.[63]

At the General Conference in 1843, Burr described *The Morning Star*'s portion of the new building:

> It is about seventy feet long and forty-six wide. Its walls are of brick, and it contains a composing room, a press room, a book room, a counting room, a room for a bindery, a paper room, and a cellar under two-thirds of the building, which is a convenient storage.

What he didn't mention was that the trustees were in dire need of the funds to pay the bills, and actually ran a notice on the front page of the *Star* Oct. 18 that they were in immediate need of $1,600 to pay for their part in the construction. A suggestion was made that patrons who hadn't paid for the *Star* or books might just do so.

Another idea of what the meeting room upstairs looked like can be gained from a description by Elias Hutchins' widow, Mrs. Marilla M. H. Hills, who joined the church in early 1847 and was a member until her death in 1901. At the advanced age of 89, "Mother Hills" recalled in 1896, when the church celebrated the burning of its mortgage for the present building:

> When I came to live in Dover near the close of the year 1846, the Washington Street church had its home in a very humble building set on the summit of the Free Baptist Printing Establishment now owned by the Odd Fellows. Entrance was gained by a long flight of outside stairs. The audience room was severely plain but neat. At a later date the wall directly back of the pulpit was adorned by a beautiful fresco painting of a large open Bible and a dove hovering over it. I do not know as a judge of paintings would have called this a picture of much merit but I can say as Mrs. Stowe said of the European galleries "If I am not a judge of paintings, I know what gives me pleasure." So to me this wall painting with its beautiful suggestions, as for years I faced it on the successive Sabbaths, was a source of delight. A small vestry underneath the Printing Establishment furnished the place for prayer meetings.[64]

THE CHURCH now was located in its own building, but there still

---

[63] Place, No. 66.

[64] *Dover Daily Republican* (DDR), Feb. 13, 1898.

was a time of struggle. Financially, it felt it was only able to pay Elder Dunn $400 for the time he was there. Though Elder Dunn was called an "enthusiastic preacher" and the church was strengthened spiritually, only 11 members were added during his one-year pastorate, 10 of them by letter from other churches.[65]

Dunn, writing later in *The Morning Star*, praised the Dover church, which he admitted was poor and small when he was there. "I always have felt thankful for the kindness of my little band of brethren in Dover. There were only 30 or 40 of them when I went there three years ago," he said. "The churches in Dover and Portsmouth both of them agreed to give me three hundred and fifty dollars per year. The church in Dover paid me in all $400, and 35 members agreed to do this; but before the year was up, the number increased to about 60 or more." Dunn, of course, was wrong in the figures he gave, the church having voted when it called him to pay him $400 for the year.[66]

It also was during Dunn's pastorate that the Millerite movement reached its peak and disrupted many churches in the Dover area and elsewhere. Those involved in the movement had set a date in 1843 in which they expected Christ to return and awaited the event with great anticipation.

The movement was so disruptive that the pastor of the old First Freewill Baptist Church in Dover actually left his pastorate and took many members of his church with him into the movement. For awhile, the Millerites even met in the Freewill Baptist church on Chestnut Street, creating a major disruption in the church for several years.

Elder Place was very discouraged by the disruption in the old church, writing in his journal:

> Eld. Hiram Stevens, the pastor of the First Church, has not been in his pulpit for 12 weeks past & seems to talk as if he never shall preach in it again until Christ comes in the clouds, and could they have [been] gratified we should have had a *Millerfied* Q. M. instead of the usual order on similar occasions. No doubt there has been very many conversions within two months past in that M. House, but there seems to be no regular order among them. Shouts on shouts from every part of the building. They may continue a few weeks longer but they cannot stand it long for human nature must give out under such continued violent exercises.
> They say that it is too late in the day for argument and that they have

---

[65] *Manual of Washington Street Freewill Baptist Church*, 1885.
[66] DBC, 1:67.

no time to spend in that way for Christ will appear in a few days—weeks at most. No one of our preachers or members made the least opposition to their tenets of Miller & Co. But I am convinced that some dreadful trials await that already much afflicted church. But at present they say that they are the happiest people on earth, or in other words none can be happier in this life than they are. In some way I have the conviction that they are doomed to disappointment. I leave it may God have mercy on those that have the error, they or me for I have greatly loved that church and have ever thought to do them good. But most of the members are at present beyond the reach of my influence, and some appear severe and cold to all but second advent believers etc.[67]

When Elder Stevens finally left the old church, the remaining members felt helpless and without leadership and begged Elder Place to minister to them. But he was reluctant, suggesting in his journal that the church always seemed to turn to him when it was in trouble when he wrote ". . . what to do with these brethren I know not, for they hang on to me like Paul's brethren at Miletus—saying come, do come and preach with us &c."[68]

The Washington Street Freewill Baptists seem not to have been infected by the movement to any great extent. The only mention of Millerism in its records is when it accepted into membership in 1860 Sophronia Wiggin, "she having embraced Millerism in 1842 . . . She has been with us for several years."[69]

When the date proposed for Christ's return passed without incident, many of those caught up in the movement gradually returned to their original churches, including the errant Elder Stevens. Others met for years and churches were formed from the original adherents to Millerism, including the Advent Christian Church in Dover, now called Hope Community Church.

Ransom Dunn had been hired for a year. Following his pastorate, Elder Elias Hutchins on May 4, 1845, was received into membership from the church in Newmarket and unanimously elected pastor of the flock at Dover.[70] He already was an editor, writer and trustee with *The Morning Star*, positions he continued to hold, and he was a leader in the Freewill Baptist denomination. He also was a controversial advocate of emancipation, bringing great wrath from some of the secular press,

---

[67] Place, No. 63, Jan. 13, 1843.
[68] *Ibid.,* No. 70, July 30, 1844.
[69] DBC, 1:105.
[70] *Ibid.,* 1:69.

especially the *Dover Gazette and Strafford Advertiser*. But he was a man of God, too, and he led the Washington Street church through 13 years of tremendous social ferment and growth.

By the time Elder Hutchins arrived, the church already was known for its vehement opposition to slavery and its involvement in the temperance movement. In the town directory, it was the only church in Dover specifically listed as such, it being described thusly: "The covenant of this church debars from its membership slaveholders and their apologists, and persons who manufacture, sell, or use intoxicating liquors, as a beverage."[71] There are instances in the church records where those wishing to join were specifically asked their views on slavery. The clerk reported on July 15, 1843, "Heard the experience of G. W. Johnson, who offered himself for baptism and membership, after being questioned by Br. Dow & W. Burr in relation to his views upon the subject of slavery, temperance & &. Voted to receive him."

The Civil War was drawing ever closer. Those in the church who for years had believed that slavery was an evil that should be opposed even if it meant the dissolution of the Union were beginning to see other churches join them. It was becoming an issue that the churches no longer could ignore as just a political question. And under the leadership of Elias Hutchins, plus the constant prodding by *The Morning Star,* the Central Street Freewill Baptist Church of Dover (for this is what the Washington Street church continued to call itself until 1855), was in the thick of the fight.

---

[71] *Norris' Dover Village Directory*, 1843.

5.
The Freedom Fight

Without at all neglecting the spiritual needs of the Central Street Freewill Baptist Church, Elder Elias Hutchins and the church leadership plunged headlong into the continuing struggle over two important social issues of the day that already had been an important part of the church's short history—freedom for slaves and the growing temperance movement.

The good news was that other churches—earlier quiet or in opposition as *The Morning Star* and some of the Freewill Baptists had sounded off about the evils of slavery—were beginning to join the call for emancipation. Rev. Root of the First Parish Congregational Church had all along been an outspoken advocate of emancipation.

For instance, in 1835 he took the opportunity to launch a long sermon against slavery, saying in part:

> Slavery like an incubus presses upon the heart of this republic. It is a cancer fastened upon the vitals of this great community. It is evil and only evil continually. It stirs the wrath of heaven, and if there be a God on high who legislates in righteousness, unless speedy repentance prevent, the days of this nation are nearly numbered and finished.[72]

But Rev. Root left for Waterbury, Ct., in 1839, before the idea of emancipation began to be popular.

The Friends [Quakers], of course, always had opposed slavery, even though some of the Dover Friends had owned slaves themselves until the time of the American Revolution.[73]

By the mid 1840s, meetings were being held in several churches in the Dover area calling for an end to the evil. Indeed, among those

---

[72] A Fast Sermon on Slavery delivered at First Parish Church, Dover, 5.
[73] *The Genealogical Record*, Journal of the Strafford County Genealogical Society, 25:55.

congregations was the First Freewill Baptist Church, where Elder Place's journal related in 1845: "We then went to the old or First Freewill Baptist meeting house to attend the quarterly meeting of the Dover Anti-Slavery Society, which was well attended by ministers and others."[74] The Franklin Street (Central Avenue) Baptists specifically decided in 1843 not to fellowship with anyone who supported slavery.[75]

The Methodists increasingly supported the movement, although apparently reluctantly at first, beginning in the middle 1830s.

Rev. James Thurston wrote concerning Dover's Methodist Episcopal Church:

> Rev. Jared Perkins was the next pastor . . . It was during this time that the great agitation of the public mind on the slavery question began to cause considerable trouble and disturbance in the M. E. church. Mr. Perkins sympathized strongly with the growing anti-slavery sentiment of the time, and readily admitted to his church and pulpit George Storrs, who came to lecture on the sin of slavery, the "vilest that ever saw the sun." It was on such an occasion that an attempt was made to mob Mr. Storrs, when Mr. Perkins and Rev. Mr. Root, pastor of the Congregational church, with their friends, led the lecturer between them safely through the raging rabble to the pastor's house.[76]

But later, when it came time for Rev. Perkins to move on to another pastorate, Thurston was able to write: "I have been informed that the church strongly desired Mr. Perkins to remain a third year because of his sympathy with the anti-slavery sentiment so predominant at that time in this community."

Perhaps it was a comment by one of the older Freewill Baptist ministers at a general conference which finally led to the formation of the denomination's own official anti-slavery organization. He remarked in 1843 that "there was a strange inconsistency in the operation of our denomination. They had a Home Mission Society, a Foreign Mission Society, a Sabbath School Society, and an Education Society, but no Anti-Slavery Society."[77]

He continued by hitting at the lukewarm support by some Freewill Baptists, saying: "Influenced by a false policy and a false standard of right, they are disposed to compromise with the dark spirit of slavery, and

---

[74] Place, No. 76, July 27, 1845.
[75] CABC Book 1, April 11, 1843.
[76] *A Historical Sketch of the Methodist Episcopal Church in Dover*, 10.
[77] *Star*, May 31, 1843.

yield a little and parley with the enemy, instead of standing forth in bold defense of the truth, with a fixed determination to live or die, stand or fall with it."

At any rate, led by William Burr and other leaders and pastors from the Washington Street church, the Freewill Baptist Anti-Slavery Society was formed just about the time the Dover church was erecting its new building in 1843. Meeting in Lisbon, N.H., 55 persons signed the constitution of the society on June 21. All the names were not listed in *The Morning Star*, but among the officers and executive committee were, from what would one day be Dover Baptist Church, William Burr as treasurer; J. C. Dow as corresponding secretary; former pastors J. B. Davis and A. K. Moulton, and future pastor Elias Hutchins as members of the executive committee. Rev. Moulton later was elected corresponding secretary of the society. Also elected were Jonathan Woodman as president, Samuel Whitney as vice president, and Silas Curtis to the executive committee. They all had been involved with the Washington Street church at various times but never were members.[78]

A future pastor, Rev. Isaac D. Stewart, would be secretary of the society in 1851, and at that time wrote a history of the denomination's push toward emancipation. (See Appendix B)

At the Franklin Street (Central Avenue) Baptist Church, it was written of Rev. A. M. Swain, who began work there in 1842: "Strong resolutions in favor of the abolition of slavery were adopted by the church during this pastorate, and a call extended to other churches to co-operate in the cause of human freedom."[79] This Calvinist Baptist church is the same church that one day would join with the Washington Street Free Baptist Church to become today's Dover Baptist Church.

Quarterly Meetings also began one by one to endorse the movement. The New Durham Quarterly Meeting was early to declare its support and had come out to join with the earlier resolution of the Rockingham Quarterly Meeting with a strong statement on the subject as early as 1841. Without coming right out and saying so, its resolution seemed to endorse the Dover church's stand by declaring the "full examination of slavery has . . . been sanctioned by the blessing of God." It declared:

> Whereas attempts to keep the discussion of slavery out of the church have caused much trouble, and whereas the full examination of slavery

---

[78] *Star*, Aug. 9, 1843.
[79] *The History, Articles of Faith and Government of the Franklin St. Baptist Church*, 4.

in the church has resulted in the most happy consequences, and been sanctioned by the blessing of God —Therefore

Resolved: That this conference, believing the anti-slavery cause to be the cause of God, recommend to all the churches and especially all the ministers of this Q. M. to bear solemn and decided testimony, in public and in private, against the sin of slavery, and to use faithfully their moral and religious influence for removing this foul stain from our nation's character, and this deadly sin from the Christian Church.[80]

The *Dover Gazette and Strafford Advertiser* continued to blast religious leaders who promoted the anti-slavery movement, accusing them of getting into politics to the detriment of their denominations. The fact that the Whigs were in favor of emancipation and the Democrats opposed probably was a bigger factor in the general Freewill Baptist support of Whigs, although William Burr's entry into the fray as a Whig candidate for state office probably added to the complaints that churches were meddling in politics.

The *Gazette,* to be sure, did not save all its venom for the Freewill Baptists or William Burr's newspaper. After one anti-slavery meeting held at the First Parish Congregational Church, the newspaper, after the usual assurance that it also was really against slavery, spewed forth one of its most scurrilous attacks against the churches involved, saying: "But the course that has been pursued by renegade fanatics in this town and elsewhere—the desecration of the holy Sabbath and houses consecrated to the worship of Almighty God, to the purposes of private invective, slander, abuse, misrepresentation, hot-headed debate, and exciting arguments and details, we do as strongly protest against . . ."[81]

What really seemed to enrage the *Gazette* was the fact that Dover, perhaps due in part to the influence of *The Morning Star,* was one of the few places in the state that favored the Whig candidates, and thus the abolition movement generally, in 1844. In a few years, the growing sentiment for emancipation brought statewide victory to the Whigs.

In its continuing opposition to *The Morning Star* and its stand, the *Gazette* at one time even offered to handle the paperwork if subscribers would leave the *Star* and subscribe to another denominational paper called the *Repository* being started in Saco, Me.

The *Gazette* at one point accused anti-slavery advocates of splitting churches over the issue, stating:

---

[80] *Star*, June 2, 1841
[81] *Gazette*, Jan. 12, 1841.

The fell spirit of Abolitionism, engendered and fostered by a hatred of democratic institutions, has so far accomplished its object of *disunion* as to effect a severance between the Northern and Southern division of the churches of three of our most numerous religious denominations— The Presbyterians, the Methodists and the Baptists.

. . . Their efforts may irritate and harass the public mind, but they cannot, we trust, so far influence public opinion at the North, as to make the sentiment general, which is now factious and fanatical.[82]

The newspaper may have been referring to a trip to the South made earlier by the Washington Street church's pastor, Elder Elias Hutchins, who met with some Freewill Baptists in North Carolina who wished to join the Freewill Baptists of the North.

After meeting with the southern Freewill Baptists, Elder Hutchins reported to the General Conference:

During one of my visits to these churches, a member, who, in everything save slavery, was among the most mild, humane, and hospitable men, and devoted Christians I have ever seen, told me that he once pursued a runaway slave—an outlaw—and, on his refusing to stop, fired at him as he was getting over the fence. And said he, 'I tracked him for some distance by his blood, but he was never seen afterwards,' intimating that he died of the wound.

Another man, who was among the most zealous members of the North Carolina Free-will Baptist churches, told me that he wanted no better sport, than to take his horse, dogs, and gun, and pursue a runaway slave whenever one came near him; and that it was no more harm to shoot such a slave, than to shoot a deer.[83]

Needless to say, the North Carolina Freewill Baptists, numbering two quarterly meetings, 45 churches, 36 ministers and a total of 3,000 members, were not welcomed into fellowship.[84]

Sentiment throughout New Hampshire was changing dramatically during the 1840s. The state Legislature, which had for several years refused to let the Book Concern incorporate because of its stand on slavery, finally let it do so in 1846 after the Legislature itself had come to favor emancipation. The Book Concern thus officially became incorporated on Oct. 1 of that year as the Freewill Baptist Printing Establishment, and the trustees who had taken on the financial burden of

---

[82] *Gazette*, May 31, 1845.
[83] *Annual Report, Freewill Baptist Anti-Slavery Society* (See Appendix B), 1851.
[84] *Ibid.*

the concern transferred all assets to the new corporation.[85]

SWIFT REACTION among Freewill Baptists came after the Fugitive Slave Act was passed by Congress in 1850. Compliance would have forced anti-slavery advocates to return runaway slaves or face fines and a possible six months in jail. They weren't about to do so.

Washington Street Freewill Baptist's pastor, Elias Hutchins, speaking for a committee shortly after passage of the measure, reported to the General Conference being held in Providence, R.I., the following resolution, in part:

> And whereas said bill is oppressive, tyrannical and odious in its nature, barbarous and incendiary in its inception and tendencies, and dishonorable to its authors and abettors, a stain upon the statute book of the nation, a reproach to humanity, and insulting to the religion, conscience and intelligence of the Christian and freeman of the free States: Therefore
>
> 1. *Resolved,* That we do deliberately and calmly, yet earnestly and decidedly, deny any and all obligation on our part to submit to the unrighteous enactments of the aforesaid Fugitive Slave Bill. Also, that regardless of unjust human enactments, fines, and imprisonment, we will do all we can consistently with the claims of the Bible to prevent the recapture of the fugitive, and to aid him in his efforts to escape from his rapacious claimants.[86]

A request was sent to the U.S. Congress to repeal the act.

DOVER'S ANTI-SLAVERY adherents must have been thrilled on March 2, 1860, when the northbound train pulled into the station just after 5 p.m. Abraham Lincoln, in New Hampshire to visit his son at Phillip's Exeter Academy, had been convinced by a local delegation to come to Dover to speak. No one could mistake the Great Emancipator when he stepped off the train, towering as he did above all those there to meet him.

Even though there had been only two days notice that he was to speak in Dover, the city hall auditorium, directly across the street from the Washington Street Freewill Baptist Church, was jammed by a standing-room-only crowd. One source described the scene as people having to ". . . elbow and crowd their way into the hall for the pleasure of standing two hours to hear Lincoln."[87]

---

[85]Strafford County Deeds, Bk. 200:89.
[86] *Star*, Jan. 1, 1851.
[87] *Abraham Lincoln in New Hampshire*, 78

Prominent among those who attended the event was William Burr. Before Lincoln spoke, the local Republican committee named officers for the occasion. Among those selected was Burr as a representative from Ward 3. Also there was church member James M. Haynes, elected representative from Ward 2. News reports indicate that those elected that evening sat with Lincoln on the platform.[88]

The meeting was opened by John R. Varney of the Republican committee, who 22 years later would lose his life in the blackened ruins of the present church building.

Speaking to the packed audience (the seats had been removed to accommodate a standing crowd), Lincoln apparently gave the same general speech he had given at Cooper Union in New York City Feb. 27, before heading to New Hampshire.

The speech, of course, was praised by the *Dover Enquirer,* the local Republican paper, and denounced by the *Dover Gazette & Strafford Advertiser*; the *Gazette* even at this late date continued to denounce those who wanted slavery abolished. It panned both the speech and the size of the crowd, saying the hall was only half-filled. It also waited a full week before printing the story on an inside page.

Lincoln spent the night at the home of George Mathewson on the corner of Locust and Nelson streets before leaving town.

SOLID PROOF has not surfaced concerning any actual instances in which Washington Street Freewill Baptists helped fugitive slaves along the Underground Railroad to safety in Canada. Records of such actions, for obvious reasons, seldom were kept. But it is known that some slaves traveled through the area on their way to Canada, and William Burr's biographer, Rev. J. M. Brewster, at that time a member of the Washington Street church and a fellow worker with Burr at *The Morning Star,* says: "Mr. Burr was, during those years, what might be termed a practical anti-slavery man. More than once the hunted fugitive found protection within his dwelling, and was speeded by him in his flight from bondage to liberty."[89]

Brewster then recounted a story he had heard about Burr:

> One morning as he was deeply engaged in business, a fugitive, who had grown gray in the service of a southern master, entered his office and gave him a letter of introduction from a Friend [Quaker] residing in

---

[88] *Enquirer*, March 8, 1860.
[89] Burr, 164-5.

Philadelphia. As the colored man passed the letter to him, he tremblingly inquired, "Are you an abolitionist?" Mr. Burr, reading the letter, at once replied, "I am abolitionist enough to take care of you." The emphasis and almost sternness with which these words were uttered, terrified the poor fellow, who feared that he had fallen into the hands of an enemy. The kindness, however, with which he was treated, and the hospitable manner in which he was received into Mr. Burr's home, soon quieted all his fears, and he came to feel and know that he had found a friend indeed.[90]

If the above anecdote is true, it would mean that at least this one fugitive slave traveling the Underground Railroad was harbored in the very building in which the Washington Street Freewill Baptists met for services, Burr's office being on the ground floor. Burr's home at the time, where his biographer says this black man and others were sheltered, was at the corner of Washington and Belknap streets, where it still stands only a block from the present church building.

In a letter years later to Rev. Brewster, former U.S. Sen. John P. Hale of New Hampshire, a resident of Dover, who had deserted the Democratic party because of its stand against emancipation, wrote concerning Burr: "He was an early, steadfast, heroic advocate and protector of the hunted fugitive, even in those days when it was dangerous to harbor a runaway slave; no fugitive was ever turned away from his door without having received the sympathy and aid which his case demanded. It is indeed difficult in these days to realize the obloquy and danger attending protection thus afforded."

So though no concrete evidence exists that Mr. Burr sheltered runaway slaves at his home in Dover, it is very possible if not probable that he did so, especially because of his extreme stand on the subject and because those who knew him seemed well aware that he did. If indeed he did so, his home would have been known as a "station" on the Underground Railroad and he would have been known as a "conductor," terms used to conceal the secretive nature of what was taking place.

Some inkling of the high esteem in which the Freewill Baptists were held during these years, especially those in Dover, can be seen in a paragraph written by Oliver Johnson in his biography of William Lloyd Garrison, founder of the American Anti-Slavery Society and publisher of the anti-slavery newspaper *The Liberator*, when, after criticizing churches in general for their lack of an early stand on slavery, he says:

---

[90] Burr, 165.

It gives me great pleasure to mention one Christian denomination, somewhat numerous in parts of New England, as well as in other states, that deserves to be excepted from the censures I have been compelled to bestow upon the rest. I allude to the Freewill Baptists, who, from the beginning refused to receive slave-holders into communion, and most of whom were prompt to espouse the doctrine of immediate emancipation. The *Morning Star*, the organ of the denomination, did much to inform public sentiment on the subject of slavery, especially in New Hampshire, where it had a large circulation . . . Its leaders refused to follow the example of other churches in countenancing slavery, and for this reason incurred much censure and some persecution. It is not too much to say that it was more through the influence of the *Morning Star* than from any other cause that the power of the pro-slavery Democracy in New Hampshire was first broken, and John P. Hale elected to the Senate of the United States . . .[91]

Johnson admitted not all Freewill Baptists were anti-slavery, "but compared to the churches around them, they were as light in the midst of darkness. If all other Christian denominations had come up to their level, the chains of the slaves might have been broken by moral power" instead of by war.

Many people fought the Fugitive Slave Act for more than 10 years, but it took the Civil War to end the need for the Underground Railroad.

SLAVERY WAS not the only issue on the Washington Street church's agenda. The temperance movement was in full swing and the church took its stand against what seemed like a national binge of drinking. Temperance speakers were allowed in the pulpit. Many members joined temperance societies springing up all over town, even in the hard-drinking riverfront area at the Landing.

No mention of it is made in any church or society records, but according to Elias Hutchins' widow, in a piece presented at the burning of the mortgage on the present building in 1896, "The church early enlisted in the temperance war and was among the first to substitute unfermented wine in the place of alcoholic wine at communion service."[92]

Indeed the newspapers are full of notices of temperance meetings on into the 1870s and the meetings often were held at the Washington Street church. One of the leaders of the women's temperance movement in Dover seems to have been Mrs. L. R. Burlingame, a prominent member of the church. Presumably she's the one who gave the notice to the

---

[91] *Life of William Lloyd Garrison*, 81.
[92] DDR, Feb. 13, 1896.

newspaper in 1869 that said the women were becoming more active in their anti-liquor moves "to induce the liquor dealers of this city to abandon a business which carries so much suffering and sorrow into our homes." That was followed by an announcement that the next meeting would be held in the vestry of the new church.

No churches and few newspapers opposed the temperance movement and it was one area where the churches all over Dover, including those considered the most liberal, were joined together in a national movement against the rampant use of intoxicating liquors. But one Dover newspaper, the *Gazette,* by the late 1860s was still voicing its opposition to the movement mostly by making fun of those involved in it.

MEANWHILE, CHURCH members continued on their spiritual journey.

Slavery and intemperance not withstanding, the Gospel continued to be preached from the pulpit. The church was involved in home and foreign missions, education and Sabbath School. But the slavery and temperance issues provided great distractions during those tumultuous years.

6.
Maturing with a mission

T hough deeply involved in the social issues of the day, the Washington Street Freewill Baptists, young and poor as a church, never neglected the spiritual mission that they had declared when the congregation first met.

Where *The Morning Star* had been a leader in moves to establish home and foreign mission societies and Sunday schools, this church so closely related to the *Star* was quick to establish its niche as a congregation with a heart for missions.

Only three years after its founding, the church sent out its first missionary, one of its own members. James C. Dow, who had joined the church by letter from a church in Livermore, Me., in May 1843, was sent out with the blessing of the church just two months later after being approved by the Foreign Missions Board.

Dow, before joining the church, had been filling in as interim pastor for quite a few weeks.

The clerk wrote: "Voted, that we shall part with Brother Dow with regret, and do it only in consideration of his feeling it his duty to go to India, and that we shall always remember him in our prayers, that God will make him a blessing to the benighted heathen."[93]

Dow had the honor of being ordained when the church dedicated its new building Sept. 1, 1843. Enoch Place, in his journal, described the event:

> . . . Bro. Dow, a young man, was ordained a missionary for our Orissa or India Station, ordaining prayer by Elder Jonathan Woodman. All was solemnity and deep feeling, and so interesting was this meeting that it seemed for the moment as if we should all be missionaries.
> An appropriate charge and hand of fellowship was given in due

---

[93] DBC, 1:66.

form, and a liberal collection made for the candidate who with his youthful wife are soon to depart for the heathen land of Hindustand.[94]

Dow and his wife sailed Nov. 18, 1843, arriving in India May 7, 1844, and served there nearly four years before leaving for home on March 28, 1848. The couple served most of their time in the city of Midnapore, about 70 miles from Calcutta. Rev. Dow's health failed and they were forced to return home.[95]

It was the beginning of a long history of missionary endeavor by the church which continues today both at home and abroad.

But that first missionary endeavor did not come easily. Elder Elias Hutchins back in February had warned that if more money was not raised for missions there were three men, including Dow, who probably would not be able to go to the mission field. "There has never been a time since the formation of our society, when we were more in want of funds than we are now," he wrote.[96]

But despite the financial difficulties, the Foreign Missions Board on June 10 appointed him to the Orissa field in India. Reported *The Morning Star:* ". . . James C. Dow, now preaching with the Central Street Church in Dover, was appointed to go out as another missionary to Orissa. It was agreed that he should sail next September, and a committee was chosen to make arrangements for the outfit, ordination &tc. of Br. Dow."[97] There followed another appeal for funds to make it possible.

THE EARLY DAYS of the church also were times of strict adherence to the rules, members being excluded for unspecified "unchristian conduct" or in some cases for conduct specifically mentioned in the records. But none seem to have been excluded before the church at least tried to meet with them, work out the problem and bring them back into the fold.

Besides cases mentioned earlier, there was the situation with Elizabeth Marston, who had left the place in what was considered an unchristian manner, and "other evidence of her want of piety being brought forward," she was considered no longer a member.[98]

Sister Christian McKenley was dropped after a committee visited her

---

[94] Place, No. 66.
[95] CRFB, 120, 244.
[96] *Star*, Feb. 8, 1843.
[97] *Ibid.*, July 5, 1843.
[98] DBC, 1:58.

several times and eventually determined she had been engaged in dancing and telling falsehoods.[99]

C. W. Jones was visited in an attempt at reconciliation between him and other brethren. The reconciliation was achieved, but Jones decided he wanted his name dropped from membership.[100]

Hannah Twombly retained her membership after a trial in which the church considered reports that she had stolen a handkerchief and lied about it. The vote was that the evidence was not sufficient. But a small group, including William Burr, entered in the records an official protest, claiming there indeed was sufficient evidence.[101]

Mary Stevens, charged with "imprudent conduct," was excluded after she confessed she had been rude at the office of a local doctor. The church felt her confession didn't go far enough.

After the first few years, actual "trials" of members for various reasons appear fewer times in the records. Only an occasional instance surfaces after the early 1850s. But the church for many years demanded strict adherence to its covenant for a member to be in good standing.

One incident that did occur as late as 1862 was when Samuel L. Gray was excluded when a committee found reports to be true "that he has been in the habit of playing slice dominos, and backgammon and of using profane language."[102]

Gray's wife, being dealt with by another committee, admitted she had not been leading a good Christian life, but she asked for a second chance, writing: "In my report I would say that I am very imperfect and live far beneath my privilege, yet I hope that through the blood of Christ I shall be an overcomer and have a seat with him at last. I am resolved to be a Christian the rest of my life by the grace of God helping me. I ask the prayers of all that love the Lord."

When she was asked to go before the church and acknowledge her shortcomings, as well as owning up to "unbecoming treatment" of the pastor, she refused. She was excluded.[103]

Some members left on their own, or at least threatened to leave, especially as the emancipation rhetoric reached its peak.

B. F. Vittum told a committee visiting him that "he would not hear

---

[99] DBC, 1:66.
[100] *Ibid.*, 1:68-69.
[101] *Ibid.*, 1:70-75.
[102] *Ibid.*, 1:113.
[103] *Ibid.*, 1:112.

political preaching,"[104] according to the records. But the committee met with him some more and he agreed to remain a member and try to attend regularly.

William Burley, when visited by a committee seeking to know why he had neglected attendance, said "he did not like [the] course of our pastor in preaching political & wish[es] his name dropped," the committee reported. But he was visited again and the records don't show he was dropped. That was in 1857 and in the next few years he again was active in church affairs. But in 1861, when anti-slavery rhetoric was reaching a crescendo, he again neglected attendance and when a committee visited him it reported back to the church that he was "tired with political preaching or preaching not in accordance with his political views" and he wanted to be left alone.[105] But after William Burr visited him again he agreed to attend at least once in awhile and the matter was dropped.

He remained a member of the church until his death in 1872.

Daniel Littlefield and his wife, who had joined in 1841, were dismissed to the old First Freewill Baptist Church in Dover for unspecified reasons in 1847. But it was at their request. An inkling of why they left can be obtained by reading records of the old church some years later when the Littlefields were miffed at action taken by a church committee and sought dismissal to return to the Washington Street church.

The problem was Mrs. Littlefield's singing. The music committee reported it was "their opinion her singing was not generally acceptable to the congregation," thus excluding her from the choir.[106] The controversy continued for months until the Littlefields asked to have their letter to return to the Washington Street church.

It was then that someone asked if he did not "remember of telling a number of brethren after he left the other church that a member in that church could not get justice done him, every thing was cooked up in the *Star* office when any business was to be done, one was appointed to make the motion, another to second it & so on & would carry any thing they wished to."[107]

It seems to be the only time in the records where there was a hint that

---

[104] DBC, 1:93.
[105] *Ibid.*, 1:108.
[106] FFBC Book 2, December 1861.
[107] *Ibid.*, September 1863.

anyone thought William Burr had too much say in church decisions. Any real control Burr had certainly hadn't been sufficient to exclude Hannah Twombly when she was accused of stealing the handkerchief, since he was one of those who protested the church's action in exonerating her.

The Washington Street church seemed reluctant to welcome the Littlefields back at first, but did so Feb. 5, 1864,[108] and he was later elected a deacon and served until his death Jan. 10, 1892.

It is not known whether Mrs. Littlefield ever sang in the choir at the Washington Street church.

ANOTHER EARLY issue in some Freewill Baptist churches was the question of whether musical instruments should be allowed in the services. One of the Strafford churches had quite a controversy concerning the subject until Elder Place—the same man who was instrumental in forming the old church in Dover—wrote in his journal that if musical instruments help get the message out to a lost world it probably was alright even though he found nothing in the Bible to support it.

The Washington Street church on July 28, 1843, discussed "the subject of having a bass viol introduced into our meetings of worship or into the singing choir." Without much ado, it was decided "it would be beneficial in promoting spiritual singing."

Ten years later the church installed its first organ, an instrument built in Boston by The Simmons Company for $800.[109] The instrument, which must have been provided through action of the society since there is no mention of it in the church clerk's records, would serve the church for nearly 30 years.

---

[108] DBC, 1:116.
[109] *Boston Herald*, Aug. 6, 1853.

7.
Hard times and sorrows

With the formation of the Washington Street Freewill Baptist Society on Jan. 8, 1855, we begin to get an altogether different view of the life of the Washington Street church. The society looked after the financial and real estate needs, leaving the elders and pastors to provide for the spiritual needs of the members.

Until the society was formed, most of what we have seen has been the spiritual and social aspects of the church and its membership.

The society was a method of organization used by many churches in the early days. Although it caused grievances in some churches, usually due to personality conflicts, and eventually was dropped, the Washington Street church and society never had problems with each other. William Burr again was instrumental in the organization of the society, as he was the church earlier, and he served as its president until his sudden death in 1866.

As pointed out earlier, the church's financial and real estate matters had been handled by the Central Street Freewill Baptist Society. The new society simply replaced the old one and all the property was transferred to the new organization, one entry in the clerk's records showing: "Whereas the Central St. F. W. Baptist Society has transferred all its property to this society, therefore resolved, that the Washington St. F. W. Baptist Society assume all the liabilities of the said Central St. Society."

It is not known why the society's name was not changed earlier. But the church hadn't changed its name, either. That is, not until five days earlier, when on Feb. 3, 1855, the clerk showed two actions by the church—the acceptance of two new members and a vote "to change the name of the church from Central St. F. B. Church, to Washington Street F. B. Church." That's all. It was the first of three changes in the church name.

The society's records show us immediately some of the costs of keeping the church open for services. By then, Elder Elias Hutchins was being paid $500 a year—he having agreed to stay at least one more year as pastor.[110] It was the custom at that time to hire the preacher for one year at a time. At the same meeting, Asa H. Littlefield was voted "one dollar per Sabbath for service as organist." At a meeting on May 7 it was voted to pay the same to a choir leader if they could find one. One of the items the society thought it needed was a new funnel for the church stove, but a committee advised against it because of the high price of funnel at the time.

The church had no extra money. The annual report from the treasurer in 1856 showed a total of $749.35 received during the year and expenditures of $747.01, leaving a balance of $2.34. Of course, that didn't count the approximately $80 in outstanding bills that hadn't been paid.[111] The next year, the treasurer reported that $8.86 was left over but also noted that outstanding bills amounted to $100.

Though never going deeply into debt, the church for many years was forced to appoint committees to solicit subscriptions to meet expenses— an early form of pledging for the annual budget. But the society was forever returning to the church members to ask them to make up a deficiency in subscriptions.

There were times when subscriptions just were not enough to meet the needs. In 1857, five members petitioned for a special meeting to see if the society might begin assessing pew owners to pay for insurance and repairs to the meeting house. But it was decided it wasn't the right time for such a move and money was borrowed instead.[112] But by 1859, it was voted to assess all pew owners an amount that would bring in a total of $300 to pay expenses. Although records aren't available for when the meeting house was built, members of churches in the 1700s and 1800s often bought pews to help pay construction and other expenses and actually owned the pews like real estate and sometimes sold them to other members. Churches assessed pew owners for various expenses usually having to do with maintenance or repairs.

At another time, a committee was asked to look into the possibility of the society hiring the pews from the owners and then renting them at a markup to help raise funds. The suggestion was turned down.

ELIAS HUTCHINS by 1858 was in declining health and on April 4

---

[110] WFBS Book 1, April 2, 1855.
[111] *Ibid.*, April 21, 1856.
[112] *Ibid.*, May 11, 1857.

resigned as pastor after having served the church for 13 years. An undated entry in the clerk's book recorded his death, at age 58, the next year:

"Rev. Elias Hutchins, who was pastor of this church for thirteen years died at his residence on Atkinson St. Sept. 10th 1859 about ten o'clock in the evening in the full assurance of a home in heaven. His last words were *trust, trust, trust.* He was buried from the meeting house on the 15th. Sermon by Rev. J. B. Davis of Lowell, Mass.—There were present thirty clergymen, twenty one F. W. Baptist." This is the same Rev. Davis who 17 years earlier had been the church's first pastor.

In a preface to the funeral sermon published later, the esteem in which Rev. Hutchins was held by fellow Freewill Baptists is indicated by the events of the day of his funeral:

> The funeral was attended at 2 o'clock, on Thursday, at the Washington street church, the place of his labors for thirteen years as pastor. Before assembling at the church, a number of ministers called at the house of the deceased, and prayer was offered by Rev. Theodore Stevens, of North Berwick, Me. The remains were then carried to the church, accompanied by Revs. D. P. Cilley, J. Stevens, S. Curtis, L. B. Tasker, J. M. Durgin, O. R. Bacheler, T. Stevens and D. Mott, as bearers. The house was crowded, even the aisles and vestibule, and many who desired were not able to gain admittance. There were about thirty ministers present, and many others would have been there had not the session of one Yearly Meeting and two Quarterly Meetings in the region called them to duty elsewhere. The occasion was one of deep solemnity, and no doubt will contribute to the cause to which the subject devoted his life, the conversion of souls.[113]

Rev. J. B. Davis in his funeral sermon noted that Rev. Hutchins was still corresponding secretary of the denomination's foreign mission society when he died. He had served in that capacity for years.

In a tribute to his standing in the community as a whole at the time of his death, Davis spoke directly to all the inhabitants. It was important because 13 years earlier Elias Hutchins had faced violent opposition to his stand on slavery. On the day of his funeral even some of the city's businesses closed. Near the end of the sermon were these words:

> Permit me to say a word to the church and townsmen of Dover; for our brother was not a sectarian, he loved all Christians, as is shown by his reply to the Congregational minister who called to see him just before he died, and when he said to him, "You are going, brother, where

---

[113] Funeral Service of Rev. Elias Hutchins (See Appendix D).

Hard times and sorrows 53

there are no differences." "There are none between Christians and myself here," said brother Hutchins. No, he loved all Christians in all churches. And the closing of your places of business, the attendance of ministers of other denominations, and crowding numbers who could not obtain admittance, all show your high esteem for one of the best husbands, most worthy citizen, and devoted minister, who has fallen in your midst. The life and death of Rev. Elias Hutchins are identified with the history of his denomination, and your city.[114]

Hutchins' ministry had been tumultuous because of his anti-slavery stance, but it also had been fruitful. During his 13 years as pastor, there were 212 members added to the church, 107 by baptism and 105 by letter.

His death just before the Civil War was a big blow to the denomination and the Dover church; another death soon after the war would strike another blow.

After Rev. Hutchins' resignation the previous year, the church and society had immediately arranged with Charles Edwin Blake to be pastor for a few weeks "on trial." Then in December the society asked Rev. Blake to remain, but with the strange proviso that ". . . he be at liberty to negotiate with another church and to accept an invitation to become its pastor, and the society to be at liberty to negotiate with and engage another minister, when he or it shall deem best . . ." The reason for such an arrangement never was spelled out. He was to be paid $500 per year.

In any event, Rev. Blake remained but a year. No entry in either the society or church records shows exactly when he departed but other records indicate he later served at the old church from which the Washington Street church had emerged, as well as in other ministries. He entered the U. S. Army as a private in 1861 and served as a chaplain during the Civil War, from which he apparently emerged unscathed.

Charles Edwin Blake was born in Exeter, N.H., in 1818 and joined the Methodist church before transferring to Freewill Baptists in 1843.

After Rev. Blake left the Washington Street church, Rev. A. W. Avery supplied the pulpit for a few months and then at a meeting on Jan. 2, 1860, the society engaged Rev. Willet Vary for the remainder of the year at a salary of $600. He actually had begun preaching at the church Dec. 1, 1859[115] and remained at the church until 1866.

Rev. Vary was born in Stephentown, N.Y., in 1827. After his conversion in 1848, he studied for the ministry and received a degree in

[114] Funeral Service of Rev. Elias Hutchins (See Appendix D).
[115] DBC, 2:3

theology from New Hampton in 1855. Before coming to Dover, he preached in Newmarket, N.H., and South Berwick, Me.

INCOME INCREASED but so did expenses just prior to the Civil War in 1861. Just 11 days before the outbreak of war, the treasurer's annual report showed receipts of $853.86 and expenditures of $846.88. But the problem of outstanding bills still plagued the society. With $6.98 left in the treasury, there were $318 in bills unpaid and pledges of $90.75 still due.[116] Still, the society raised the pastor's salary from $600 to $800.

The war for a time brought extremely tough sledding financially. By September 1861, five months after the outbreak of hostilities, a special meeting was called to confront the increasing debt as people were unable to pay the amount they pledged.

One way to raise a little money was to rent the church auditorium to "the friends of the slave" one night a month.[117] Dover had its own anti-slavery society.

A committee was formed to see if members would agree to pay certain proportions of debt coming due or make other arrangements to meet the payment deadline. And after having voted earlier to pay the pastor $800 annually, a committee headed by William Burr was asked "to see if some such arrangement as the hard times would seem to require can be made with our pastor, Rev. W. Vary."[118] Burr made a favorable report at the next meeting, but what he reported is not recorded. Apparently Rev. Vary either took a pay cut or agreed to forego remuneration for awhile so the church could get back on its feet financially.

But it was not that easy. With the nation already at war for a year, in April of 1862 the society—and thus the church—was still in debt and finally decided to borrow money so Rev. Vary could be paid what was owed for the past year. Then he agreed to stay for the next year at a $300 cut in salary, receiving only $500.

By 1864, society finances had improved some, so Rev. Vary's salary had been raised back to $600. The treasurer reported that $1001 had been raised and $891 expended, leaving $110 in the treasury. With $300 in outstanding bills, the society was less than $200 in debt.

THE SUMMER of 1864 brought home to the church the reality of the Civil War with the news that one of its own had been killed in battle.

---

[116] WFBS Book 1, April 1, 1861.

[117] *Ibid.*, Oct. 28, 1861.

[118] *Ibid.*, Sept. 2, 1861.

Church records mention that Nathaniel Brown, who joined by letter from the Barrington church in 1851, on July 30, 1864, was "killed in the charge before Petersburg, Va., was shot thro the breast."[119] He had served in Co. K, 11th New Hampshire Regiment. But that is the only mention in the records of a member of the church losing his life in the conflict, despite the fact that 93 Dover men died in the war.

The next year, Rev. Vary decided he'd stay another year if the society would pay him $700 and give him four weeks vacation. It did. But Pastor Vary resigned in January 1866. Although times had been tough, his pastorate was considered a success and 147 were added to the church, 94 by baptism and 53 by letter.

Just a month after resigning, Rev. Vary was accepted as a member of the Central Avenue Baptist Church (Calvinist) and a council was formed to see if that denomination would recognize him as a minister in its churches. The entry in that church's record book indicates that the Washington Street church probably knew he was considering the change.

The entry in the Central Avenue church's records for Feb. 15, 1866, reads as follows:

> Church met by appointment of the Pastor, and a letter was read from the Freewill Baptist Church in Washington Street dismissing the Rev. Willet Vary "and recommending him to the fellowship of God's people." Mr. Vary himself was present and gave an account of his conversion and his change of views from those held by the Freewill Baptists to those held by us, and also requesting to be rec'd as a member of this church.
>
> On motion, it was voted unanimously that Brother Willet Vary be rec'd as a member of this church.
>
> [Council to meet] to consider the propriety of recognizing as a Baptist minister, the Rev. Willet Vary, lately pastor of the Washington St. Freewill Baptist Church.[120]

Rev. Vary was somewhat ahead of his time, since more than 50 years later the Washington Street and Central Avenue churches combined to form Dover Baptist Church. A week after he appeared before the church, the clerk penned on Feb. 22, "Council met, as notified as above, and after a full and very satisfactory examination of Brother Vary's views of Christian doctrine, it was voted that he be recognized as a minister of this denomination."

---

[119] DBC, Book 1, Member List No. 3, back of book.
[120] CABC, 2:28.

Rev. Vary then on April 13, was dismissed to a Calvinist Baptist Church in Randolph, Mass. He later preached at churches in Ohio and died in 1870.

EVENTS THAT FOLLOWED the resignation of Rev. Vary probably brought the society and church to their lowest ebb since they were organized.

Attempts to get Rev. Vary to stay had been unsuccessful for obvious reasons. Records show that only $55.13 was raised to pay for someone to supply the pulpit in the interim. When Rev. J. M. Bagley was asked to become pastor, he declined. The society then invited Rev. A. H. Heath to be pastor at a salary of $1,000, despite the fact that he was still in college. He declined, too.[121] Rev. E. A. Stockman declined to fill in as interim pastor, and Rev. O. T. Moulton declined a pastoral call in January 1867.[122]

Several meetings were held in which the society's clerk wrote that the "welfare of the society" was seriously discussed. The wardens were actually instructed to sell the stove and funnel in the vestry to raise some money.

Finally, on April 1, 1867, it was announced that Rev. I. D. Stewart, the outspoken advocate of the now-successful fight for an end to slavery, had agreed to become pastor of the Washington Street Freewill Baptist Church and Society. His would be a successful ministry, and following his pastorate he would remain a member of the church and go to work full-time for the Freewill Baptist Printing Establishment, eventually becoming publisher of *The Morning Star.*

PERHAPS THE most devastating event that occurred during these years of deepest discouragement, while the church still was searching desperately for a new pastor, was the sudden death of church and society founder William Burr. The end came almost without warning.

Burr died on Nov. 5, 1866. He had lived to experience victory in the greatest struggle of his career—emancipation—but had succumbed to the greatest enemy of all—death—and was ushered into the presence of the God he had loved and served for so many years.

Just the year before, at the general conference, his official report had said:

Since the last Conference the *Star* has had the unspeakable joy of

---

[121] WFBS Book 1, Oct. 15, 1866.
[122] *Ibid.*, Jan. 28, 1867.

announcing the most important event of the nineteenth century, viz.: the overthrow and, as we hope in God, the final death of American slavery, for which it has so long and arduously labored, and ardently hoped and prayed, but which at times it has almost despaired of living to see. [123]

Burr had been busy on two fronts. He was helping search for a new pastor and his final report to the society in October was that he was unable to obtain the services of Rev. A. H. Heath. He also had been working on a committee of five men to "take into consideration whether it would not be for the interest of this society to sell their present house of worship and build a new one . . ."[124] The committee was to have reported at the next annual meeting Jan. 7, 1867.

His final day has been described by his biographer and fellow worker at *The Morning Star*, Rev. J. M. Brewster. Also a member of the church, Rev. Brewster described Sunday, Nov. 4, as a beautiful cloudless day of late autumn and said Burr had both prepared and helped serve communion at the second service, it being the first Sabbath of the month.

Brewster says several who saw him at church that day remarked that he seemed even more chipper than usual. After church, he went to his nearby home and spent the afternoon with his daughter and her husband, who had stopped by on their way home to Bangor, Maine.

Then in a long and vivid report Brewster described that evening:

At prayer-meeting in the evening, he was in his accustomed seat, and joined in the exercises, both by prayer and exhortation. In the former he was more than usually fervent. Referring to the future world, he said, — "We have friends there; some of them have passed the river only just before us." With the utterance of these words, his feelings overcame him and he paused, to recover himself in a few moments. In his exhortation, later in the meeting, he referred to the Christian warfare, to which the sermon of the afternoon had special reference, and urged upon Christians the importance of "fighting the good fight of faith." He also spoke of the shortness of time and the importance of improving it. Speaking of his own life, he said that it seemed to him he had accomplished but little, and he desired to renew his consecration, and thereby pledge himself in increased fidelity. In closing, he appealed to the large number of young men present to consecrate themselves to Christ, that they might become useful in his service and thus accomplish the great end of life. He believed that God designed some of them for the ministry. His remarks were a noble testimony for Jesus, and in every

[123] Burr, 127.
[124] WFBS Book 1, April 2, 1866.

way was worthy to be the dying words of such a man and Christian.

A few minutes before eight o'clock, he rose and attempted to remove his overcoat, but sank back upon his seat. Some who had observed that his movements were not entirely natural, went to him and learned that he was sick and wished to retire. It was soon discovered that he had been seized with what might prove to be apoplexy, yet all hoped that the stroke might not be fatal.

He was soon carried by his brethren from the church to his grief-stricken family. He spoke but few words after he was seized, and these with difficulty. On his arrival home he seemed to recognize his wife and daughter, but soon became unconscious. Every means in human power was used for his relief, but to no purpose. He grew worse, and about two o'clock in the morning it became evident that his end was near.

During the hour following, there stood around him his devoted family and a few long-tried but now weeping friends. Angels hovered over that dying scene, and all could not but rejoice in view of the prospects which awaited him who was about to depart to his eternal home.

At three o'clock, his convulsions ceased, and it became apparent that his time had fully come. He breathed easily once or twice, and then his spirit took its departure. The gates of heaven opened widely for its entrance, and there was joy at its advent.[125]

The church clerk recorded the event:

> Dea. Wm. Burr, one of the original members of the church, died of apoplexy after an illness of only seven hours—He was attacked in the Sabbath evening prayer meeting having been as well as usual during the day—and prayed and exhorted in the meeting with more than usual feeling and in a few hours had passed to the better land—In his death the church sustained a very great loss.[126]

The society's records were more business-like, saying only on Dec. 10, 1866, "Meeting was called to order by the Sec., who announced the death of Wm. Burr the late president—and Dea. Daniel Lothrop was chosen president for the evening."

But at its annual meeting, the society adopted a resolution that in part said:

> Whereas it has pleased Almighty God since we last met in annual meeting to summon from among us by death our beloved Brother

---

[125] Burr, 190-194.
[126] DBC, 1:122.

William Burr, who was the instrument in the formation of this society, who has always been its efficient president, had labored most zealously for the interest and has been one of its main pillars of support, therefore

> *Resolved*, that while we greatly miss his wise and judicious counsel, and deeply lament his sudden departure, we will ever cherish in our memories his noble Christian example and the valuable services, and will seek in our future efforts for the welfare of the Society, to perpetuate his spirit and fill the place made vacant by doing individually more to promote the cause in which he was so deeply interested.[127]

In contrast to what had transpired when Burr had fought so hard for the cause of emancipation, it seemed as if the whole city turned out for his funeral. The mayor and other city officials were at the service in the packed Washington Street church.

According to his biographer, stores in downtown Dover closed between 10 a.m. and 3 p.m. and many businessmen attended the funeral. Even some of the newspapers which had lambasted him for his stand on slavery wrote glowingly of his achievements and his life.[128]

He was buried in Pine Hill Cemetery in the same plot in which six of his children had preceded him. His beloved wife Frances would follow in 1895.

ALTHOUGH THE SOCIETY already had decided to study the possibility of constructing its own separate church building, the death of William Burr was an event that seems to have accelerated a gradual loosening of the ties that bound together the Washington Street Freewill Baptist Church and the Freewill Baptist Printing Establishment.

Not that the ties were broken—several church members and pastors and former pastors continued to work at *The Morning Star* until it moved to Boston in 1885.

So 1866 was the beginning of new things for the *Star*, which soon would own and expand the building in which it had shared quarters with the church for 23 years; and for the church and society which soon would have their own building just up the street.

---

[127] WFBS Book 1, Jan. 7, 1867.
[128] Burr, 195, 199

8.
Going it alone

A t a special meeting Sept. 16, 1867, of the Washington Street
Freewill Baptist Society, a committee assigned to study the
possibility of selling the church's interest in its building and
constructing a new one reported it thought the time for such action had
arrived.

After adding a new member to the committee to fill the vacancy left
by the death of church founder William Burr, a resolution was
unanimously adopted that "in view of our present information upon the
subject, it is expedient for this Society to make an immediate and earnest
effort to sell its present house of worship and build a new [one]."[129]

They even went so far as to assign a committee the job of consulting
with architects and builders.

No time was wasted. Just three days later the society met again and
was told that the Freewill Baptist Printing Establishment was willing to
buy the property at a fair price.[130] So without the least delay, the meeting
instructed the committee to offer "the lot of land on which the house sits
on & house to the trustees of the F. W. Baptist Printing Establishment for
forty five hundred dollars, reserving the privilege of taking out the pews
& pulpit, fixtures of the church, or leaving the price to be stated by three
disinterested men . . ."

The Printing Establishment balked at the $4,500 price, offering
$4,000 instead. That seemed acceptable to the society, but since some
persons who owned pews also were involved in ownership of the
building, they were consulted before a final decision was made.

All pew owners present then voted in favor of the move and in a
decision that would mean a great deal to the future of the Washington
Street Freewill Baptist Church and Society, it was resolved "That we

---

[129] WFBS Book 1, Sept. 16, 1867.
[130] *Ibid.*, Sept. 19, 1867.

accept the sum of $4,000 offered this Society from the board of Corporators for the interest this Society owns in this church and land, provided they consent that the Society shall remove the pews and fixings of the church."[131]

Several possibilities for a new church site were discussed at this and subsequent meetings. One suggestion was that a committee see what price the Unitarians would want for their church on Locust Street, a building then standing on what now is the site of the Greek Orthodox Church of the Annunciation. The Unitarians at that time were somewhat in disarray over who should be preaching at their church, but they weren't ready to give up and the committee was told the church was not for sale. There was some early talk of building the church next to the printing establishment, with only a common right-of-way between the buildings, on land then owned by John S. Glass, a local carpenter and builder. The lot already had wooden buildings on it.

After some thought, the society decided it actually would sell its interest in the building only if it felt it could raise enough money to build the new one, adding to its earlier resolution the proviso: "provided we obtain funds sufficient to build a new house."[132]

Raising the money wasn't that easy. The first plan was to solicit funds by voluntary subscription, both from inside and outside the church membership. By the middle of October the committee reported it wasn't making much progress under that plan.

But the committee which had been formed to look into the matter continued on in faith planning for a new church building. The committee divided itself into three areas—soliciting subscriptions, selecting a lot and securing plans and estimates.

After the first 1867 financing plan failed, a new plan sought to sell pews at auction and the committee reported Nov. 4 that it had raised $1,200. Those owning pews in the old building would continue ownership in the new building, though their portion of ownership in the old building would not purchase a whole pew in the new building. The society's records indicate this method brought subscriptions totaling $15,718.90.[133]

At that same Nov. 4 meeting, the society gave final approval to its sale of rights in the old building for $4,000 and ordered the wardens to begin a campaign to raise funds for the new building. Strafford County

---

[131] WFBS Book 1, Sept. 27, 1867.

[132] *Ibid.*, Oct. 18, 1867.

[133] *Ibid.*, Jan. 25, 1868.

records show transfer of the old property was recorded Jan. 28, 1868.[134]

At the annual meeting Jan. 6, 1868, the same one at which the society called Rev. Isaac D. Stewart as the next permanent pastor of Washington Street Freewill Baptist Church, three things were decided: to store the organ and other church furniture pending completion of the new meeting house, find a place to meet while the church was being built, and have the committee find a lot on which to build the new church.

Events moved rapidly. By the next meeting on Jan. 20, the wardens reported that Rev. I. D. Stewart had accepted the call as pastor, the committee reported it had bought the Towle & Dame lot at the corner of Washington and Fayette streets, and action was set in motion to name a building committee of three and designate the powers and duties with which it should be entrusted.

The lot which the committee bought for the new church was owned by Almanzor R. Towle and his wife Emma. The land was part of what had been two lots, one of which Towle purchased on the same day he sold the land to the society. Towle originally owned 88 feet of land along Fayette Street, property he bought from Levi G. Hill in 1866.[135] The lot he purchased from Daniel P. Dame Jan. 16, 1868, abutted the earlier purchase, and it ran an additional 66 feet along Fayette Street.[136] Both lots were 67 feet in depth from Fayette Street.

The lot Towle sold the church was not large. Snuggling up to the western corner of Fayette Street it ran the full width of his land—67 feet—westerly along Washington Street, but to a depth of only 101½ feet of the 154 feet Towle then owned along Fayette.[137] The new church would nearly cover the lot, leaving only seven feet on the west side between the church and land of John B. Stevens, and 16½ feet in the rear. The real estate transaction stipulated that Towle had "the right to enter upon said land to take and remove" the buildings, stone and fence that ran along what had been the boundary between the two lots as long as he did it by the first of April. By the middle of March he had moved the "large dwelling house" from there to Belknap Street next to what had been Folsom's carpet factory, which had burned a few years earlier. It is believed to be the house still standing opposite the intersection of Belknap and St. Thomas streets.

---

[134] Strafford County Records, Bk. 242:407, 441.

[135] *Ibid.*, Bk. 238:431.

[136] *Ibid.*, Bk. 242:377.

[137] *Ibid.*, Bk. 242:395.

The building earlier had been a tavern, according to John B. Stevens, who at the time lived in the house west of the lot bought by the society. In a paper read in 1916 before the Northam Colonists, Dover's historical society, Stevens declared: "On the site of the Free Baptist meeting house was the 'Farmer's Tavern,' not many years ago moved to Belknap street, the final resting place of a good many old houses. Thomas Hough, father of Major Andrew J. Hough, was the landlord. He was very popular. Old men have told me that the meat was excellent, served direct from the grid-iron, and the postprandial [after meal] punch left nothing to be desired."

Stevens also noted that between the tavern and his house was a bowling alley.

Thomas Hough, a transplant from Manchester, England, who originally came to Dover to work in the Cocheco Print Works, died at the old tavern in 1840, according to Stevens. Available records indicate Hough was the proprietor of the tavern, but not necessarily the landlord, since he actually lived on Fifth Street. The 1838 town directory is the only other mention of his operating the tavern, the entry reading: "Thomas Hough, taverner, Washington St."

Real estate records show that James W. Hayes of Barrington bought the land and building in 1834 from Joseph Ham Jr. of Dover. Hayes died and the land was sold in 1842 to Thomas H. Cushing as part of a plan to pay off the debts of Hayes' estate. Cushing sold the land to Levi Hill in 1863, and it was owned by him until Towle bought it in 1866.

Washington Street in 1868 was not the wide and busy street it is today and there were few buildings west of the new church site. It had some gas street lights but was still unpaved, as shown by early pictures of the church. The street had been laid out in the 1830s to make it easier for those traveling from Barrington to Dover via Tolend Road to get to Dover Landing. Earlier, they had to travel across what now is Arch Street to Silver Street before turning toward the center of town.

When James Hayes bought the land in 1834, it was described as "situate in said Dover on the new road leading from the Dover Bank to Tole End Road so called."

A BUILDING committee consisting of Henry A. Chesley, John Mason and Daniel Ham was named at a meeting Jan. 25, 1868, and its instructions were that it was ". . . empowered to erect a house of worship for the society on its lot, under the direction of the executive com., said building committee shall be & hereby are authorized to issue proposals, make contracts, approve bills & draw on the treasurer for money. They shall have full authority to perform all necessary acts in building said house that the executive committee may approve."[138]

By Feb. 3, it was reported that Edward Blaisdell had been hired to draft a plan and make estimates to build a brick meeting house and the building committee was authorized to seek bids on the project. The society was emphatic only in that it definitely wanted a brick meeting house.

The *Gazette* made a more complete report of a Feb. 24 meeting than found in the clerk's notes, stating:

> The Building committee recommended through their chairman, the building of a brick church, which was adopted without a dissenting voice. Proposals are at once to be issued for building, which are to be closed March 20. It was said during the discussion that brick would cost but $2,000 more than wood, and $1,000 had been subscribed conditionally, that the building should be built of brick and it was thought expedient that it should be built of that material. The different styles of contemplated pews was brought to the notice of the meeting— sofa pattern, all black walnut, the other style of chestnut back, with black walnut arms. The whole matter was referred to the building committee."[139]

The bids, duly submitted, were opened March 20.

Several plans were submitted and placed on file, according to the clerk's records of March 23, but those plans have disappeared. The proposals were turned over to the executive committee, which was told the whole matter was in its hands, but again stipulating that ". . . nothing in this resolve should be construed to repeal a former vote of this society to build a brick house of worship."

The clerk's report of the above meeting, which was held at Ham's Hall just down the street, was less complete than the one in the *Gazette,* which was as follows:

> It was voted to build a church of brick 85 by 60 that the executive committee consisting of ten members, be empowered to commence the work at once. The lot on which the handsome building (judging from the plans already drawn), will be built lays on the "sunny side" of Washington at the foot of Atkinson street, and has a front of 67 feet, and is in depth 100½ feet. It is a fine location and the house which will be modern in style, will be a great improvement in that part of the city. The Society deserves great praise in thus subscribing liberally for such a

---

[138] WFBS Book 1, Jan. 25, 1868.
[139] *Gazette,* Feb. 28, 1868.

place of worship in which not only the parishioners may well take pride, but the citizens generally.[140]

The church held its last services in the old building on Jan. 26, 1868. The *Dover Enquirer* colorfully described the events as follows:

> On Sunday morning, Rev. Mr. Day preached an able and impressive sermon, and in the afternoon, Rev. Mr. Stewart, the pastor, gave a very concise and interesting review of the past history of the church, drawing from it lessons of hope and encouragement for the future. The prayer meeting in the evening closed the public religious services in what has for more than twenty years been known as the Washington St. church.[141]

The paper didn't stop there. It related that "[o]n Monday morning early the carpenter's axe and hammer were heard in the building, and before noon everything giving the room the appearance of a church was removed. The work of preparing the premises for the enlargement of the *Morning Star* printing office is being pushed rapidly forward." The Printing Establishment would spend $27,000 to renovate and expand the two-story building to four stories and buy new equipment for the printing business.

Six months later the *Enquirer* reported the outside of the *Star*'s building was finished and was receiving the last touches of paint, and said the building "stands out in all its beauty, an ornament to the city, an honor to the denomination, the admiration of all, and a compliment to the good taste and enterprise of Mr. Burlingame, under whose immediate super-vision the work has been done . . . In addition to two first rate stores, they have one of the best arranged printing offices in the state, a splendid suit of rooms for offices, and above all a light, airy and commodious hall . . ."

With their access to the old building gone, the church and society held meetings at the two Congregational churches in the city, plus with the Charles Street Freewill Baptists, before voting April 13 to begin holding meetings in the brand new city hall across the street from their old building. The city hall had just been rebuilt after a devastating fire. The church clerk's records show that:

> . . . for more than two months, we worshipped with the first Congregational Church on the Sabbath, holding our prayer meetings Sabbath eve with the Charles St. F. B. Church and Friday eve at the

---

[140] *Gazette*, April 3, 1868.
[141] *Enquirer*, Jan. 30, 1868.

Belknap Vestry and then on the Sabbath we went into the City Hall, where we continued until we went into our vestries in our new church the last Sabbath in Dec. 1868.[142]

CONSTRUCTION BEGAN on the new church almost immediately after the final decision was made to go ahead with the project, but little information is included in any church records concerning specifications or decisions on what materials to use. The building committee apparently made most of the decisions and acted as overseers during construction.

It is known that the church originally had no cellar; much of it still has no cellar. The foundation of the four walls and the supports were built on solid blue clay which comes nearly to the surface in the area. The granite foundation sits atop stone footings on the east, west and south sides of the building, but only stone footings set into the clay provide the foundation at the rear. The ground floor beams are just a short distance above the clay in some areas. But the clay has acted as a solid foundation for more than 140 years even though a partial cellar was carved out when furnaces were installed years later.

The local newspapers continued to show an interest in the project, and from time to time contained small items on its progress. The *Gazette* on July 24, 1868, had the following:

> The foundation of the new church on Washington Street of the Freewill Baptist Society was completed last week, and has been exceedingly well done by Daniel Murray, master mason. No better spot so near the heart of the city, and yet outside the din of business, could have been selected by this large and rapidly increasing church for their new forthcoming place of worship . . .

Then the *Enquirer* reported on Aug. 20:

> The work on the New Washington Street church is progressing rapidly, the first story having been completed and the flooring timbers for the audience room put in position—The work is being done in the most substantial manner; and under the direction of the Chesleys as master builders and Aaron Roberts as master mason, the work goes forward as if by magic.

By Dec. 18, the *Gazette* reported: "The Freewill Baptist Church contractors are busily at work finishing the vestry in their new house of worship, to obviate any further occupancy of the City Hall, where the

---

[142] DBC, 1:127.

Society has been holding weekly religious services for the past six months. They propose to occupy it at the earliest practical moment."

Then on Dec. 25 it was announced that the first services would be held two days later in the 57- by 40-foot vestry of the new building, and would continue to be held there until the audience room was complete. It was said that the vestry would seat 400. The *Enquirer* noted that worshippers were surprised when they arrived and found 100 new hymnals inscribed "Washington Street F. B. Vestry, Dover, N.H.," a gift of member John E. Goodwin. The ground floor also included two smaller rooms—another vestry on the northeast side of the building used for prayer meetings, and a ladies parlor in the northwest corner. Both measured 28-by-28 feet. All three rooms were connected by either regular or sliding doors, and until the whole building was complete people used a door on Fayette Street opening into a small entry way with access to both vestries.

The new vestry, which had a ceiling 12 feet high, was put to full use. At the first worship service, the room was packed. The Sabbath School that first week held its annual "tree" as part of the Christmas program. And the temperance society began using the vestry as its main meeting place. Sunday morning, afternoon and evening services were held each week.

CONSTRUCTION WORK slowed during what turned out to be a severe winter, but resumed in the spring. By May 27, 1869, the *Enquirer* could report: "The spire of the new Washington Street church is fast acquiring form and comeliness, in its heavenward aspirations, under the skillful management of 'the Chesleys' who thoroughly understand their business in all its branches, and will doubtless furnish in this a masterpiece of their skill."

By early July, the staging around the steeple was removed, the *Gazette* reporting July 9 that it had been taken down the week before and that when people got a glimpse of the new steeple ". . . our citizens generally agree in its being one of the neatest and best proportioned in town." It then described how someone with powerful field glasses had been atop the staging and reported they were able to see a distance of 35 miles.

By then, workmen were "busily at work on the interior of the edifice, which ere long will be ready for occupancy." We find little in the church records concerning what the main auditorium would look like, with the exception of the placement of the pews and aisles. We get that information from a printed sheet used the following November when the pews were put out to bid.

So again, we have to rely a great deal on newspaper accounts of the dedication of the completed building Oct. 28, 1869. The *Gazette* had reported on the 22nd that the ceremonies would be held at 7:30 p.m. and that "the ladies connected with the parish are busily engaged this week in preparing their new carpet of a unique, pretty pattern, containing about 500 yards. The church is a credit to the society and an ornament to the west end of the city."

When the big day came, for the first time those attending entered through the giant central front doors rather than from Fayette Street. The front doorway was 20 feet high and 9½ feet wide. From a vestibule inside the entrance, there were two doors into the large vestry. Stairs to the right and left, 5½ feet wide, led up to what still was called the "audience room," although in later years it would be decided that "sanctuary" was a better description. The upstairs room covered the entire second story of the building except for a narrow vestibule across the width of the church with three entrances into the room.

That first crowd filled and overflowed the room, the ceiling of which was 24½ feet high. They sat beneath a large central chandelier lighted by gas. A smaller chandelier was beside the organ, which until then had been in storage since being taken out of the old church. Then on either side of the pulpit was "a cluster of burners" to help with the lighting.

There were six sections of pews in the main part of the room. Single rows of pews were against both outside walls of the building. An aisle went the length of the room beside each of those rows. Then toward the center of the room were two double sections of pews, with another aisle between them in the exact center of the room. Additional sections of pews were on either side of the small platform, these facing inward toward the pulpit. A newspaper account when describing the seating capacity as 840, also mentioned that number was "besides the gallery,"[143] presumably meaning there was some sort of balcony. If there was indeed a balcony, it would seem it must have been above the vestibule at the back of the room. No other mention of it has been found.

Furnishings in the audience room included fully cushioned pews. The newspaper described the pulpit as "small, plain and tasty,"[144] presumably meaning tasteful, and it was built of black walnut with chestnut panels.

---

[143] *Enquirer*, Oct. 28, 1869.
[144] *Ibid.*

The pulpit chairs were described as "of walnut, with open and carved backs, and the upholstery is of an entire green color." The floor, as mentioned earlier, was fully carpeted. The woodwork in the whole auditorium was of chestnut, with black walnut trimmings.

Also adding to the decor were a number of frescoes done by P. A. Butler of Boston, who was paid $350 for his trouble.[145]

The building committee itself consisted of 10 persons: Henry C. Chesley, J. C. Hutchins, Daniel Lothrop, Daniel Ham, J. M. Haynes, John Mason, I. D. Stewart, J. E. Goodwin, G. K. Nealley and R. E. Clark, Chesley actually being the agent for the job and who with his brother did the carpenter work. Daniel Murray put in the foundation, Aaron Roberts did the brick work, Morris D. Palmer the plastering and Smith and Laskey the painting.

MAYBE EXCITEMENT over being in their new church building contributed to the event that followed closely on Nov. 2, when the "choice" pews were sold to the highest bidders. Bidding for the choice of a pew did not bring in a lot of money (the two highest bids both were $19). But when a person won the right to a particular pew they also obligated themselves to actually purchase that pew at its assessed value. Although the best seats in the house were assessed at the highest amount, the total assessment of all pews approximated the cost of the new building. Winning ownership of the pew also brought an obligation to help in upkeep of the building. Owners clearly understood they were agreeing to that obligation since the bidding conditions included the statement that "[t]he pews will be sold, subject to such tax or taxes, as the society may, at any time hereafter, at any legal meeting, for that purpose, vote to assess, for the sole purpose, of keeping said church in repair, and insuring the same; which tax or taxes, whenever assessed, shall be apportioned on the pews, according to the appraisal."

One of the highest bids on that first day of bidding was from William Burr's widow, who continued to attend the church until her death in 1895. She obviously didn't like to sit down front and her $19 bid for the privilege of buying pew 123 meant she also had to pay the assessed value of $200 for the pew itself. Its location was nine rows back from the front right against the wall on the Fayette Street side of the church. L. R. Burlingame, who had replaced William Burr at the *Morning Star,* bid $19, too, but the location of his pew is not known. The highest priced pews

---

[145] WFBS Book 1, Jan. 3, 1870.

were next to the center aisle, the 5th through 11th rows back from the front. Each cost $250.

The least expensive seats were a couple of pews against the wall in the back of the auditorium, each assessed at $40.

The location of J. T. S. Libbey's pew is known since the deed he received Nov. 3 from the wardens shows he had paid $200 cash for pew No. 36, located about two-thirds of the way back in the left center section.

The sale of the pews raised about $700 the first day.[146] Additional sales sessions were held, and by Jan. 3 the society treasurer reported that 95 pews had been sold, including 73½ that had been paid for and the deeds delivered, and 21½ for which deeds had not yet been delivered. That left 43 pews, worth $5,890.00, unsold.

But the treasurer reported that the sale of the 95 pews had raised a great deal of the money needed to pay for the new building—$16,800.[147]

At least one pew was purchased by Strafford Bank, where the church now had a $4,000 mortgage. But some pews remained unsold, and it later was decided that the society would try to rent them and funds raised from the rents would go toward mission work, which at that time was called benevolences.

To help raise the additional funds, the wardens were authorized to sell some of the remaining pews at below their assessed value.

THE CHURCH and society rejoiced when the entire building project was finished and came in $2,300 below the estimates of $25,000. The society resolved "That this Society, in view of the marked success which has attended its efforts to erect a house of worship, in view of the skill and fidelity of those who have had immediate charge of the undertaking, and of the unity, the mutual sympathy, and the enterprise that have so generally distinguished its members throughout the entire work, would there gratefully recognize the favor of God and find fresh reasons for encouragement and fidelity in the future."[148]

The names of persons and companies from outside the church who had helped then were listed, including such local companies as Cocheco Mfg. Co., Boston & Maine Railroad and Strafford Bank.

In his final accounting of the whole construction project, building

---

[146] *Enquirer*, Nov. 4, 1869.
[147] WFBS Book 1, Jan. 3, 1870.
[148] *Ibid.*, April 25, 1870.

committee treasurer J. C. Hutchins gave the figures as follows:

Lot	Cost	$4,000.00
Plans and specifications	275.00	
Excavations	140.67	
Foundation	762.00	
Underpinning	230.96	
Hewn stone work	99.00	$1,507.63
Bricks	2,329.77	
Laying the same	2,446.00	
Plastering	441.08	
Frescoing	350.00	$5,506.83
		$11,074.48
Lumber	3,695.71	
Carpenter work	4,827.42	8,523.13
Nails & iron work	724.17	
Rail Road Freight	284.64	
Cartage	292.01	
Gas-piping	72.49	1,473.31
Painting & glazing	987.17	
Tinning the bell deck	78.39	
Vane	65.00	1,130.56
Interest on borrowed money	99.10	
Insurance	75.00	
Enameled cloth	8.25	
Numbers for pews	30.60	
Grading &c. estimated	200.00	
Incidentals	85.57	498.52
TOTAL COST		$22,700.00 [149]

Soon the church would try to improve the neighborhood some more by asking the city if it would put in sidewalks, in front and on the side of the church, even though the streets still were not paved.

The city agreed to put in the curbing and pave the sidewalk in front, either with bricks or with a new pavement with which they had been experimenting—concrete. Sidewalks on Fayette Street came later.

FINANCIAL STRUGGLES did not end with the completion of the new church building, even though its reality seemed such a miraculous victory. Current expenses also had to be met. And it seemed as if there was a constant call for more funds to meet the shortfall. Funds fell $300 short of the money needed to pay the bills in April of 1870. Membership

---

[149] WFBS, Book 1, Jan. 3, 1870.

at the time was just under 300. But as the financial struggles continued, so did the expansion of the church's outreach made possible by the new facilities.

As often occurs following events that have brought growth and blessings, there ensued a time of discouragement when even the pastor called for a revival of interest and participation in the spiritual and social activities of the church. It turned out that the lull was temporary and the church continued to reach out to Dover, surrounding communities and through missions around the world.

9
𝔄lways a 𝔖truggle

An imposing new brick church building now stood on the western edge of downtown Dover. With the new building came new opportunities for the Washington Street congregation. There also were new struggles, some financial, some otherwise.

With the new facilities, the church was able to increase its outreach to the community. That resulted in increased costs. By the time the society's treasurer made his report on Jan. 1, 1869, it was noted that cash on hand amounted to only $1.94. Needed by April just to pay the pastor, Rev. I. D. Stewart, was $575. If everyone who had pledged an amount toward the budget paid up, the church still would be $200 short of what was needed.

It was voted to take an extra collection every two weeks to help make up the difference.

It was a time also of great confusion as several of the old-timers died. In early 1871, with everything else that was going on, someone somehow lost the records of the Society's annual meeting. There had been a gap of about nine months in the clerk's entries. So six members of the society went to court to have a judge order that the meeting be held once again.

There also seemed to be some hard feelings when long-time organist Asa H. Littlefield was replaced by Carrie Gray.

CHURCH MEMBERSHIP began to change. New members came from other communities as the population of Dover shifted. Many of those who had worked for years in the mills were being shifted to factories in other cities—especially other manufacturing towns like Haverhill and Lawrence, Mass., and Manchester, N.H.

Others were following Horace Greeley's admonition to go West.

But membership in the church and society remained fairly stable. By 1871, there still were just under 300 church members, and about one-third of them were listed as non-resident. Many who removed to other towns for work never moved their membership and were listed as non-resident members. Non-residents were not counted when the church paid its annual dues to the state society.

Some things didn't change at all. The church still was dealing with reports "unfavorable to the Christian character" of members. In 1872, committees were set up to deal with Bros. Daniel Emerson and Henry Meserve, both reportedly imbibing a little too much. One quit, claiming the church was trying to get rid of him; the other was given a second chance.[150]

Henry Lothrop was quickly dropped when he ended up in police court after a Sunday evening drunken brawl and gambling event. That came only a couple of months after he was given a second chance following an admission that he had played billiards and danced, and promised not to do it again.[151]

Asenath Caverly was expelled when it was learned she was living with a man without benefit of marriage.[152]

In addition to having to deal with such matters, for the first time the church records show it also still was dealing with "unpleasant feeling existing among members of the church." The exact problem was not spelled out, but it must have proved hurtful because in his annual report in May of 1873, Rev. Stewart noted that things were not going well:

"The labors of the past year have been continued thro' hope & fears, the use of means has been regular & consistent, but the results have been less than our hopes. The changes have been less marked than in some former years, & in some respects the trials have been greater."

He continued:

"It is sad, painfully so, that members of the church absent themselves from the prayer meetings almost as regularly as the weeks pass by. Perhaps a change in the pastorate would bring relief to some of this class."

By that time, the membership had decreased, partly because a committee had reviewed the membership and dropped those names where the persons were no longer known. Total membership was 243, and 73 of those still were listed as "non-resident."

Rev. Stewart first tendered his resignation to the Society in a communication April 5, 1873, but the Society declined to accept it. It

[150] DBC, 1:137-38.
[151] *Ibid.*, 142.
[152] *Ibid.*, 141.

voted instead, on April 21, to ask him to reconsider. The vote was not unanimous, though, nine voting in the negative. But those nine then adopted their own resolution, declaring that in the name of unity they would change their vote so that the request to reconsider would be unanimous, 25-0. [153]

Rev. Stewart, in his wisdom, declined, issuing the following communication:

> Gentlemen: Your committee appointed to confer with me on the withdrawal of my resignation have presented me with a copy of the resolutions adopted by the Society, and the one adopted by the minority. These resolutions have been carefully considered in connection with the whole subject as I understand it.
>
> You ask me to withdraw my resignation. I thank the Society for this additional expression of confidence, and desire only to do what may be for the best. Just before the adjourned meeting of the Society, early in April, it was stated in a meeting of the Official Board of the church, that some of those desiring a change to the pastorate claimed that more than one half of the church and Society desired it, and one of them said that he believed that two thirds would vote for it. I was also told by three different persons that they understood from some of them anxious for a change, that the desire had ripened into a purpose, and that the effort would probably be made at the Society meeting to effect it. Under these circumstances, to save the church, Society and myself from such a contest, my resignation was presented.
>
> Instead of accepting it, as I expected it would be, you have taken counsel of the church, and now ask me to withdraw it. I acknowledge my obligations to respect the wishes of a majority of the church and Society, as well as the wishes of a minority. I would not grieve or alienate either, but I cannot please both.
>
> With the facts before me that there is a desire for my removal, a desire that has been privately and openly urged by a few, and is much prominent in the very paper that promises cooperation if I remain, indeed, that paper begins by saying "We, the minority of the Washington Street Society cannot agree with the majority in requesting Rev. I. D. Stewart to withdraw his resignation" — with these facts before me I cannot avoid the fear that this oft repeated and continual design for a change, would so develop itself, as to make it exceedingly embarrassing for me, and it would be likely to be both unpleasant and unprofitable for both church and Society — For these reasons I do not see my way clear to comply with your request. [154]

---

[153] WFBS Book 1, April 7-May 7, 1873.
[154] *Ibid.*, May 7, 1873.

When Stewart later tendered his resignation to the church body, acceptance of it was put off when not enough members could be gathered together for the monthly meeting. It was decided to take it up the next Sunday when more members would be present, and on Sept. 5, 1873, the church released him from the pastorate, but also adopted a resolution indicating it had complete confidence in his integrity and faithfulness.

After resigning, Rev. I. D. Stewart never left the church. He remained a member for the rest of his life, and served faithfully in various capacities. He died 14 years later on June 7, 1887. During those years, he worked at the *Morning Star*, part of the time as editor.

Following the disruptive days that brought an end to Stewart's pastorate, the subject of a new pastor languished a few months until in December five members of the society petitioned for a meeting to take up the matter of "settlement of a pastor." The meeting was held but no action was taken. For nearly a year there was no pastor and the annual budget's largest single item was for "pulpit supply."

When action finally was taken, the first candidate, Rev. DeWitt Clinton Durgin of Newmarket, refused. Some correspondence was undertaken with a Rev. Bickford of Lewiston, Maine, and Rev. Granville C. Waterman of Lowville, N.Y., and finally the pastorate was offered to Rev. Waterman. He accepted, and commenced his pastorate the first Sunday in July 1874.

Rev. Waterman was born in Booth Bay, Maine, May 4, 1835, the son of a Freewill Baptist minister. He was educated at Litchfield Liberal Institute in Litchfield, Maine, and at Bowdoin College, and was ordained in 1869. Dover was only his second pastorate, and from Dover he went to Laconia.[155]

Rev. Waterman tendered his resignation to the Society in September 1879, leaving it up in the air as to when it would take effect, suggesting a meeting with the wardens to discuss the matter. He declined to state his reason for leaving. But for some reason he announced to the church Oct. 3 that his resignation would take effect immediately, and the Society was again left with the task of finding a new pastor.

His had been a successful ministry in that it drew 47 new members into the fold, but in the end the removal of old members had left the church membership about the same as when he arrived in Dover.

But Rev. Waterman was back in Dover by 1881, when both his family and his father became members of the Washington Street church.

---

[155] FBC, 681.

Granville was working at that time at the *Morning Star* office, in charge of the denomination's Sunday School quarterlies. He also for a time was president of the Washington Street Freewill Baptist Society. Then in 1886 he took a pastorate in Littleton, N.H., and his father soon after took a pastorate in Carroll, N.H., ending their connections with the Dover church.

For a few months, the pulpit was filled by the Revs. Owen, Rev. O. T. Moulton and Rev. Frank K. Chase. By the first week in January 1880, Rev. Chase had agreed to become interim pastor at least until April. The church voted officially on Jan. 2 to ask him to be pastor, and in a letter dated Jan. 10, he accepted. But for some reason the Society never changed Chase's status, and it was noted in the Society records April 4, 1881, that he still was being paid as interim pastor, even though he had officially joined the church Jan. 24, 1880, from the Freewill Baptist Church in West Buxton, Maine; joined the Society April 5.

Rev. Frank K. Chase was born in Lawrence, Mass., Sept. 3, 1848, son of Stephen J. and Caroline E. (Kimball) Chase. He studied at New Hampton four years, and also at Andover, Mass., an additional three years. He was licensed to preach in 1875 and ordained at West Buxton two years later.[156]

His arrival in Dover began a time of renewed interest and growth in the church. With the membership having dwindled to just over 240, Rev. Chase began the demanding job of bringing renewed unity to the members of the church and reaching out to the community as a whole. His yearly reports recounted the hundreds of calls he made in the community, including with Christians from other local churches. He even took on the task of raising the final amount of money needed to pay off the church debt.

In the long run, the demands he placed on himself began to wear on his health, and before he left Dover he had spent many weeks absent because of sickness.

But the church was looking forward to a promising future during the first years of what would be a long ministry by Frank K. Chase. Membership again was beginning to grow, the debt had been quickly paid off on the new church building, and the future looked prosperous.

No one could have foreseen what would come next.

---

[156] FBC, 111

10.
Tragedy and passing the test

O n April 3, 1882, the pastor reported the last payment had been made on the debt of the Washington Street Freewill Baptist Church. Membership was growing. The future looked bright.

Rev. Frank K. Chase said he often stood on Washington Street across from the church and looked over at the beautiful red-brick building. He saw nothing but great days ahead.

Some time later, he wrote:

Again and again as I have passed our beautiful church home in the evening, I have stood and looked upward to the tall spire lifting its summit gracefully toward the shining stars, and my own heart has been thrilled with tender emotions, and tears of thankfulness have come all unbidden to my eyes. We had assured ourselves that now, after a long struggle, we had reached a place where, unhindered by any financial embarrassments, we could engage more earnestly in that work which lies so near all our hearts,— the gathering in and saving of those about us, and we were glad. There was a song of joy and thanksgiving in our hearts and upon our lips. How little we knew what was before us. [157]

What was before the church would test the very resolve of its members.

It was Tuesday, May 2, 1882. Many people already were at work in the factories and the nearby downtown area of Dover. The time was 7:40 a.m. and there was a good breeze blowing from the west.

Suddenly, workers on the first floor of Lewis Laskey's brush factory to the rear and left of the church noticed that brushes hanging from the ceiling had begun to drop from their places. Checking for the cause, it was discovered that the entire attic was ablaze.

The fire spread fast.

Within minutes, the dwelling directly behind the church was ablaze.

---

[157] Sermon at Belknap Church, May 7, 1882 (See Appendix G)

Soon after, flames spread to the church. What followed was described by the *Dover Enquirer*:

> . . . flames were discovered issuing from under the eaves of the church, and soon had spread to its roof, a large portion of which was almost instantly ablaze. The whole upper story of the structure, including the tower, was one unbroken sheet of flame. The fire in the church continued steadily to burn and increase in magnitude, the tower being completely enveloped in flames, which were now burning with increased fury, while above their roar and crackling was heard the crash and boom of the upper floor as it descended to the one beneath with a terrific report. The fuel thus added caused the flames to shoot high in the air, the tower began to show the effects of the suddenly increased heat and swayed perceptibly. The boards began dropping from its sides until the bare frame of the tower and steeple were all that could be seen, and this gradually weakened and finally tottered over into the flames which filled the interior of the church where it fell with a heavy crash.[158]

Within a short time, the church building was nothing but a shell, even though all four walls—minus the steeple—were still standing. The fire had been so fierce that several houses, some as far away as Second Street on the other side of the Cochecho River, were in danger of being set on fire by the embers.

If the church records were in the building, someone saved them. They still are in existence. "We saved all we could," explained Rev. Chase, "and then we stood looking on with heavy hearts and tearful eyes."[159] He and those members who watched were stunned. It was only a couple of weeks after the final payment was made on the debt incurred when the church was built in 1868.

But the church building was not the only loss that day.

Curiosity got the best of people, as it often does. They began to visit the ruins, some even going inside the burned-out hulk to see for themselves the extent of the damage. Suddenly, about 4 p.m., the rear gable wall and two chimneys crashed down with a roar inside the ruined church.

It came down as several persons gazed up at the damage done by the morning fire. With it came a small portion of the upper floor that had been clinging to the wall.

---

[158] *Enquirer*, May 4, 1881
[159] (See sermon, Appendix G).

The *Portsmouth Journal* described the scene:

> An alarm was at once given, and hundreds of citizens rushed to the aid of the sufferers. Four persons were taken from the debris in a badly mangled condition, but not dead. Their names were Mrs. Whitney, Mrs. Stewart Clifford, J. H. Burleigh and a lad named Peters. When found, they were with difficulty distinguished from the ruins beneath which they fell, and from which they were with great difficulty extricated.[160]

The *Dover Enquirer* reported:

> Among the severely injured were Mrs. Stuart Clifford, residing on Washington street, who had a leg broken, and was badly injured otherwise.
>
> Mrs. Jed Whitney, who had a leg broken and also one arm, and was otherwise jammed, cut and bruised.
>
> Job H. Burleigh, blacksmith, on Locust street, who was badly jammed, but had no bones broken.
>
> A Dominique lad, employed by G. W. Tash, was injured on the head and leg, but was able to walk away. The injured were with difficulty got out from under the debris, and removed to their homes, where the best of treatment was provided, and this morning seemed better, although some of them are not out of danger.[161]

All felt thankful that those pulled from the debris were not badly hurt. But by night the joy had turned to horror when an anxious family reported that Judge John R. Varney, editor of the weekly *Enquirer* and the *Daily Republican*, had not been seen since noon. The boy who had been pulled from the ruins offered a description of a man who had been at the site that afternoon, and the search began.

Reported the *Dover Enquirer*:

> At first no one supposed Mr. Varney to be in the building at the time of the crash, and no efforts were made to find him. As he did not go home to tea at the usual hour, his daughter came down town to learn the cause. The door of his office was locked, but he could not be found. Upon this being known inquiries were raised, and it was soon learned that he had been seen in the church about the time of the crash. The Dominique lad was interviewed, and he described Mr. Varney so accurately, although not knowing his name, that search among the ruins was at once instituted, under the direction of Mayor Murphy. Many willing hands, some unused to such work, volunteered to help

---

[160] *Portsmouth Journal*, May 6, 1882
[161] *Enquirer*, May 4, 1882

remove the blackened timbers and rubbish, and at 11 o'clock the body was found prostrated upon the face, with a large stick of timber lengthwise upon it, and above this several feet of rubbish. He was taken up and carried to the court room, and delivered to the care of John A. Glidden, who prepared the remains to be taken to his late residence, which was done this morning. Coroner Pray was called, but deemed an inquest unnecessary. From the position in which he was found, and other circumstances, it is evident he must have died instantly.[162]

And from the *Portsmouth Journal*:

Mayor Murphy ordered a strict search to be made by the police, who in about an hour came upon the body of the unfortunate man at the entrance of the small vestry. The body was lying upon its face, which was mangled beyond recognition, and was with great difficulty removed from between two timbers. [163]

Rev. Chase, present during the search, reported: ". . . at length the word passed from one to another, 'We have found him.' And there he lay—in our room of prayer, on our night of prayer, on the very spot where some of us have bowed in prayer—there he lay, himself a man of prayer. And when at length we raised the great, noble form, still now in the silence of death, raised him and bore him forth, is it any wonder that strong men looked upon that pale, death-stricken face, and wept like children?"[164]

The tragedy even made the papers in New York, the *New York Post* reporting, in part:

DOVER, N.H., May 3 — Yesterday afternoon while a number of persons were standing near the Washington Street Baptist church, which had been burned in the morning, the walls fell, burying five persons in the ruins and injuring five severely, killing one outright . . ."

The loss of Mr. Varney was felt throughout the city. For years, he had been one of the leading men in city, county, judicial and political arenas, as well as editor of two of the city's major newspapers. At one time, he was a partner with John P. Hale, Dover's famed anti-slavery U.S. senator. Area leaders along with ordinary citizens packed the First Parish Congregational Church when his funeral was held a few days after the fire.

---

[162] *Enquirer,* May 4, 1882.
[163] *Portsmouth Journal,* May 6, 1882
[164] (See sermon, Appendix G).

The exact cause of the fire never was found. Some thought it was from spontaneous combustion, but the brush factory operator claimed no combustible material was near the place where the flames broke out. The factory was owned by John B. Stevens Sr., an official with the Cocheco Manufacturing Co., who lived in his house next door to the church on Washington Street. This is the same house the Stevens family sold to the church in the 1920s for future expansion of church facilities.

The loss to the church was great. The *Enquirer* published the following figures on damage and insurance:

> The church, which is partially destroyed, was built in 1870 at a cost of $23,000, the last installment on the church debt having been paid within the past fortnight. The building was insured for six thousand dollars, half of which was placed with the Royal, of which Geo. B. Prescott is agent, and the balance with the Fire Insurance Co. of Philadelphia, H. A. Redfield, agent. The insurance was apportioned as follows: church $5,000, organ $500, furniture and fixtures $500, but it is thought the total loss will be $12,000.[165]

The church clerk simply noted that "our meeting house was burned together with the organ. Insurance on the whole six thousand dollars."[166]

The devastation left the Washington Street Freewill Baptists without a home. Almost all the churches in town immediately offered their facilities. The Belknap Congregational Church was chosen, it being without a pastor and not holding regular services at the time, and by the next Sunday, only five days after the fire, the Baptists held services at that church on Central Square. Rev. Chase preached a sermon from 1 Kings, 19, giving examples of Elijah and others who had pressed on during terrible times of adversity.

"There is a work for us to do in the direction of repairing our beautiful church," he told the grieving members. "It means toil; it means sacrifice on the part of all, but it can, it will, be done. I consider it a marvelous thing—but I have not met with one single man or woman who has expressed an accent of doubt in regard to that, and as I look into your faces, saddened, it is true, by the memories of the past, I read there only one sentiment; and that is that each and all of us are ready to work and sacrifice as we never have before, if need be, that once again we may have a church home of our own."[167]

---

[165] *Enquirer*, May 4, 1882
[166] DBC, 1:169.
[167] (See sermon, Appendix G).

And he added, "With the blessing of God not many months shall pass before that church shall rise remodeled, improved, a beautiful house for a glad-hearted and thankful people."

But, he warned, "The next few months will test our strength as a church, the strength of our Christian courage, as they were never tested before. By the grace of God, who is our strength, we shall not fail; and this Christian community shall see that our heroism is of that kind which bears the banner aloft even amid the thickest of the fight, a courage which knows no such word as defeat."[168]

He shouldn't have worried. The church and society members already had met at the First Parish Church chapel to discuss the future of the Washington Street building. The clerk simply wrote: "Decided to rebuild."[169]

But the actual decision to rebuild had to come from the Society. The Society met the day after the fire and appointed a committee to look into rebuilding the structure. On May 16, a meeting was held at city hall, and it was reported that the debris from the fire had been removed from the hollow shell of the church and half of the insurance already had been paid, the rest to come in 60 days. Total insurance paid was $5,000 on the building, $500 on the organ, and $400 for furnishings.[170]

The committee appointed to look into rebuilding the church reported at this meeting that plans and projected costs already were in hand, only 14 days after the fire. The cost was set at about $11,000. No time was wasted. The clerk reported "that it was in the interests of the Society to have a meeting house, and a unanimous vote was passed to rebuild the meeting house as soon as practicable."[171]

By the next meeting on May 22, architect Charles E. Joy's plan for rebuilding was chosen and a committee of seven was named to oversee the project, with specific instructions that it "shall not exceed eleven thousand dollars . . ."[172]

By June 29, the committee reported it had awarded the contract for rebuilding to Beede & Shaw, local builders, for $8,500. The amount included all except frescoing, gas fixtures, pews and the organ.[173]

On Nov. 13, a committee appointed to buy a new organ reported it

---

[168] (See sermon, Appendix G).

[169] DBC, 1:169.

[170] WFBS, 2:47.

[171] *Ibid.*

[172] *Ibid.*, 2:50.

[173] *Ibid.* 2:53.

had obtained one for $1,300, and it would be installed by the first of January 1883.[174]

At the same meeting, the building committee was instructed to obtain plans and costs for frescoing the "audience room." It reported at the next meeting that both the auditorium and vestries could be frescoed for $400. The committee got the go-ahead.

It seemed as if all was going splendidly. But amidst all the progress toward rebuilding there appeared a dilemma. It must be remembered that the pews in the destroyed church were owned by individuals who paid what amounted to taxes on their property for upkeep of the church. Were they entitled to some of the insurance money paid after the fire? Some said they were; others said no. The Society tried to solve the problem by offering to take on the responsibility of upkeep if the pew owners would give up ownership. Some agreed; others did not.

There also was discussion as to whether the Society might rent pews.

In the end, it was impossible to come to an agreement and a request was made to Judge Jeremiah Smith to rule on the best way to solve the problem.

The following decision, a surprise it seems to everyone, came on March 3, 1883:

> My understanding is that your church was substantially destroyed last May, and that what the Society has since done is to build a new church, not to repair an old church.
>
> Assuming this to be so, I am of opinion that no pew holder in the old church has, as such, any right in the new church. When the old church was substantially destroyed by fire, the pew holder's right ceased. He had no ownership in the ruins, nor in the insurance money.
>
> The Society owns the new church, and can sell pews, rent pews or make it a free church, just as they please.
>
> Should the Society conclude to sell the pews at an appraisal, it might be desirable (to save all chance of legal controversy) to appraise the house and pews at the cost of rebuilding over and above the insurance, viz. if the new church cost $20,000 and $5,000 of this was paid from insurance, appraise the pews on the basis of $15,000.
>
> Respectfully,
> Jeremiah Smith[175]

That settled it. The Society decided it would rent the pews in the rebuilt church. But no, it reversed itself again and decided to sell them,

---

[174] WFBS, 2:58.
[175] *Ibid.*, 2:71.

with the owners of pews in the old church given first choice in buying the new ones, with the price being 10 times the price it would have gotten for annual rental. Pews not sold would be rented by the Society. It wasn't until 1895 that the Society decided the best way to raise money for property upkeep and salaries was a weekly offering. The days when people owned or rented pews was over, and from then on the Washington Street church was known as a "free church."

THE NEW structure would not take on the exact shape of the original. Most noticeable was that the tall spire on the original structure would be replaced by a lower tower on the east side of the building rather than in the center. Gone were the huge center doors at the front of the church, to be replaced by smaller double doors on the east and west sides of the front.

But some of the original designs remain to this day. The walls between the ground and the auditorium level remain. The first floor side windows are the same. Above these windows is an ornamental ridge of bricks, above which the rebuilding of the outside walls took place. The telltale evidence of this is in the slightly different color of the bricks above the ridge, especially on the west side of the building.

The brickwork in the front corners of the building was not destroyed in the fire and is retained to this day with its original indentations and designs. But there are stained-glass windows and a large rose window replacing the original entrance design and window in the center of the building.

Much of the lower floor was rebuilt as it was in the original building, with the exception of the front entrances.

The auditorium and roof designs were completely different, as were the entrances on each side. A raised section of seats at the rear of the auditorium replaced the original vestibule. The design of the auditorium was greatly altered, the original being one large section. The new design is of a large high central section, with lower sections on each side. The new design is of arches and columns, dividing the room into three sections. The main roof is held aloft by giant gothic arches of natural wood. Four lower arches along each side of the main section of the auditorium, separated by thick Corinthian columns, provide support for the main roof and arches, plus the lower, flatter roof of the side sections.

Aisles on the sides of the main section, as well as outer aisles against the east and west walls, replaced the three interior aisles which had been in the original building.

As the rebuilding progressed, some changes were made, boosting the costs a few hundred dollars. One of the changes, apparently, was to excavate a section of cellar beneath the building. This was authorized in anticipation of placing furnaces under the building, which before the fire had been heated by stoves.[176]

Because of the questionable status of the pews, assessments could not be made in the regular manner, so the Society voted to mortgage the church property to the tune of $3,600 to finish paying the reconstruction costs.[177]

Interestingly, there never was mention of some important items in the new building. No mention is made of installing the many stained-glass windows. There is no mention of the huge rose window, with its centerpiece of an open Bible, which graces the front of the church. Despite all the talk about ownership of the pews, there is no mention of the pews being installed, although apparently they were included as "furniture" in the final report of the building committee. They hadn't been included in the building contract. We do find in the building committee's final report that the Ladies Circle provided $250 for installation of gas fixtures.[178]

SOME QUESTION as to the quality of the brickwork seems to have cropped up during re-construction. The Society wanted to withhold the final $1,000 until it was found that the brickwork was acceptable. Beede & Shaw wanted the money put in a savings account so it could accrue interest while the matter was being negotiated. The Society finally authorized appointment of a referee to decide the question.[179] The result is not stated, but the building committee was given a rousing vote of thanks on Jan. 7, 1884, for a job done well and with discretion.

The final report of the building committee showed the cost to be $14,188.02, with all bills paid. But the church was left with that $3,600 mortgage with Dover Five Cents Savings Bank.[180]

Whether intentional or not, positive evidence of the fire remains in the building today. About halfway up the present tower is a section of charred woodwork from the conflagration. It still clings to the inside of the front wall retained from the original building. Beside the creaky tower

---

[176] WFBS, 2:54-55.

[177] *Ibid.,* 2:79

[178] *Ibid.,* 2:83.

[179] *Ibid.,* 2:65.

[180] *Ibid.,* 2:84.

stairs, it is a grim reminder of what occurred on that fateful Tuesday morning in 1882.

11.
Community outreach

With the dedication of the rebuilt church in 1884, the society again was faced with debt. The Dover Five Cents Savings Bank owned a piece of the church building—at least temporarily—having loaned the Society $3,600.

The society never had been awash in money, and annual costs always were on the minds of church and society leaders. On May 4, they got a report from the society treasurer for the year ending March 31, 1884. He reported receipts of $1,575.59 and expenditures of $1,574.79, leaving a mere 80 cents in the hands of the treasurer.

By January 1885, the treasurer reported that a $457 shortfall was facing the society. A committee was appointed to raise the balance, reporting only a short time later that all but $40 had been raised. The committee was asked to devise some plan under which the society would "not be obliged to raise a balance every year as we have had to do for several years."[181]

Then came a move that eventually would phase out pew ownership and rental. The committee recommended that the society institute a weekly pledge system of paying church expenses, a system that would give a general idea of the income for each year. The system was instituted. By the time the treasurer gave his report for the next year, the results were deemed favorable and the system was adopted permanently and was used with some variations for many years.[182]

Although there never was an excess of money in subsequent years, the ending balance through most of the years leading up to the turn of the century showed a small balance.

The bank, however, did have to remind the church in 1895 that it had

---

[181] WFBS, 2:94.
[182] *Ibid.*, 2:103

missed a payment on its indebtedness. Its straightforward notice in March said simply: "Your note for ($264) two hundred and sixty four dollars was due Jan. 2, '95. Please pay this."[183]

Enthusiasm for eliminating the debt gradually grew. A committee was appointed to devise ways the society could become debt-free. Even Sunday School children participated, with each child receiving a certificate when he or she gave as much as $1 toward retiring the debt.[184] Two bequests, one from Robert Christie for $1,000,[185] and another from long-time member Mrs. Abra Caverly for $300,[186] gave the impetus to pay off the debt, and went a long way toward the goal. Robert Christie never was a member of the church, although financial reports show he had given money for several years before his death. Mrs. Caverly had joined the church way back on March 20, 1841, little more than a year after it was organized. A push to pay off the rest of the debt resulted in a payment of $2739.20, and by Dec. 31, 1893 it had been reduced to $400.[187]

On Jan. 27, 1896, society Treasurer Charles L. Ricker reported "the note against the society had been paid."[188] It was time for a celebration and a committee was named to begin plans for it.

On Feb. 12, the doors of the church were thrown open for one of the greatest celebrations any of the members could remember.

The new pastor, Rev. R. E. Gilkey, was there. And Rev. Chase, pastor when the church burned and instrumental in re-building the church and its membership, was there to be a part of the joyous occasion.

Vienna Hill gave a history of the church. She told how discouraged the people had been at first, including the pastor, when they saw the ruins. But that didn't last, she said, when:

> Very soon after the loss the heart of the pastor was greatly encouraged by receiving a silver dollar, all that a child of 12 years possessed, enclosed in an encouraging letter, looking towards the building of a new church home.[189]

The long program neared an end when Florence V. Steeves stepped

---

[183] WFBS, 2:172
[184] *Ibid.*, 2:157.
[185] *Ibid.*, 2:135.
[186] *Ibid.*, 2:188.
[187] *Ibid.*, 2:155.
[188] *Ibid.*, 2:190.
[189] *Foster's*, Feb. 13, 1896.

forward and, laying the mortgage on a large tray, gave a humorous speech as she consigned it to the flames.

Said she:

> Mortgage, Oh Mortgage, we have nothing but bonds of kindness and love for you tonight. What a blessing you have been these many years. You are an instrument of high repute and have been of great value to us. On your authority, at your command money has come to us to make it possible to complete this beautiful edifice which we can now call our own church, our Sunday home. How bravely you have stood the test of time never for a moment faltering, never flinching, but ever and always you have stood at your post.
>
> But mortgage, our kind Father has given us the money to pay the indebtedness for which you have so long stood, in short we have no further use of your service. We appreciate the mission you have filled, and lest you should fall into the hands of someone who would deal harshly with you to me has been committed the task of consigning you to the flames. Your ashes will be carefully preserved and let us hope that unborn generations will rise and call you blessed.[190]

As the mortgage burned, the congregation sang "Blessed Be the Tie that Binds." After which, continued a newspaper account, "Rev. F. K. Chase pronounced the benediction and all went away delighted that the church was free from debt."

Perhaps the above ceremony is why the church has no original copy of the mortgage in its records.

It was announced during the program that all pews in the church had now been "emancipated" and were free to all. It had been suggested two weeks earlier that the name of the church be changed from Washington Street Freewill Baptist Church to Washington Street Free Baptist Church. But the clerk noted at the next meeting, Feb. 28, that "no action was taken on the proposed change of name." No further mention ever was made about any such action, but it was usually called the Free Baptist Church in its own and other records.

By 1898, the church had voted to approve the proposed constitution and by-laws of the Rockingham Association of Free Baptist Churches, the new name of the denomination's regional association. The Washington Street society kept its Freewill designation until it disbanded on March 21, 1911. The society never even discussed the name change.

One of those mysteries that defy solution crops up in the church

---

[190] *Foster's,* Feb. 13, 1896.

records in September 1894. It was reported that a man named Abner Moses of Wisconsin had died in 1871 and left all his property to the church. The report was that the administrator "by alleged fraud" had disposed of the property without even notifying the Dover church.[191] There is no indication as to how the church received this information.

A committee reported dealings with an Atty. Buckner in Wisconsin in an attempt to find out what had happened to the Moses property, but in 1895 the lawyer was paid $35 for his trouble, a letter from him was placed on file, and the matter dropped.[192] The letter, of course, now is nowhere to be found.

A search of Wisconsin records indeed shows that a man with that name, who died in 1871 in Grant County, left a will in which he wrote: "My past debts being paid, I do hereby devise and bequeath all of my property personal & real, of which I may be seized or be possessed, or be in any way entitled to, whether such estate real or personal be in the State of Wisconsin or elsewhere, or whether I am possessed or seized of the same at this time, or at any time hereafter; all such real and personal estate I do hereby devise & bequeath to "The Washington Street Freewill Baptist Society of Dover, New Hampshire"; said society and corporation to own, possess & enjoy said real & personal estate, subject to my debts if any, to them, their successors and assigns forever."

There is no indication that the man had any connection with the Dover church. The only possible hint of a connection is that he named Joseph T. Mills as his executor. There was a man and wife named Mills—but no Joseph Mills—who had been members of the Washington Street church years earlier. No record of probate for the man's estate is found in Grant County, so the mystery of who the man was and what happened to his estate remains just that—a mystery.

Another mystery appeared in 1874, when it was noted that the society had procured a $100 scholarship (No. 210) at Hillsdale College in Hillsdale, Michigan, which one student from Dover could use at any given time. At the time, the college was operated by Freewill Baptists. And in fact several of Dover Baptist's early pastors trained at Hillsdale. But no subsequent record indicates the scholarship ever was used.

A check with the college in 2003, brought the following response from Linda Moore, public services librarian at the college: ". . . regarding the history of the perpetual scholarships. They were

---

[191] WFBS, 2:159-160.
[192] *Ibid.*, 2:174.

issued at a time when the major source of college revenues were fees and not tuition. We think it unlikely that anyone used the scholarship. Several years ago, the board of trustees passed a resolution that these scholarships were not to be recognized any longer."

THE SUGGESTION to make all pews "free" in the church had been made at a society meeting Dec. 4, 1895[193]; then at a meeting Dec. 11, it was made official that ". . . we discontinue our present pew rental system and raise our money by weekly offerings."[194]

But the church would not remain debt-free for very long. By Oct. 20, 1896, discussion began on the possibility of building a church parsonage. By December, a parsonage building fund had been started.

The late 19th century was a time during which the church operation was modernized and expanded. Besides the new, simplified, method of raising money by the use of annual pledges, there began a more organized method of funding missions and other projects. But still there was no fixed budget for the year. The Sunday School, which although connected with the church was not an actual church organization, was made an official function of the church so the church not only could elect those to run it but also be responsible for its welfare. After all, there often were more people on the Sunday School rolls than on the church rolls.

One event noted in the records was that on Sept. 30, 1883, the Rev. Chase used the new baptistry for the first time. In the rebuilt church, it was located in the floor of the platform. No longer would the church have to cut through the ice of the Cochecho River for baptismal rites.[195]

Many societies were formed for various groups and reasons. The Hills Home and Missionary Society, later the Hills-Garland Missionary Society, was formed in January 1895, a tribute to Mrs. Marilla (Turner) Marks Hutchins Hills, a long-time missions advocate and widow of the church's fourth pastor, Elias Hutchins. Still alive in 1895, she would live until Nov. 28, 1901. Five years before the mission society was formed, the young adults of the church formed the Advocates of Christian Fidelity, which later had a junior society and took on special needs of the church (such as a new furnace) and various other projects, mostly educational. This eventually became known as Young People's Society of Christian Endeavor and continued well into the 20th century, as did the Hills-Garland Missionary Society.

---

[193] WFBS, 2:183.
[194] *Ibid.*, 184.
[195] DBC, 1:173.

Then, and during the next few years, there were the Young People's Union, the Ladies Circle, the Young Men's Christian Society, the Women's Missionary Auxiliary, the Young Men's Christian Association, the A.M.S. Club, the Men's League, the Ladies Aid Society, the King's Daughters, the Lend-a-Hand Class, the Friendship Class; there was a Boys Orchestra and Boy Scouts, and others. There also were outside organizations that met at the church, including temperance societies, in which many of the church members and pastors were involved.

But a significant change through the 1880s and 1890s came with a growing realization of the importance of prayer in the life of the church, something which seems earlier to have been neglected to some extent. When first organized, members often met several times a week for prayer. Now, the church noted that the young people had, on their own, begun a weekly Friday night prayer service. So the church voted to make it an official church meeting for the young each Friday, except for the night when the church held its monthly meeting.

Pastor Rev. Frank K. Chase noted that the regular Tuesday night prayer meetings also had seen an attendance larger than in the recent past. [196]

He said at the annual meeting in April 1886 that "[t]here has been on the whole a prevalence of kindness through the year. You do not need that I do more than to refer to the series of special meetings held during the past season. At no time since my connection with the church have any special services been so largely attended nor has there been so much of spiritual interest developed."

In December of that year, a special week of prayer was held, with meetings Tuesday through Friday evenings. [197]

BUT THESE also were years of sadness and loss. The Rev. Isaac D. Stewart, formerly pastor and in 1887 the president of the Washington Street Freewill Baptist Society, died. [198] After resigning his pastorate in 1873, he had worked for *The Morning Star* in various capacities for the rest of his life.

Rev. Chase himself, who had worked so hard to keep the church and society "steadily on their way," had become sick and was kept from his duties from November 1888 to the first of March 1889. [199]

---

[196] DBC, 1:189
[197] *Ibid.*, 1:196.
[198] WFBS, 2:109.
[199] DBC, 2:9.

Rev. Chase had striven diligently to find a way to pay off the indebtedness. He was active in the community as well as making hundreds of calls on parishioners. He reported in May 1888 that he had made 600 calls during the year, and commented on how united the membership had become and how well things were going. The next year he apologized for his sickness and lack of ability to "perform the duties of my office." But by 1891 his annual report showed he was again pushing himself to great lengths as a pastor. He took no vacation that year and had begun publishing "Our Church Visitor," sending out 400 copies each month. He'd made another 500 calls on parishioners, and again noted the great unity he found in the church.[200]

After more than 12 years, Rev. Chase resigned his pastorate effective the last Sunday in March 1892, leaving undone his dream of making the church debt-free. He felt called to a pastorate in Concord, he said, and the church and society reluctantly released him.[201] His departure was only temporary. He left the church in good shape. It was growing spiritually and in numbers. There were many active groups and there was great unity.

Rev. Chase would return for a year in 1907, coming here from a church in Somerville, Mass.

Finding a new pastor was not the hardship it had presented in some of the earlier years. In fact, the society actually received applications for the position before a search got under way. But the committee appointed to find a new pastor reported it had heard good reports about Rev. Ransom E. Gilkey, then of Richmond, Maine, and he was invited to supply the pulpit the first week in April. On April 4, 1892, a call was issued, with promise of a salary of $1,000 per year.[202]

For some reason, the next meeting of the society, supposed to have been held May 2, is missing from the records, but Rev. Gilkey must have given an answer in the affirmative, because at the next recorded session he was elected a member of the Washington Street Freewill Baptist Society and became a member of the church May 29. He had preached his first sermon as pastor on May 10.[203]

Rev. Gilkey came originally from Sharon, Vt., where he was born March 21, 1857, the son of John and Ann T. (Currier) Gilkey. His father was a deacon in the church.

---

[200] DBC, 2:60-61.
[201] WFBS, 2:137-138.
[202] *Ibid.*, 2:140.
[203] DBC, 2:66.

The Free Baptist Cyclopædia gives the following summary of Rev. Gilkey's life before he arrived in Dover:

> He prepared for college at Lyndon Institute, graduated from Bates College in 1881, and from Bates Theological School in 1887. He was converted in Saco, Maine, April 28, 1884, and entered the Theological School and began to preach the following autumn. He preached at New Gloucester, Maine, from April, 1885, to May, 1886, when he began his present pastorate at Richmond, Maine. He was ordained at the June session of the Edgecomb Q[uarterly] M[eeting] at Parker's Head, in 1887.[204]

Again the church had a pastor who with his wife worked fervently to free the church from debt. They were successful. But the biggest change in finances that came during his pastorate was that vote on Dec. 11, 1895, to end pew rental and raise money by weekly offerings. At the mortgage burning in 1896, Vienna Hill mentioned that fact and said: "Now we worship [with] free seats, in a free church, on free soil, free from debt, with none to molest or make afraid."[205] Even today, most of the metal plates containing the numbers for the old pews still are in place, a reminder of days long gone.

Rev. Gilkey was pastor until the fall of 1901, when he tendered his resignation. When the church demurred, having found their pastor to be a good man, Rev. Gilkey told a meeting he'd already accepted a call to Auburn, Maine, and it would be useless to delay his departure. His resignation was accepted with "deep regret."

THE LATE 19th century also was a time of great sadness in the church, despite the grand outlook for the future. Some of its oldest members, several there since the early years, were giving up their church offices and gradually dying off.

At the burning of the mortgage in 1896, only two of the original members were there. Both Edward B. Chamberlain and Asa H. Littlefield attended, but Mr. Chamberlain died Feb. 17, 1901, and Mr. Littlefield on Sept. 12, 1903, he being the last of the original members who first met together Feb. 4, 1840.

Mrs. Marilla Hills, for many years the leader of the church's missions program and the author of a book on missions, died Nov. 28, 1901. She also wrote a biography of her first husband, David Marks, who was an elder and active in the publication of *The Morning Star*.

---

[204] FBC, 231.
[205] *Foster's*, Feb. 13, 1896.

Renselaer Clark, who served nearly 20 years as treasurer of the society, gave up the job Oct. 2, 1892, because of poor health, and died Oct. 28.[206] Deacon Daniel Littlefield and his wife, Mary, died within 19 days of each other in January of that same year. The wife of the founder of the church, Mrs. Frances M. Burr, died Nov. 25, 1895.[207]

And soon after the turn of the century, the Rev. Amos E. Wilson, who had accepted a call to replace Rev. Gilkey in December 1901, died on March 1, 1907, at age 67, the first of the church's pastors to die while serving the Dover pastorate.

Rev. Wilson was born in Gilbert's Mills, N.Y., April 8, 1840, the son of Rev. Joseph Wilson. His mother, Ruth (Thomas) Wilson, was a descendant of Benjamin Randall, founder of the Freewill Baptist denomination.[208]

Amos Wilson attended Valley Seminary in Fulton, N.Y., and Mexico Academy in New York. He was ordained in 1869. He pastored several churches in New York before coming to Dover. His wife was the former Frances M. Parker, who always was active with him in his ministries. [209]

Following Rev. Wilson's death, Frank K. Chase returned as pastor for a year, resigning in November 1908 because of poor health. Within a month, a call was issued to Rev. Albert E. Kenyon, then serving a church in Lowell, Mass., and he began his ministry in Dover on Jan. 2, 1909. Before he left Dover, he would witness the consolidation of both Baptist congregations in the city, leaving the Washington Street church as the only Baptist church in the community.

ALONG WITH the losses, there appeared new leadership among the membership. In 1885, Cyrus L. Jenness, one of the church's great lay leaders and benefactors, was first elected a deacon. He had joined the church by baptism back in 1877 (first called Lyordly C. Jenness in the records).[210] He held several other church posts. And from 1878 to 1894 he also was clerk of the Washington Street Freewill Baptist Society. Though an enterprising Dover businessman—he owned a well-known hardware store in town—the church was the center of his life and that of his wife. For many years after his death he was memorialized by the C. L. Jenness Men's Bible Class, which met each Sunday morning.

---

[206] WFBS, 2:144.
[207] DBC, Book 2, membership list.
[208] FBC, 704-5.
[209] *Ibid.*, 704.
[210] DBC, 1:156.

When Deacon Jenness died Oct. 29, 1929, and his wife died only 11 days later, they left to the church the sum of $40,000 to be used as an educational fund for students from what by then had become Dover Baptist Church. The fund still is used to help Dover Baptist students attend colleges.

Melvin A. Galucia, another long-time church leader, joined in 1897 from the Congregational church in Dedham, Mass. He immediately became active, and by 1901 he had been elected both clerk and treasurer of the church. At that time, the "standing rules" called for the clerk also to be the treasurer.[211] He served as treasurer until 1915 and as clerk until the church united with the Central Avenue Baptists in 1918 and became known as Dover Baptist Church.

As the church crossed into the 20th century, there were others who took over the reins of the older generation. Dr. Roland J. Bennett, who was baptized May 1, 1904, was for many years treasurer and deacon. Others came after him, including deacons Richard L. Williams, Lewis A. Miles and others; always someone to take up the leadership positions when others left or succumbed to the ravages of age. And after Mrs. Hills died there always were women in the forefront of foreign and home missions. Mrs. Garland, whose name later would be added to the Hills Missionary Society, was one. Louie Wiggin was another. In fact, a renewed interest in missions beginning in the 1940s saw the mission budget actually peak in the 1960s at almost half of the entire annual church budget.

So the church was in capable hands as the new century commenced. Growth continued and the outreach expanded during the early 1900s.

But big changes were coming. The early setup of quarterly meetings to which all Freewill Baptist churches belonged, was fading away. State yearly meetings also were becoming less important. The differences between Freewill and Calvinist Baptist churches were less pronounced, both realizing that central duty transcended issues that had kept them apart.

At the same time, because of economic and social conditions—as well as conditions unique to the Dover area—there were changes coming that in the end would leave the Washington Street church as the only Baptist church in the whole city by 1918. At the turn of the century there had been three.

---

[211] DBC, 2, 25.

12.
Consolidation

The 20th century came in at full speed for Dover's Washington Street Freewill Baptist Church. New things were begun and old things were set aside. There were wins and there were losses.

By the end of the first decade, the First Freewill Baptist Church of Dover, from which the founding members of the Washington Street church had come, would no longer exist. With dwindling membership, it had given up its building at the corner of Chestnut and Lincoln streets and bought a smaller building on the site of what now is the Central Fire Station on Broadway. The struggle continued for awhile, but in 1900 the small congregation held its last meeting and disbanded.

Several members already had transferred to the Washington Street church, but when the congregation was disbanded others were welcomed there as well. The only real mention of the demise of its sister church was when the Washington Street church voted to buy its 75 remaining hymn books and a like number of Psalm books for $5.[212]

The old church's building on Broadway was moved across the street, converted into a commercial building, and the city built its fire station on the old church site.

A grand idea that never got off the ground was proposed on Sept. 10, 1901, when Mrs. E. B. Chamberlain thought it would be appropriate to note the new century by establishing the Twentieth Century Fund.

So at the annual meeting on Oct. 7, members of the society approved the following:

> We, the undersigned, agree to pay the sum affixed to our names, for the purpose of creating a fund, to be called the Washington Street Free Baptist Twentieth Century Fund, which is to be permanent, the contributions of said fund which may occur at the convenience of the

---

[212] WFBS 2:246

giver, shall be deposited in a bank or some place of safety, as may be designated by the Washington St. F. W. B. Society, and nothing of it used until it amounts to one thousand dollars ($1,000.) and after that the interest only in aid of the above named Society.

It is the intention of the donors that first of all the keeping in perfect repair of the church edifice shall be considered and effected. When the church building is in the above named condition the interest may be used for purposes most needed by the society.

Any violation of the above preamble, by those who in the future may constitute the above named Society, shall be considered an agrievance and the fund shall be theirs no longer, but shall be turned over to the Free Baptist General Conference Board to be used as in their judgment seems most needed.[213]

By April of the next year Mrs. Chamberlain reported $6 in the fund. A year after its establishment she noted an additional $25 from the estate of the late Mrs. Marilla M. H. Hills and an unpaid pledge of $10.[214]

The fund has been listed in the society and then the church financial records ever since. For some years the small amount of interest was mistakenly put into capital improvements until it was noticed that the money was supposed to stay where it was until the principal reached $1,000. So the fund never reached that level until a member of the church, toward the end of the century, decided to add $749.87 to bring it up to the desired $1,000. By then, the amount of interest on $1,000, was little help toward the annual needs for upkeep of the property, but at least it now could be used for that purpose.

On Sept. 26, 1901, Rev. Gilkey submitted a letter of resignation, having served the church since 1892. At the very next meeting on Oct. 7, his resignation was accepted and a committee named to look for a new pastor. The exact time of his leaving was left up in the air for the moment, but it was announced Oct. 22 that he had requested to be released on the first of November.

Little more than a year into the new century, the Washington Street Freewill Baptist Society, seeing its purpose as having been fulfilled with all debts finally paid, was preparing to turn over full operation to the church and go out of existence. The church, newly incorporated, took over all responsibilities on March 20, 1911, and the society was soon disbanded.

The action came on the following recommendations:

---

[213] WFBS, 2:261-2.
[214] *Ibid.*, 2:274-5.

First. That the Washington Street Freewill Baptist Church, the Association, hereby agrees that all of its Real Estate and Personal holdings shall be surrendered to the Washington Street Free Baptist Church, the Incorporated body, said body to have legal control of the same, including its interest in the so called Susan Littlefield Estate, Mechanic Street, Dover; the so called Christy Fund invested, the 20th Century Fund so called invested and also all other properties both personal and real, together with all its records.

Second. Upon the adoption of this recommendation by the Washington Street Free Baptist Church Association the transfer of the aforesaid holdings shall be considered effected.[215]

But before going out of existence, the society had taken one more step at the behest of the pastor and other members of the church who thought it would be a good idea to have a church parsonage. On Oct. 20, 1896, it first had been suggested that a parsonage should be built.[216] A committee was appointed to look into the matter, and the project still was being considered in 1902 when it was reported that the Nathaniel Hobbs property on Lexington Street would fit the bill. James Y. Demeritt of the committee reported it would cost $5,000; however, it was not for sale.

C. L. Jenness, chairman of the committee and long an advocate of a parsonage, finally had a solid recommendation on Oct. 14 of that year when he reported the best thing to do would be for the church to build its own parsonage. He said property was available on Richmond Street, and

We recommend that the Washington St. F. W. B. Society of Dover, N.H. authorize the purchase at once of the Faxon lot, so called on Richmond St., at a price not to exceed twelve hundred dollars ($1200.), and that the Society give their note, signed by a sufficient number of members that are real estate owners, to satisfy the present owner, until the money is raised to liquidate the same.

The said lot is 70 ft. more or less on Richmond St. and runs back 175 ft., more or less to land owned by Frank Corson and Ephraim H. Whitehouse and is at present owned by Chas. A. Faxon of said Dover.[217]

The purchase was authorized. The deed was in hand by a meeting on Jan. 6, 1903, and a plan for raising the money was in place.

Records of the society from that point on are lost. But from the

---

[215] DBC, 2:176-7.
[216] WFBS, 2:196.
[217] *Ibid*, 2:277.

church clerk's records we see on Oct. 10, 1905, the following:

> We can . . . report that we have contracted for a parsonage, and the same is now nearing completion, it will cost when completed nearly $4200. and all will be paid except a small mortgage of $1600, at the present time the committee needs about $150.00 to complete all contracts and by the time the building is completed expect to have raised same.[218]

Although the society didn't disband until 1911, the church began to take over some of the actions formerly handled by the society. For instance, in 1904 members voted to buy a second-hand bell for the church. It was decided March 14, 1904, to spend $150 for the bell, then located in Biddeford, Maine.[219]

THE BELL'S OWN history turns out to be interesting, since it came from a former Congregational Church in Biddeford that had its beginning in the 1850s during the dispute over churches getting involved in the anti-slavery movement. The Pavilion Congregational Church was founded by 37 dissidents who left the Second Congregational Church when they didn't like the minister's pro-slavery sentiments. The church disbanded in 1900 and sold its building. Now, minus its steeple where the bell was located, it is known as the McArthur Public Library.[220]

The bell was made by J. Regester & Sons, Baltimore Bell Foundry, in Maryland in 1884. Besides that information embossed on the bell are the words "Pavilion Society," indicating the name of the church society founded by the dissidents. The Baltimore company was in business at least by the end of the Civil War, as it appears in the Baltimore city directories of 1865 and 1892. The firm's biggest claim to fame apparently was that it cast a huge bell, weighing more than three tons, that was placed in Baltimore's new city hall in 1875.[221] The bell that came to Dover in 1904 still hangs in the Washington Street belfry.

With the demise of the Washington Street Freewill Baptist Society, the church was on its own—it was in charge of all property matters, as well as the spiritual life of its members.

So it started a new book of records on Jan. 17, 1911, and titled it "Washington Street Free Baptist Church Corporation Records." It lists the articles of incorporation on the first pages, then the system of government

---

[218] DBC, 2:147.
[219] *Ibid.*, 138.
[220] Archives, McArthur Public Library, Biddeford, ME.
[221] *History of Baltimore*, 178.

under which the church would operate. At its first meeting a committee charged with drawing up a new church covenant asked for more time, but at the next meeting it was decided to continue under the old covenant.

It was noted April 4 that all legal actions transferring properties and liabilities from the society to the church had been completed.[222]

It didn't take long for the church to be faced with some major capital expenditures. By June 1911, the trustees were looking at installation of new furnaces. In the early days, the church had been heated by stoves located in the vestries. A new hot-air system, with two furnaces, had been installed before the turn of the century, but by 1901 the furnaces were described as "practically of no use."[223]

One large furnace was installed, but the wardens decided the smaller old furnace could be repaired. They reported the job completed by cold weather, including cementing the floor of the area which had been dug out under the church so the furnaces could be installed. The new heating system didn't reach the kindergarten area, though, so it got its own stove.

But now 10 years later the church, saddled with all capital expenditures, already was talking about a new heating system at the same meeting in which it voted to accept all the properties of the now-defunct society. After later voting that they didn't want a steam heating system, members left it up to the trustees as to what hot-air system it should be. The big question was whether the new system should be a "Kelsey" or a "Walker and Pratt" system.

It turned out to be a Kelsey.

Then, of course, came a leak in the roof that had to be fixed. Since it was mid-winter, it was decided to make temporary repairs and then make permanent repairs in the spring. Also, the new parsonage had to be painted, so $100 was voted for that job.[224]

The first indication of what would materialize in the next few years came in 1911, when Rev. A. E. Kenyon "introduced the subject of the two Baptist churches of our city getting in closer touch with one another."[225]

It was not the first time such a suggestion had been made and Dover was not the first location to discuss what would in the end result in many mergers of Freewill Baptists (who now called themselves Free Baptists for the most part) and regular Baptist (or Calvinist) churches. The

[222] DBC, Bk. 3, April 4, 1911.
[223] WFBS Book 2, Oct. 7, 1901
[224] DBC, Bk. 3, Oct. 17, 1911.
[225] *Ibid.*, Dec. 10, 1911.

Rockingham Quarterly Meeting records show that it opposed mergers. As early as 1908 a rather strong resolution was introduced at the May 21 meeting, mandating that "the delegates to the New Hampshire Yearly Meeting are hereby instructed to Work and Vote against the proposed union with the Baptists." [226]

There was some discussion of the resolution before the delegates watered it down a bit and came up with: "Resolved that in our opinion the time has not yet come for the Free Baptists to unite with the Baptists."

Eventually, the Quarterly Meeting—by then officially having changed its name to Rockingham Association of Free Baptist Churches— agreed that it was a good idea for Free Baptists and regular Baptists to unite their mission outreaches, both at home and abroad. But opposition to actual union with the Baptists still was strong as it was resolved ". . . that we favor unity of action by the entire denomination and deplore any attempt on the part of any church or association or Quarterly Meeting to independently affiliate with the Baptists."[227]

But circumstances were working against the Freewill Baptists in their attempt to remain a distinct denomination. In 1908, Bates College announced it was shutting down its divinity school. The denominational newspaper *The Morning Star* faced insurmountable financial problems. Despite all attempts to keep it going, the Rockingham Association on Oct. 11, 1911, found itself issuing the following resolution:

> Whereas the financial problems of the "Morning Star" has made it impossible to continue its publication and has made it advisable for it to unite with the "Watchman"
>
> Resolved, that we as a people, hereby express our sorrow at thus losing this our denominational organ, which has been a friend in all our homes for more than 80 years, and have it merged with the Watchman.

Then the resolution, perhaps admitting that the denomination's days were numbered, continued:

> Resolved, as circumstances have made this [newspaper merger] imperative and because of the present status of union between the Baptists and Free Baptists denominations. We would heartily recommend that our pastors and churches give to the united paper "The Watchman," continuing the "Morning Star," our most loyal support and pledge ourselves to do all that is possible to induce our people to subscribe for the united paper.

[226] Rockingham Quarterly Meeting Record Book, 4:337.
[227] *Ibid.*, 4:347.

In Dover, already under the pastorates of Revs. Chase, Gilkey and Wilson, there had been a closer working relationship with some of the other protestant churches, including some joint evangelistic campaigns. It was a change from earlier days when there was little or no relationship between the Washington Street church and others in the city.

There were especially good relations with St. John's Methodist Episcopal Church, the First Parish Congregational and Belknap Congregational churches. When Rev. Wilson died in 1907, the Dover ministerial association, noting Rev. Wilson's "helpful co-operation in Christian labors," sent a special resolution to the church signed by:

George E. Hall, pastor, First Church (Congregational)
Ward R. Clarke, pastor, Unitarian Church
W. Weir Gilliss, rector, St. Thomas Episcopal Church
J. E. Cunningham, pastor, Central Avenue Baptist Church
Benjamin F. Eaton, pastor, Peirce Memorial Church
Albert Justin Northrup, pastor, St. John's Methodist Episcopal Church
Harry E. Shattuck, pastor, Advent Christian Church[228]

But the goal suggested by Rev. Gilkey on Dec. 10, 1911, was for a closer working relationship with the Central Avenue Baptist Church, now the only other Baptist congregation in Dover. So at the pastor's suggestion, it was voted to see if arrangements could be made with the other church's pastor to have "union meetings" during the annual Week of Prayer, plus perhaps a couple of joint Sunday evening meetings.

The Central Avenue church also was thinking along the same lines. It's not indicated whether the above suggestion resulted in joint meetings, but by the next July the Central Avenue church voted to extend an invitation to the Washington Street church to hold joint worship services during the August vacations of their pastors.[229] The records of both churches are rather skimpy for the summer of 1912, so there is no record of whether they actually met together. The Washington Street Baptists had earlier voted to close the church during August and meet only with the Christian Endeavor Society on Friday evenings.

Both Baptist churches had joined other churches in town to hold evangelistic services. In the next few years, members of both churches were increasingly switching to the other for one reason or another. The reasons which at first had held them apart seemed to be disappearing quickly.

---

[228] DBC, 2:153.
[229] CABC, 3:88.

The final merger of the two churches may well have been speeded by the tough times brought on by World War I. In any case, on Oct. 2, 1917, in what the clerk called a "practically unanimous" vote, the Washington Street Free Baptist Church adopted the following resolution:

> Resolved. That the members of the Wash. St. Free Baptist Church invite the members of the Central Ave. Baptist Church to meet them in a union meeting, at such time and place as the Baptist Church members may select, for the purpose of finding out how many members of each church are willing to open negotiations looking toward a union of the two churches.

On Oct. 16, 1917, the Central Avenue Baptist Church records indicate its first move toward union. It says:

> In response to an invitation from the Washington St. F. B. Church, a union service was held in the church to consider the possibility of uniting the two churches. Resolutions offering a possible basis of union were discussed and it was then agreed to appoint a committee of seven from each church to make more definite plans.[230]

ANOTHER MEETING of just Central Avenue church members was held Nov. 12 at which a vote showed 30 in favor of union, two opposed.

Meanwhile, a committee from the church consisting of Charles E. Cate, E. E. Kidder, W. C. Swan, G. H. Mills, Luke McEwan, A. E. Bickford and Irving Young began meeting with a similar committee from the Washington Street church. That church's committee of seven is not named in the records, but later entries indicate C. L. Jenness was its chairman.

A letter had been sent out to members of the Washington Street Church explaining the basis of the union. Responses, both in person and by letter, indicated 93 members in favor of the move and one against.[231]

The two churches, when joined, would operate under a new organization. Each church would urge all of its members to join the newly incorporated, re-named church, and a joint committee would work out the constitution and by-laws under which it would operate.

The joint committees continued their work and on Feb. 12, 1918, Dover Baptist Church was officially incorporated, and at a special adjourned meeting of the Washington Street Free Baptist Church, it was

---

[230] CABC, 3:118.
[231] DBC, Bk. 3, Nov. 13, 1917.

decided that the entire membership of the church would be "elected into full membership of the Dover Baptist Church."

On the same day, The Central Avenue Baptist Church voted "that the entire membership of the Central Ave. Baptist Church as enrolled upon its membership book, be, and hereby is, elected into full membership of the Dover Baptist Church."[232]

By March 26, the last entries in the Central Avenue church's records are as follows:

> Luke H. McEwan introduced the following resolution.
>
> "I would move that all of the property of the Central Avenue Baptist Church of Dover, N.H. be transferred to the Dover Baptist Church, and that the chairman of the trustees be authorized to sign deeds and papers necessary for such transfer.
>
> Voted To accept and adopt this resolution.
>
> Voted To adjourn.[233]

On April 9, the Washington Street church treasurer, Roland J. Bennett, issued his final report, and the following recommendation was adopted:

> That the Washington St. F. B. Church Inc. hereby agrees that all of its real estate and personal holdings shall be transferred to the Dover Baptist Church, Inc., said body to have legal control of the same, including its interest in the so called Susan Littlefield Est. on Mechanic St., Dover, the so called Christy Fund invested, the Gear Fund invested, the 20th Century Fund so called and also all other properties both real & personal together with all its records.
>
> Upon adoption of this recommendation by the Wash. St. F. B. Church, Inc. the transfer of aforesaid holdings shall be considered effected.
>
> A motion was then made and 2nd that the recommendation be accepted and adopted. Carried.
>
> No further business, meeting adjourned.[234]

A new Dover Baptist Church record book was begun, beginning with the incorporation agreement. Its records begin even before the final dissolution of the merging church, when on Feb. 12, at its first meeting, it voted to accept into membership all the members of the Central Avenue and Washington Street churches. Strangely enough, the meeting was held in the chapel of the Central Avenue church, not at Dover Baptist Church.

---

[232] CABC, 3:123.

[233] *Ibid.*

[234] *Ibid.*, 3:123-124

But it was called the first annual meeting of Dover Baptist Church.[235]

The membership list now included all those who had been members of the two churches prior to the union. A few, mostly from the Central Avenue church, never became part of the congregation on Washington Street. Eight former members of the Central Avenue church had already asked for, and received, letters of dismissal in the month before the merger. But a total of 159 persons listed as members of the Central Avenue church were listed in the first membership rolls of the consolidated Dover Baptist Church.

Lucy J. Gould had been a member of the Central Avenue church for the longest time when she transferred to Dover Baptist Church. She had joined that fellowship by baptism March 7, 1852. She remained a member of Dover Baptist for the rest of her life, dying Oct. 21, 1921, at the age of 86 years, 5 months.[236]

With the merger of the two churches, and the resignation of both pastors so the combined membership could choose a new pastor, the future was looking prosperous. Both pastors stayed on awhile, Rev. A. W. Clifford of the Central Avenue church leaving for a new pastorate in Natick, Mass., Feb. 26, 1918, and Rev. A. E. Kenyon leaving a year later for a pastorate in Bridgeport, Conn.[237]

---

[235] DBC, 4:4-7.

[236] *Ibid.*, 4:272-273.

[237] *Ibid.*, 4:268-269; 274-275.

13.
𝕷ooking forward

With both of Dover's Baptist churches now united, the first
matter of business was to find a pastor. While the search went
on, Rev. William J. Twort, a native of England who for many
years had held pastorates in Maine, filled the pulpit on most Sundays.

It was not until May 14, 1918, that a call was extended to Rev.
Arthur L. Snell of Mt. Vernon, N.Y., who at the time was secretary of the
Foreign Mission Society, District of New York. He accepted, and began
his Dover ministry on June 16.[238] But his ministry got off to a slow start
when the church and many of the city's public buildings were virtually
closed down for four weeks "owing to the epidemic of Spanish
influenza."[239] Only two short meetings were recorded between the time
Rev. Snell arrived in May and Oct. 29. In fact, the pastor, his wife and
two children were the only persons received into membership until the
next year.

But in 1919, there were 21 new members, 28 the year after that, and
14 more in 1921 before Rev. Snell died on Sept. 16. The clerk recorded
that "Our pastor, Rev. Arthur Lincoln Snell died suddenly after a few days
illness. Funeral services were held at the parsonage Monday, Sept. 19, and
the next day he was carried to rest in his native city of Lawrence,
Mass."[240]

His family moved a short time later to West Somerville, Mass.

It had been a successful year at the church, despite the pastor's death,
with the church reporting at the Portsmouth Association meeting an
abstract of the year's changes at the church as follows:

> Baptisms 13, letters 15, experience 1; dismissed 8, death 5, net
> gain 16. Total membership 372. Resident members, male 78, female

---

[238] DBC, 4:12.
[239] *Ibid.*
[240] *Ibid.*, 4:36.

185. Home expenses total $11,712.78, apportionment $4,531.88, other objects $515.42.

Bible School officers and teachers 45, scholars 280, average attendance 180, Home Dept. 60, cradle roll 42, members in S.S. uniting with church 25.[241]

THE CONSOLIDATION of the churches had left Dover Baptist with several properties that were not needed by the church, most having been bequeathed to the Central Avenue Baptists. So during the next few years houses on Central Avenue, New York, Ham and Mechanic streets were sold.

Other items that became surplus because of the consolidation also were disposed of, including the platform furniture and pulpit that had stood at the front of the Washington Street church since it was re-built after the 1882 fire. The church apparently began using the platform furniture that had been in the Central Avenue church. Trustees were authorized to present the "discarded pulpit furniture" to the Third Baptist Church of Strafford.[242] Although nothing is in the records to show when this was done, the Strafford church on Feb. 15, 1919, thanked the members of the Dover church which "generously presented a much-needed pulpit set to the Center Strafford Baptist Church."[243] In 2008, the Strafford church still was using the same pulpit and platform furniture.

First sale of the "inherited" houses and church buildings came in 1920 with the sale of property at 27-29 New York Street, then a house and land on Mechanic Street in 1926, the old church and its annex at 526 and 528 Central Avenue and another house and property at 652 Central Avenue, all in 1929, just as the Great Depression hit. The old Central Avenue Baptist parsonage on Ham Street was sold in 1931.[244]

The Ham Street sale was more complicated than the others since the house, at the corner of Park Street, had been left to the Central Avenue church by Mrs. Betsy Weed, in memory of her husband John, to be forever used only as a parsonage or it would become the property of the American Baptist Foreign Mission Society. Since the Washington Street church already had a parsonage on Richmond Street and didn't need a second one, it was decided to sell the house. The church was willing to name its own parsonage in memory of John Weed if it could work out an

---

[241] DBC, 4:37
[242] *Ibid.*, 4:14-15.
[243] Strafford Third Baptist Church Record Bk. 2, Feb. 15, 1919.
[244] Strafford County Deeds, Bk. 447:81.

agreement with the Mission Society. So the society and church met and agreed that the $2,500 realized from the sale would establish a "John Weed Fund" from which half of the income each year would go to Dover Baptist Church for upkeep of the Richmond Street property, and the other half would go to the mission society's budget and be credited as a contribution from the Dover church.

So the parsonage was named the "John Weed Parsonage" and received income from the fund until it was sold many years later. After the sale, the John Weed Fund's income went solely to the mission society.

The Central Avenue church building itself, along with an annex, at the corner of Fourth Street, remained part of the church's property for 11 years and was used extensively for meetings and young people's events. It eventually was called the "recreation hall."

THE NEXT major move by the church was to join the Northern Baptist Convention. The convention's confession of faith was read at a meeting Jan. 10, 1922, and approved. A copy of it is pasted into the clerk's book. At the same time, the church remained a member of the Portsmouth Baptist Association and the United Baptist Convention of New Hampshire.

Two months later, on March 14, 1922, having been without a pastor since the death of Rev. Snell the previous September, a call was issued to Rev. Lester C. Holmes, then leading a church in Biddeford, Maine. He was to be offered $2,000 a year plus free use of the parsonage and one month annual vacation. He began his pastorate in Dover June 4.[245]

The next few years were ones of great activity and community participation. Though some of the earlier church organizations had gone by the wayside, organizations still active in the church included the Hills-Garland Missionary Society, Ladies Aid, King's Daughters, Christian Endeavor Society, A.M.S. Club, Lend-a-Hand Class, C. L. Jenness Men's Bible Class, Men's League, Ever Ready Class and Busy Bees Class. The Mothers Club came a couple of years later. All were in addition to the Sunday School and young people's activities.

Young people's groups were greatly expanded during those years, when they had available the former Central Avenue Baptist Church building for many activities. A large committee directed activities there until it was decided 11 years later to sell the property.

In 1923, when Dover celebrated the 300th anniversary of its settlement, the church and Bible school entered one of the scores of floats

---

[245] DBC, 4:40-41.

that wended their way down Central Avenue in a huge parade of celebration. The church singled out the E. J. York Co. for its help in furnishing horses and personnel to man the parade float.[246]

During the next few years, the church continued to grow, with almost every recorded meeting containing names of new members. By 1926, the treasurer's annual report showed regular budget receipts of $7,367.66 and almost identical expenditures, leaving only 85 cents to begin the new year. Mission receipts, then still called benevolences, were $3,589.06.[247]

Despite slow but steady growth during these years, there were times when it seemed the whole congregation was dying off. In a period of about nine months in 1926 and 1927, deaths were so common they were listed in the clerk's notes. Between October 1926 and June 1927, Augusta W. Caverly, Millie L. Hobby, Clara Taylor, Calista Foss, Laura A. DeMeritt, Nellie A. Seavey, Lillian Ella Kimball, Thomas L. Slater and Martha Demeritt, all died.[248] Normally deaths, if listed at all, were noted in the membership list at the back of the book.

But, with total membership having reached 421 by 1926 and still growing, and with the Sunday School quickly expanding, church trustees began looking toward the possibility of expanding the facilities. Next door was a large house owned by two brothers, sons and heirs of John B. Stevens. If the property could be purchased, it would be the first step toward expansion of the church building.

During 1927, one of the brothers, Herman Stevens, sold the church his half interest in the house and lot for $2,000.[249] The other brother, Frank, finally relinquished his half ownership a year later for $3,000.[250]

The building on the lot was of good size, wrote Dr. Roland Bennett, a trustee at the time, and it consisted of two tenements. The dwelling was quite old, in poor condition, and was not fit to be rented. He further explained years later in his memoirs:

> At this time, the church did not have any funds to immediately do any new construction. What should be done with the house until such time enough funds could be raised for the needed expansion? A highly favored suggestion was to put the house in good repair and rent it. The tenements were of such size that some thought it would be advisable to make four apartments.

[246] DBC, 4:52.
[247] *Ibid.*, 4:79.
[248] *Ibid.*, 4:82, 88.
[249] *Ibid.*, 4:89.
[250] *Ibid.*, 4:99.

By this time I was chairman of the trustees, and it was my responsibility to investigate as to what should be done and how much it would cost. The trustees decided to have an architect draw some plans dividing the house into four apartments, the thought being that having four apartments might bring in more revenue than just having two tenements.[251]

The architect made a sketch showing four moderately-sized apartments. The house needed painting both inside and out. Nearly all the rooms needed new wallpaper. The roof needed re-shingling. The wiring was inadequate, among other needed improvements.

When all the cost estimates were in, the trustees determined the building was not worth repairing since it never would pay for itself before the church demolished it to construct a Sunday School addition to the main church building.

Since the church was planning to build the addition as soon as it was able to raise the necessary funds, it would be a waste of money to spend any more upon the Stevens house, noted Dr. Bennett. Without any reservations or doubts, the trustees opted to get rid of the house. Someone was found who would demolish the structure and cart it away for the second-hand lumber it contained.[252] The men of the church filled in the cellar hole, seeded the lot, and it was maintained as a lawn until the addition finally was built in 1950.

But there were additional major plans adopted during 1930, in what the trustees called a move "to better provide for worship."[253]

TRUSTEES RECOMMENDED the first major alterations to the church building since it had been rebuilt after the devastating fire of 1882. The plans were to make major changes to the platform and pulpit areas and to re-build and update the old organ that had been installed after the fire.[254] A separate organ fund already had been set up and a pulpit fund now was contemplated. The trustees were specific in their recommendations:

> The alterations would consist of locating the new organ in the open space at the left of the pulpit. The pulpit-platform would be changed in that there would be at the rear an elevated baptistry with a stained window back of it, or with a gold cross hung on a rich dossal background. Just below would be the communion table with perhaps a

---

[251] Memoirs of Dr. Roland J. Bennett (Bennett), 69.
[252] *Ibid.*, 70.
[253] DBC, 4:117-118.
[254] *Ibid.*

tankard and goblet upon it. Thus the symbols of the two main ordinances of the Baptist Church, immersion and communion, would always be plainly in sight. In front there would be steps leading to the platform.[255]

The fund for a new organ had been set up earlier. Deacon Melvin Galucia had reported by 1929 that various sources, including public professional musical programs held at the Dover City Opera House, had raised a total of $3,834.68. This included $80 profit brought in by an appearance of the famous John Sousa's Band. Other attractions that came to Dover to help raise funds for the organ were The Bostonians and a group called the Duartells.

But unforeseen circumstances occurred that slowed plans for the church alterations. Though not abandoned, the plans took second place to fears for the very fiscal survival of the church.

The church, along with everyone else, was hit hard by the financial collapse of October 1929. One of the actions the church took that month was to authorize the sale of the old Central Avenue Baptist Church building, with its annex which at that time was being rented to the Dover Chamber of Commerce, in addition to selling additional property further north on Central Avenue.[256]

BY THE END of the year, the church had on hand a balance of only $44. Total income for the next year was less than $4,000. With the deepening Depression, in 1931 it totaled less than $3,500 and at the end of the year the church treasurer, Dr. Roland J. Bennett, reported a deficit of nearly $560.[257] A short time later, Dr. Bennett reported he expected the deficit to grow to nearly $730 by March 31, 1932.

But during 1932, there seemed to be some improvement and a budget totaling $6,000 was adopted, in addition to what had been coming in for Organ and Pulpit-Platform funds.

Then came an announcement from the pastor, Rev. Lester C. Holmes, which the clerk, when he read it, called "not a pleasing duty." It read in part, "Another church has sought me as pastor; and after much prayer and waiting upon God, it seems His will that I yield to their desire." He asked to be released on July 2, 1932, to become pastor of the

---

[255] DBC, 4:117.
[256] *Ibid.*, 4:111.
[257] *Ibid.*, 4:140.

Pleasant Street Baptist Church in Worcester, Mass., having served in Dover for 10 years.[258]

In leaving, Rev. Holmes, in his final message to the congregation, offered hope for the future:

> . . . I am confident that with Christ and in Him, the best is yet to be. I trust that definite steps will soon be taken to install the new organ and make the necessary alterations in the auditorium. There are many in the parish who are anxious to see these delayed plans carried out.[259]

He also mentioned that he hoped steps would be taken to provide more space for Sunday School, a project that would never see completion until several years after World War II.

THE CHURCH moved quickly to find a new pastor and by Sept. 16, 1932, it met and voted unanimously to call Rev. Buell W. Maxfield, then pastor of the Bethany Baptist Church in Roxbury, Mass., to minister to the Dover flock.[260] By Oct. 30, he was in Dover preaching his first sermon.

Plans were set in motion to get rid of the deficit in finances as quickly as possible and by July 1933, the treasurer was able to report balances of approximately $146 in current expenses, $412 in the charity account, $1,966 in the pulpit-platform account and $434 in the real estate account.[261]

The pulpit-platform project was undertaken about the middle of August and the major part quickly completed, although complications surfaced in the rebuilding of the organ. But the church didn't wait for completion of the organ before beginning to use the auditorium. Having met in the crowded vestry for more than three months, it was decided to move back into the auditorium when most of the work and painting was completed by the end of the year. Re-dedication of the project was put off until the organ work could be completed.

Minor items and the organ were still left to be done. The minor work was completed, but then a major holdup came when the agreement with the organ contractor fell apart and it looked for awhile as if the church would end up paying a lot for something it never was going to receive.

It seems a certain organ man said he would give the church an organ practically as good as a new one—and for much less money. He even

---

[258] DBC, 4:145; 288-289.

[259] *Ibid.*, 4:147.

[260] *Ibid.*, 4:149.

[261] *Ibid.*, 4:157.

offered to furnish most of the wood paneling for the chancel. His price for the two was $5,000. Total combined estimates for the organ and platform project was $8,000.

All went well until problems surfaced with the organ contractor.

The $5,000 agreement with the organ man was that one-fourth of the amount, $1,250, should be paid before each quarter of the work was started, except the last quarter, which should be paid when all the work was finished. The furnishing of the wood paneling was sublet by the organ contractor to a firm in Providence, R.I.

When the delay on the organ work began, the new electric organ console had been made and delivered and the wood paneling from the firm in Providence had been installed. The old organ had been completely dismantled and the pipes were piled on the floor.[262]

Dr. Bennett, in his paper, recalled the following:

The time had come, according to the terms of the contract, when the church should make the third payment of $1,250. However, there were articles in the Boston newspaper that this organ man was suing a famous actress for one million dollars, as he claimed that his name was involved in an alleged kidnapping attempt and as a result, he charged slander and libel in connection with a declaration made by the actress.

There were other articles in the newspapers of how this organ manufacturer had moved from place to place, and each time left a lot of unpaid bills behind . . .

. . . We felt certain he would not do anything more toward finishing the rebuilding of the organ. Legally, the church was obligated to pay the third installment of $1,250 on the contract. Mr. Richardson, our architect, got in touch with the firm in Providence which had furnished the wood paneling, and although they had finished their part, they had not received any money.

The trustees received a letter from the organ man, stating the installment of $1,250 was due the first of the month and demanded that we pay it on time. I was very much against paying any more money to this character. But, what could we do? No question about it, we were legally bound to pay. Anyhow, the check for the amount was not sent for 10 days. Then the check was mailed and we said "Good bye" for we did not have any hope at all of getting anything for it.

Three or four days later the unexpected happened, praise the Lord! The envelope containing the check was returned by the Post Office Department, marked "Moved, address unknown."

Two days later the wood-working firm in Providence, R.I. placed an attachment on the church's bank account so that the church could

---

[262] Bennett, 73-74.

not pay the organ man any money until the wood working firm had been paid. Praise the Lord again! Now, no more worry about paying the organ man for awhile.

In a few days the trustees received notice that the organ man was going to sue the church for the money. . . .On the date set for the trial the organ man never showed up and this ended any further dealings with him.

William Laws, of Beverly, Massachusetts, an organ builder, was made acquainted with our plight and he offered to finish rebuilding the organ for $2,500, the same amount remaining from the previous contract.[263]

The rebuilt organ was completed and installed by Laws and finally on Oct. 1, 1933, the church was able to report:

In the morning the chancel and equipment were dedicated with a fine service prepared by our pastor, Rev. Buell W. Maxfield, and a sermon by Dr. Byington of Gordon College, Boston.

At 3:30 our new organ was dedicated and another sermon, "The Organ and the Soul," by Prof. Edward H. Byington, Prof. Robert W. Manton, professor of music, University of New Hampshire, gave an organ recital which was very fine.

In the evening at seven the baptistry was dedicated and three went down into the waters and were baptized by our pastor . . .[264]

THE NEW CHANCEL area was much changed from earlier. Where there had been pews to the left of the original platform, there now was an enclosed area on the left for the organ pipes and equipment. There remained an anteroom on the right. Rather than a pulpit in the center of the platform, there was a lectern on the right side and a large pulpit on the left that extended from the platform out into the auditorium.

The console of the organ, on the right side at the rear of the platform, was placed in a depression to avoid conspicuousness. The organ pipes were screened from view on the left. The church had decided in 1932 to rebuild and upgrade the organ already being used, authorizing the trustees "to have the present organ rebuilt and electrified, including a new console, new blower and generator with additional stops, making an up-to-date modern organ."[265]

Though the church had undertaken the whole project as the nation

---

[263] Bennett, 74.
[264] DBC, 4:159.
[265] *Ibid.*, 4:148.

was coming out of the Great Depression, it was reported little more than a week later that there were balances in all church accounts except the Pulpit Platform Account, which showed a deficit of about $847.[266]

But by the quarterly meeting in April 1934, pastor Maxfield reported all bills had been paid.

Growth during the ensuing years was slow but steady; the financial situation as the nation recovered from the Depression caused the church to put off projects it felt were needed to provide better facilities. But with careful planning the church managed to make ends meet during most years of the 1930s.

The 1930s also was a time when the church held or participated in evangelistic services from time to time. Included were services in 1938 by "The Bonny Workers," a husband and wife team,[267] and in 1939 by southern evangelist Bob Jones. He was appearing in Portsmouth and the church skipped the Sunday night service so the congregation could attend. Dr. Russell Brougher held an evangelistic campaign at the church in 1940.

Special sessions on church growth and outreach were held. For awhile, the church also broadcast morning services on a local radio station as part of its community outreach. Having contacts with other pastors and churches in the city was a part of Rev. Maxfield's ministry. He announced that Easter union services would be held by the Dover Ministers Association. The services were held during the week at the Methodist, Congregational and Episcopal churches, as well as Dover Baptist.

By the Easter morning service of 1939, the attendance was reported at 457.

BUT THEN came a national crisis that disrupted the life of the church. When word arrived in Dover on that Sunday afternoon in December 1941, the church, the city and the nation began a four-year struggle like no other in memory. World War II would change many lives, but also would provide new opportunities for the church.

The church even became a designated air raid shelter at one time during the war because of fears of attack from across the sea. But Dover and the church building survived unscathed.

After an eventful and difficult first century, there were hopes that the second century in the church's history would provide new victories and new opportunities. Looking back—despite all that had befallen the congregation—members could rejoice. A lot had been accomplished since

---

[266] DBC, 4:160-161.
[267] *Ibid.*, 4:200.

the day in February 1840 when the first 13 persons had met in an upstairs room near the Cochecho River on Central Street, to form what would become Dover Baptist Church.

Epilogue

The years following World War II were ones of great growth and expansion for Dover Baptist Church as it entered its second century.

The church had bought a home on the west side of the present church and cleared the lot in the late 1920s, but it wasn't until the 1950s that the property was used when a four-floor educational wing was attached to the west of the main building. It went a long way in alleviating conditions in the crowded Sunday School, in which several classes were at times forced to meet in the same room or the main auditorium because of lack of space.

Since the church was limited in further expansion by the fact that the building itself took up much of the small lot, by the late 1950s its leaders were again thinking of expansion. On April 17, 1957, the church purchased houses at 10-12, 14-16 and 18-20 Fayette Street behind the church. One of the properties was used for Sunday School classes for a time, and there was talk of another addition at the back of the church. But in the end the church, finding that renting the properties was a losing proposition, demolished them and created a church parking lot. Nothing further came of expansion plans at that time.[268]

Eventually the property behind the church was taken by the city of Dover as part of an urban renewal project, was reconfigured somewhat and then deeded back to the church, which before the 20th century ended owned all property bounded by Washington, Fayette and Green streets.

Further expansion of the main building came in 1995, even as the church was without a pastor. The first phase of planned construction resulted in a new main entrance, kitchen, restrooms and elevator at the rear of the building adjacent to the parking lot. The second phase of the project, a large meeting room that also was intended to be used as a gymnasium-type facility, was postponed near the turn of the century at a time of high costs and dwindling resources.

Dover Baptist has spawned other churches over the years, so never outgrew its present site. Church works were begun both in nearby Durham and in Eliot, Maine, where congregations continue to prosper.

---

[268] Church manuscript notes left by Willis E. Littlefield, deacon and architect.

The church now owns a house on the property it uses as a home for missionaries on leave or preparing for the mission field, and while many churches have moved to more convenient sites outside downtown areas, Dover Baptist has determined, at least for now, that its mission continues to be downtown, where it has been for nearly 170 years.

Church attendance and membership blossomed after World War II, and the missionary programs that always had been a large part of the church's ministry expanded way beyond anything that had been possible earlier. In 1960, with attendance at about 350, and with 400 deemed the maximum "comfortable" seating in the auditorium, thoughts for awhile again turned to expansion. Mission expenditures increased and during the 1960s at times were approaching 50 percent of the church's total budget; in the 1967-68 budget being $31,000 for current expenses and $24,000 for missions.[269] Yearly week-long missionary conferences brought speakers from across the nation and from foreign fields and were probably the major events of the year for many seasons.

Attendance for awhile taxed the auditorium to the extent that extra seating had to be provided. Monthly events that included other churches and other denominations in the area were singular gatherings in which all the churches got together for what was called "Singspiration."

A compilation of membership over the first 100 years shows nearly 1,900 persons were members at one time or another. Hundreds more have been members since that time.

But the bell that once tolled for church services Sunday morning and evening, and Tuesday or Wednesday evenings for prayer meeting, is no longer heard on a regular basis. It tolls mostly on special occasions. The Sunday evening service, as in many other churches, has been discontinued. The prayer meeting, once drawing enough members to fill the large vestry, now meets in a small parlor in the Sunday School annex.

The church became affiliated with the Conservative Baptist Association of America in 1948, and eventually severed its connection with the Northern Baptist (now American Baptist) Convention. It has remained a member of CBA ever since.

The Gospel still is preached and missions, though much changed over the years, still are a vital though reduced part of the church's program. The building itself stands as a living reminder of the significant influence its founders had on the history of Dover and, yes, even of the nation in its early struggle to see an end to the institution of slavery.

---

[269] Littlefield.

Appendix A

Dover Gazette and Strafford Advertiser
March 17, 1840

"THE FIRST
FREEWILL BAPTIST CHURCH
IN DOVER."

Mr. Gibbs:

Knowing the liberality of your sentiments toward all religious societies, and your determined support of freedom and equal rights, we the FIRST FREE WILL BAPTIST CHURCH IN DOVER, ask of you the favor of your columns for the purpose of making to the public the following true and candid

STATEMENT.

It is much to be regretted by us, as well as by all the lovers of Christianity and peace, that is well known to the community in this region and somewhat extensively through the country that some unpleasant difficulties have for some time existed in the First Free Will Baptist Church in Dover, which commenced about the latter part of the year 1838 in regard to the Ministry of their Pastor Elder A. D. SMITH, which difficulties like all others of a like kind, have by circulation been misrepresented and exaggerated much to the grief of the sincere friends of Zion, bringing a stigma upon that holy cause which should be kept pure as the light which emanates from the third Heavens. We would therefore in a concise and summary manner, with a strict regard to truth and the cause of Christ, state the circumstances to the Christian public and to the world, that the obscuring veil of darkness and error may no longer rest upon the unpleasant subject, and that all may form correct ideas and judge for themselves.

Though we are decidedly of opinion that all the difficulties which arise among brethren of any Church should be amicably adjusted and kept within the pale of the Church, without the opprobrium always arising from its being bruited to the world, who are indeed too apt to magnify the apparent dereliction of professing Christians from the path marked out by the great head of the Church, even Christ.

Neither should we have taken this course of publishing to the world these few remarks, had not some disaffected, ambitious, and we must say, unchristian members of our Church, amounting to some fifteen or sixteen, recently published a pamphlet stating that the majority of the First Free Will Baptist Church in Dover had rejected certain terms imposed upon them by the Rockingham Quarterly Meeting, as requisite for their retaining their fellowship, and were therefore *expelled*   from said Quarterly Meeting; accusing them of "neglecting necessary discipline, and in countenancing and *laboring to uphold an impure Ministry;"* and that they, this small minority, had, contrary to both civil and ecclesiastical law, formed themselves into a Church to be *known as the first Free Will Baptist Church in Dover !* in words following: "And whereas the said minority is the regular Free Will Baptist Church in Dover and the only Free Will Baptist Church in fellowship and standing in the connection, in this place." Also publishing in the Morning Star of the 19th ult. a communication purporting to be the doings of the Rockingham Quarterly Meeting of January last, containing among other things the following clause: "The Conference then met the Church and presented their decision. The minority agreed to comply with it; but after much time had been spent, the majority refused to comply, and consequently was disfellowshipped."

This minority having thus done, leaving the subject in the dark, accusing us of the heavy and unbearable imputation of "countenancing and laboring to uphold an impure Ministry;" assuming our rights and immunities as a Church and as a Society, incorporated by Statutable enactments and shielding themselves before the public under the sanction of an illegal and unecclesiastical decision of the R. Quarterly Meeting, we feel in duty bound to assert our rights both in a Religious and civil point of view, and give a fair explanation, as far as may be done in the columns of a public periodical, the nature of the case; fearing neither the envy nor maledictions of the "carnal heart;" the criticisms of those possessed of "much learning;" the ecclesiastical ambition or oppression of any, though it might vie with the Inquisition of Spain; the shafts of slander or "any other creature."

Neither time nor room would allow of our going into a minute detail of every particular of the rise and progress of those difficulties which have for some time disturbed the quiet of our Church, and afflicted the hearts of its members, "who would live godly in this present world; neither would it be interesting or beneficial to community, further than to give a general and impartial statement of facts, which will go to exonerate the "majority" of the Church as they are called by the "minority" and the Quarterly Meeting, and in fact so known to the world, from the grievous, heinous and false charge of "countenancing and laboring to uphold an impure ministry."

Sometime in the latter part of 1838, sundry disaffected and envious individuals then members of the Church, and some we regret to say in high standing, began to agitate and pretend to feel aggrieved at certain reports which they said were in circulation detrimental in their tendency to the Christian and ministerial character of Elder A. D. Smith, then Pastor of the Church and whose labors had been blessed among us. Those individuals are of that minority to which we have alluded, and shall frequently allude. They named them to several members of the Church, and the said reports were discussed, and they were not thought to be of sufficient consequence in reality to deserve a serious labor of the Church, and were to the satisfaction of this minority amicably adjusted, and Elder Smith continued to labor amongst us received by *all*, as a minister of Christ. Even the community at large were satisfied that the improprieties of which he had been charged were unfounded or did not [*unreadable*] in any intention of evil.

One of the individuals who had been most busy in retailing the aforesaid stories against Elder Smith, was by the Church called to an account, which was the bounden duty of the Church. This renewed the hostility of some of the minority, and they proceeded to hold secret meetings under the guidance of Mr. William Burr and Mr. Enoch Mack, for purpose of privately devising measures to sustain the character of the member justly impeached in traducing the character of Elder Smith, and for the purpose of raising an excitement to get rid of Elder Smith, in some way. We have in our possession full proof of those secret meetings and the manner in which they were conducted in two Affidavits of respectable members of the Church who were induced by Mr. Burr and his party to attend, and which we would publish, were they not too lengthy, in order to show the spirit which moved this uneasy minority, and who did not name to Elder Smith or his friends the majority of the Church, the trials under which they professed to be laboring. The records of the Inquisition would hardly furnish a parallel of so unfair and unscriptural conduct. We extract the following from one of the Affidavits: "Mr. Burr said the Church was in a very bad condition that the church or the deacons of the church were misusing, or were about trying to turn out of the church, the individual before referred to, which he thought was wrong, and the object of the meeting was to contrive some plan by which they might defend her against the charges of the Church, and to prevent Elder Smith from preaching longer in the place. After some time spent in conversation, a suggestion was made to appoint a select committee of final *decision*, but no conclusions were come to that evening. The meeting agreed to adjourn to Mr. Masons (?), because they thought they might be *detected* if they should have their meeting at the same place again. They also said the meeting must be kept secret; so they agreed to pass out, some at one door and some at the other door, that a few only should go out at a time, that they might not be discovered and their plans frustrated." At another meeting of this singular kind, he says: "it was finally agreed to appoint the above named committee and refer the above named matters to them, by so doing they could carry their points; for said Mr. Burr, it will be of no use to present these things to the Church, for the *majority of the Church would be with Elder Smith*, the Deacons, &c." In another part of his Affidavit he says further: "Some brother said, he should be opposed to Elder Smith's going away; Mr. Burr said it would be much easier to get rid of Elder Smith then, than it would be if he should stay his year out, for the longer he stayed, *the more his friends or the Church* (this large "majority" some ways back alluded to) *would be attached to him,* and the harder it would be to get rid of him." Did ever any one versed at all in the proceedings of Christians or churches, or Ecclesiastical History, ever meet with just such a kind of dark and inquisitorial proceedings? Did their self-sufficiency lead them to suppose, that they, some twelve or fifteen were to draw wires to manage a whole church of more than two hundred and twenty members? were they to be the sole judges of the case whether this two hundred majority in sitting under the preaching and supporting Elder Smith, were "countenancing and laboring to uphold an impure ministry"?

But this minority, did, by dint of maneuvering and perseverance so represent the case to the Quarterly Meeting, as to obtain without the request or coincidence of the Church, a Council to examine into the existing difficulties. The Council did convene, and all the charges that could be found, were brought before them by the minority who had requested the assembling of the Council, and investigated thoroughly all the matters in relation to Elder Smith, and they reported thereon accordingly, which report was accepted by the Church.

We would here observe, that in the account of the proceedings of Rockingham Quarterly Meeting holden Jan. 30th, 1840, as published in the Morning Star of the 19th ult. it is stated, that—"the subject of the difficulties that have existed for a long time in the Church at Dover (on which several Councils from the Q. M. had previously set, with whose decisions the majority of the Church had refused to comply) came up by postponement from the preceding session. After a protracted sitting and a patient hearing of the whole case, Conference came to a decision similar to the decisions of the Councils which had previously set upon it, and decided further, that if either division of the Church refused to comply with it, such division should be disfellowshipped by the Q. M." This leaves the subject much in the dark, and needs explanation, for it carries the impression to the world that we did not accept or comply with any report of the Councils; whereas we did accept the first and only impartial and proper report as touching the affair at issue, which was in substance, that he had been in a certain instance, guilty of rudely or improperly talking to sundry poor children; and in unguardedly using some loose and lascivious expressions; equivocating in some degree when questioned by sundry individuals in regard to his conduct; and some other equivocal "appearances of evil" which were improper in a minister of Christ and calculated to bring an evil report upon the holy cause of Religion; which were however adjudged to be imprudences resulting more from constitutional frailties and inadvertencies of speech and manners than from any evil propensities of the heart, and that for those things he should make a proper acknowledgment to the church, which if to their satisfaction, we considered would be an end of all the difficulties and trials. The church and congregation held a meeting; and in order to satisfy other religious churches and the world at large, a disinterested and impartial committee was chosen from other churches in town to hear the report of the council and the enjoined explanation, and confession of Eld. Smith. Eld. Smith accordingly made his confession fully to the satisfaction of the church, the congregation and the said committee, agreeably to the report of the Council, and as the Committee observed, "not only in the letter, but in the spirit." At an adjourned meeting of the council held a few days afterwards they decided that, "as Elder Smith's confession in the following words, viz. "I sincerely regret all my past conduct by which the cause of the Redeemer may have been injured," and as he has asked the forgiveness of God, his brethren and the world, we think no further confession necessary. The council further voted, "that we are decidedly of the opinion that under existing circumstances Elder Smith should *for the present* entirely desist from public labors as a preacher of the Gospel."

Here we supposed was a final end and disposition of the troubles. Elder Smith did desist from his public labors for nearly 3 months, being out of health; and at about the end of that time he came and preached with us, and we attended freely his ministrations; this gave umbrage to the minority, and shows the unforgiving and unchristian spirit with which they were actuated, that aristocratic spirit which has ever more or less infested the church, and which we as an order, did in our first organization, set steadfastly our faces against, where an ambitious few perhaps possessed of more talents or learning wish to rule, direct, or coerce the many. Other councils came by the undue influence exerted with the Quarterly Meeting, and hence the gross charge of "countenancing and laboring to uphold an impure Ministry," which we most solemnly disclaim, and think we have fully substantiated as being without a shadow of foundation against us as a church of Christ. For these, their unchristian, unfair, unusual and unscriptural conduct, for the manner in which they obtained the first council, without communicating their grievance in regard to Elder Smith either to him or the church; for although Mr. Burr did state to the Quarterly M. that he could not have a hearing in the church, it is without a shade of truth as is abundantly proved from the Affidavits of those who attended their *secret meetings* and by the testimony of the Church; for this, and for their persevering and anti-Christian attempts to cause approbrium and an unfounded and calumnious charge upon us as a Church we have proceeded to call Mr. Burr and his adherents to an account, to labor with them, but finding them contumacious and obstinate against every scriptural measure we have taken in regard to them, we have expelled them from the church.

We now would call the attention of the reader to the course they have taken in their appeal to the Q. M. whom they, by such representations as they saw fit to make to that body, induced them to pass, at their session in January last the following vote, "Agreed that the majority should confess to the minority of the church, that they have taken an unadvisable and improper course in dismissing A. D. Smith from the church, and in countenancing him in preaching and laboring with them after he had been suspended from the ministry, and for having fellowship with him after such incontestable evidences of his wickedness." This the church have agreed they can never do, as it would virtually be confessing an absolute falsehood, for we have above shown that we have *not* taken an unadvisable and improper course in regard to Eld. Smith, for he was only directed by the council to desist from his labors "for the present," which was an indefinite time, and he did desist for nearly three months, and was then, by any construction that may be put upon it, the decision of the council and his confession full and satisfactory to all, but this restive minority, at liberty to preach, and we at liberty to hear him, and was we say never legally "suspended from the ministry," neither have we had "incontestable evidence of his wickedness."

It is but justice here to remark that the Quarterly Conference consisted of 38 members of whom on the passage of the above vote 17 were in favor and 20 against the church, a majority of only 3, and from what we have since heard, we have no doubt, that could this Q. M. have the subject again before them, which in all probability they never will, there would hardly be this 3 majority.

In regard to the Q. M. disfellowshipping the majority if they did not comply with their requirements, we would barely remark, we do not know, nor do the best judges of ecclesiastical powers and duties, of any right or power by which a Q. M. can sever a Church, or cut off a part without cutting off the whole; or of any power by which they can transfer the name, rights, act of incorporation and immunities both civil and ecclesiastical from a church to a minority of the same church or to any other persons whomsoever; the Church of Rome in her proudest days hardly would have assumed such power.

That 16 individuals under the protection of sundry Q. M. resolves, should, from a church of 220 members, take their name, assume all the powers of said church, and claim to be the "regular Freewill Baptist Church in Dover, and the *only* Freewill Baptist Church in fellowship and standing in the place," is a most curious anomaly among the transactions of the world, an attempt truly ridiculous and absurd, an act of audacious ambition; over sight and consummate folly, especially reserved to be recorded in the annals of Church History for 1840.

We would further say in regard to the accusation made by the Q. M. of "dismissing A. D. Smith from the Church," as well as hearing him preach, we suppose they must mean that when he went away, we gave him a letter of recommendation to a Church in Vermont; where he was received and is now preaching; which we sincerely believe we had an undoubted right to do as well as attend his ministration after he had made the requisite confessions to God, the Church and the world; abstained from preaching "for the present," the terms used by the council, and strictly conformed to all the requirements of the council, and was to all intents and purposes then a member in full connection, and an accredited minister of our order, nothing to the contrary standing upon the Church or Quarterly Meeting records, the council deciding in words following: "We therefore consider him still a member of the Church."

In regard to the fulsome mockery of this "influential" minority assuming to be the First Freewill Baptist Church in Dover, we have little more to say, nor need but little more be said to any reader of common sense and a decent share of knowledge of matters and things, to convince him of the illegality and absurdity of such an attempt.

We were, agreeably to an act of the Legislature of this State, Incorporated Nov. 9th, 1830, to be known as the "First Freewill Baptist Church in Dover," we elected our officers accordingly, and received a deed bearing date the 15th day of Nov. 1830 running to the "First Freewill Baptist Church in Dover," "and their assigns, to their use and benefit forever," conveying a certain tract or parcel of land on which to erect a Building for public Worship, which building we did erect and finish about the month of June 1832, and have since occupied it for the above purpose; have all the proper church officers, such as Deacons, Clerk and Wardens; the Deed, papers, Church Records, &c. and we are well assured that we "the First Freewill Baptist church" can hold, occupy, and control the said House for religious purposes without hindrance or interruption from stockholders, or from Quarterly Meetings, or from any other source. Some few of the Pews are owned by the "minority," but it matters nothing if every Pew was owned out of the church—it would alter nothing—the design of the House is for the proper use and benefit of the church, and the control of all its affairs and use is subject to, and discretionary with the church, whether the church is owned or disowned by the Quarterly Meeting. Quarterly Meetings of our order have certain control in ecclesiastical matters, over churches who have united under their jurisdiction, but no control as it regards their civil affairs; no power to divide or create a Church; no power to authorize a church or a part of a church to assume the corporate name of another church, or annul or take away the corporate rights and jurisdiction of any church.

All this, if they have not already understood with sufficient clearness, we would have this "minority" and the Rockingham Quarterly Meeting, distinctly understand. And so auger all the attempts of intriguants to disunite us as a church, or all the opposition of the ambitious or designing, we shall maintain our rights, property and privileges as a church, hoping to have our arms strengthened and our path lighted by that strength and that light which cometh down from the Father of lights; being well assured if our cause, course and conduct be right, we shall receive the all-powerful aid of the Great Head of the Church.

Thus have we endeavored to set forth to the public, a just and true statement of all the difficulties we have encountered and the ground on which we stand. If we have in reference to papers, reports, affidavits, &c. in any case omitted to mention names, where names might have been expected, it has been done only through courtesy, but which we have on file, together with some other matter in relation to this subject; all which we can publish if thought advisable, necessary or beneficial, and which we shall do if driven thereto. We close for the present, and respectfully submit all the above to the candor and judgment of our brethren and the public.

Appendix B

FIFTH

ANNUAL REPORT

OF THE

FREE-WILL BAPTIST
ANTI-SLAVERY SOCIETY

READ AT

LEBANON, MAINE, OCTOBER 9, 1851.

DOVER:
WM. BURR, PRINTER
1851.

OFFICERS OF THE F. W. BAPTIST
ANTI-SLAVERY SOCIETY.

President, Eld. SILAS CURTIS.
Vice Presidents, ELDERS H. WELLINGTON,
          M. W. BURLINGAME, M. J. STEERE.
Recording Secretary, D. P. CILLEY.
Corresponding Secretary, I. D. STEWART.
Treasurer, WM. BURR.
Executive Committee, ELDERS D. S. FROST, WM. HURLIN, E. G. KNOWLES, L. B. TASKER, E. TRUE.

REPORT

The freedom of the will is one of our denominational characteristics. But our faith stops not here: it includes the freedom of the entire man; ever subject, however, to the restraints of the "higher law." We claim this freedom for ourselves, and we grant it to others. Aye, more, we *demand* it for others; and for *all* others. Especially do we plead for the enslaved of our race in this boasted "land of the free and home of the brave."

We do it, because they are not allowed to speak for themselves. We do it the more earnestly, because the rod of oppression is held by the American people.

The same year that our Pilgrim fathers landed upon Plymouth Rock, and founded institutions that have blessed the world, *the same year* came a cargo of slaves to Virginia's shore; and then commenced an institution, that, like the serpent in the garden, has beguiled the people, and cursed the land. For more than two hundred years it has been growing with our growth, and strengthening with our strength.

Within its coils more than 3,000,000 of victims are now held, and its slimy folds encircle both Church and State. White laborers feel its sting, and free blacks the poison of its fangs. It now claims to be the corner-stone of our republican edifice, and the *sine qua non* in every well regulated government. It threatens the dissolution of our Union, if a free State is admitted, or the door closed against its entrance into territory now free. It enslaves every free black that enters its enclosure, and hunts its fugitives in all our domain. It now makes the kidnapping of freemen as feasible in our own land as in that of Africa, so far as national laws can do it. And more than all this, it calls upon us to disobey God in the return of fugitives, and threatens us with fines and imprisonment, if we obey Him rather than men. O slavery! "full of all subtlety and all mischief, thou child of the devil;" may our right hand forget her cunning, may our tongue cleave to the roof of our mouth, if we do not resist thy wicked encroachments.

It has been our purpose to devote the principal part of this Report to

THE HISTORY OF SLAVERY IN THE FREEWILL BAPTIST DENOMINATION

The position we now occupy in the Anti-Slavery cause was not attained without struggles, fierce and obstinate. The record of our movements, the opposition we encountered, and our continued advancement in the enterprise, is found in every department of our denominational action. It has been suggested that the *facts* are worthy of collection and preservation. As the wasting hand of time will be vigilantly placing them beyond the reach of our successors in life, we now seize some of the more important ones, and solicit attention to a historical Report.

The origin of the emancipation cause is assigned, by different men, to different periods of time. Drs. Franklin and Rush were emancipationists and officers of an Abolition Society *seventy* years ago. The Friends and Covenantors have been emancipationists, with no connection with slavery, for more than *half a century.* About the year 1820, Mr. Lundy, of Baltimore, commenced the publication of a paper, advocating the abolition of slavery. But it was *gradual* abolition, and rather favorable to Colonization. During the years 1829 and '30, Wm. L. Garrison was associated with him, and was the principal editor. Garrison then inscribed upon his banner *"immediate emancipation the right of the slave, and the duty of the master."* Because he published the fact that a man from Salem, Mass., had shipped a cargo of slaves for the South, and made some truthful comments upon the transaction, he was thrown into prison, and there lay for *forty-nine days.* Being discharged, he returned to Boston, and, Jan. 1st, 1831, issued his first number of the Liberator. The next year was formed the New England Anti-Slavery Society. The meeting was held in the vestry of a colored church in the city, and only twelve men united at its organization. In December, 1833, was organized the American Anti-Slavery Society, in Philadelphia. — This soon became an efficient organization, having as many as *sixty* agents in the field at a time. Slaveholders were alarmed. With the fury of enraged demons they exclaimed, *"Let us alone."* And, *let us alone,* was the echo of their Northern allies.

Down to the time when this agitation commenced, truth compels us to say that we were no more Anti-Slavery than other denominations; unless our profound silence can be termed Anti-Slavery, when compared with the apologizing, justifying efforts of others. The Fathers of our connexion were called forth for a peculiar work.

The return of peace, at the close of the Revolutionary war, found us nationally free, but with vitiated morals and a formal religion. The great doctrines of the Bible were so explained as to savor much of fatalism, and the people were famishing for the bread of life. God raised up flaming heralds of the cross, who "went forth and preached everywhere," proclaiming a *free salvation* for all that would come, and a *free-will* on the part of man to accept or refuse it. Sinners were converted; churches organized; and a denomination formed, that was "earnestly contending for the faith," systematizing its action, and consolidating its influence. This was the appropriate work of many years; and if the slave was not remembered as he now is, who can find it in his heart to say that our fathers did not faithfully "serve their own generation?" Occupied by other duties, their attention seems not to have been directed to slavery, but when it was called to the subject, a majority of our ministers soon saw the path of duty and immediately walked therein. Some had their attention arrested by the lectures of George Thompson and other philanthropists, some by reading an article occasionally on the evils of slavery, some by reading the slanderous attacks upon abolitionists, and others by merely hearing that the subject was in agitation. It is singular coincidence that in almost every Yearly Meeting, extending from Maine to Mississippi, some of our most eminent men were prepared, in the onset, to take uncompromising ground against slavery. Like Luther, Swingle, and other Reformers, they commenced operations in their respective locations, without consultation with those abroad, and in some instances, without the least knowledge of the question's being agitated in any other part of the connexion.

In 1834, an editorial appeared in the Star, headed — SLAVERY AND ABOLITION. It took the position that slavery was an evil, but immediate emancipation was a *greater* one. It was an unjust demand upon the master, requiring such a sacrifice of his property, and cruel to the slaves, in turning them out into the world, incompetent to provide for themselves. Like pro-slavery everywhere, it feared that the cause of freedom would suffer more from the rashness of abolitionists, than be benefited by their good intentions. The effect of this article, written in a kind spirit, was like every similar production. It tended, for the time, to keep at ease those who had hitherto been so; to soothe the feelings of those who were beginning to be disturbed; and it *aroused* to redoubled effort those who were already awake. Upon the whole, it was doubtless overruled for good, as it elicited discussion, and led to investigation. Then, and then for all, was the light of our Star darkness. And, under the noontide splendor of our present light, we are ready to exclaim, "how great was that darkness!" But the palliating circumstances of that day should not be overlooked.

A few weeks after this, the junior editor was called from labor to rewards, and a change was then effected in the editorial department, by which its management since that time has devolved upon our present resident editor.

The first *recorded* action in the denomination that has come to our knowledge, was the adoption of a series of resolutions by the Rockingham Quarterly Meeting in March, 1835.

The resolutions were five in number, of which the following is one: —

"*Resolved,* That we will, as Christians, and Christian ministers, use our influence to promote the doctrine of immediate emancipation; in doing which we wish to treat the oppressor and the oppressed in the spirit of the gospel."

The Records of the Farmington (Maine) Quarterly Meeting show no action till 1837, but some brethren are confident that resolutions were there adopted before the time of those passed by the Rockingham Quarterly Meeting. Be this as it may, a brother in the Quarterly Meeting was deeply anxious to procure an expression of opinion; and expecting opposition, at his request a minister came forty miles to second the effort. A resolution, expressive of the sinfulness of slavery, was introduced, and for an hour apiece, they labored to show the great wickedness of the system, and why Christian bodies should speak against it. They were followed by brethren, who labored with equal zeal, and for as long a time, to show that the resolution was dabbling in the turbid waters of politics, that we had nothing to do with slavery, and that agitation was all wrong. The resolution, however, was adopted by an overwhelming majority.

In 1835, Eld. Marks attended the Annual Meeting of the N.H. Anti-Slavery Society, and reported the speeches for the Star. In June, the same year, the New Hampshire Yearly Meeting, the oldest and most numerous in the connexion, held its annual session under circumstances peculiarly interesting. It was understood that Dr. Cox, from London, and Rev. Amos Sutton, returned missionary to India, would be there. That our first missionary to India, and one to the Mississippi valley, would there be ordained. These circumstances called out such numbers as had never before attended a Yearly Meeting. They came up from every hill and glen of the Granite State, and both Maine and Vermont were fully represented. By that vast concourse of people the following action was taken:

"Whereas the system of slavery is contrary to the law of nature, and the law of God, and is a violation of the dearest rights of man, therefore,

"Resolved, That the principles of immediate abolition are derived from the unerring word of God; and that no political circumstances whatever can exonerate Christians from exerting all their moral influence for the suppression of this heinous sin."

The resolution passed the Yearly Meeting *unanimously,* and the *whole congregation* rose to its support. The Record says, "While the subject of Slavery was before the meeting, the greatest attention was apparent. Deep sympathy for the poor degraded slave was expressed by many a swelling bosom and falling tear." The speeches made by Elders Marks, Woodman, and Place, and Drs. Sutton and Cox, were reported for the Star, and, being the first *published argument* from members of the denomination, it doubtless had as much influence as any one effort in thus early turning our minds in the right direction.

Anti-slavery resolutions were adopted by the Penobscot Yearly Meeting the same month, and by the Vermont and Holland Purchase Yearly Meeting in August, following. For three years prior to this, the Printing Establishment had been under the control of the denomination, and managed by an Agent under the direction of a Publishing Committee, chosen by the General Conference. At a meeting of the Publishing Committee in September, it was

"Resolved, That the Morning Star shall not take any position, nor advocate any sentiments on the subject of slavery for political purposes; but as the conductors of the Star do believe that *slaveholding is a sin,* we cannot consent that the Star shall be silent on the subject. We believe that no political circumstances can excuse us as *Christians,* and conductors of a *religious paper,* from using all the *moral influence* within our power to *reprove sin.* Still, under the present critical circumstances of our country, we believe that it is our duty to treat the subject with caution, and to reprove the sin of slaveholding with great kindness."

In October, the General Conference convened at Byron, N.Y. The whole denomination was here represented, and the following resolutions were adopted, *no one voting against them:*

"(1.) *Resolved,* That slavery is an unjust infringement on the dearest rights of the slave; an unwarrantable exercise of power on the part of the master; a potent enemy to the happiness and morals of our slaveholding population; and, if continued, must ultimately result in the ruin of our country.

(2.) *Resolved,* That as Christians, patriots, and philanthropists, we ought to exert our influence to induce all slaveholders to use their best exertions, in their respective states, to procure the abolition of slavery.

(3.) *Resolved,* That a candid discussion and mutual interchange of views, on the best method of abolishing slavery, is loudly called for by the present crisis.

(4.) *Resolved,* That it is the duty of Christians to frequently and fervently *pray* that the evil of slavery may be removed from our beloved country.

(5.) *Resolved,* That we have abundant cause for gratitude to God that, as a denomination, we are so generally united in our views on the distracting subject of slavery."

For the first time, we here find the *denomination* speaking in calm but decided condemnation of slavery. As we contemplate this action from our present stand point, we discover nothing worthy of remark. But placing ourselves back *sixteen years*, to a time when political influence exerted its utmost power to suppress discussion — when popular feeling was boiling with indignation against abolitionists — and when mobs, imprisonment, and death had been the fate of some, and still threatened others, it will be seen that no small degree of moral principle and courage was then requisite to take the position we did. And especially at *that* time, as the same Conference instructed the Trustees of the Printing Establishment to procure an act of incorporation from the next session of the N.H. Legislature — a Legislature never partial to abolitionism — policy dictated a conservative course, but *duty* called for action. And, *thank Heaven,* "noble, sublime, god-like action" was then taken.

Conference adjourned, and time rolled on. But every revolving sun witnessed some new struggle with the apologists of slavery. It was one thing to adopt the resolutions they did when together, and quite another thing to defend and sustain them single handed, in their respective churches. Here came the "tug of war." But, "remembering them that are in bonds as bound with them," they faltered not.

Their conversation, prayers, sermons, and lectures, were not in vain. Accompanying these efforts were 5000 rays of Star light, weekly diffusing their illuminating influence throughout the connexion. The result was, that before the next General Conference, every Yearly Meeting, almost every Quarterly Meeting, took *high* Anti-slavery ground.

But there is a dark side to this picture.

Disaffected members were here and there showing themselves in every direction. If a minister alluded to the vile system of slavery, and called upon men to give it no support; or even if he fervently prayed for the enslaved, some, in almost every church, would be incessantly complaining, and do nothing for his support. Others would absent themselves from meeting, and not unfrequently he found it necessary to remove to another field of labor. A few ministers were grieved because others, and particularly the Morning Star, sympathized so deeply with the poor slave; and thus trials arose in the ministry as well as in the laity.

Nearly $15,000 were due the Printing Establishment for books and the Star — a debt of more than $6,000 was resting upon the Trustees personally,—and in their next Report they say, "We petitioned the N.H. Legislature for an act of incorporation, but our prayer has not been granted."

The times were unparalleled for pecuniary embarrassment, and with the arrival of every mail came requests, sometimes twenty in a letter, vile and abusive, for the discontinuance of the Star, because of its anti-slavery character. And so numerous were these requests, that for two years the subscription list was gradually decreasing. Such was the state of affairs when the General Conference assembled at Greenville, R. I., in 1837.

To avert from the denomination the public odium heaped upon abolitionists—to reconcile the disaffected members—to secure an increased circulation of the Star and an act of incorporation—and more than all, to prevent the utter failure of the Printing Establishment, a *retraction* of our strong anti-slavery ground was demanded. Not a few in the connexion thought some modification essential to our prosperity. From *without,* the mandate came with *imperious authority.*

As our patriotic fathers, in their struggle for liberty, stood undismayed through the darkest gloom of our country's adversity, so the body of the denomination at this time proved themselves worthy of their noble ancestry, in opposing a system of oppression, with which British aggression bore no comparison.

In the early part of Conference, it was *unanimously*

"*Resolved,* That we *approve* the course which the Star has taken on the subject of slavery, * * * and we recommend that it continue the same mild, but decided course."

The Committee on Slavery reported a series of resolutions, of which the following is a specimen:

"*Resolved*, That American Slavery is a sin of such exceeding enormity and magnitude, that every minister of the gospel should loudly testify against it, and every Christian should decidedly rebuke it.—That it is an outrage upon the rights and happiness of fellow countrymen, so cruel, so flagrant, and prevailing to so great an extent, that it becomes the duty of every friend of liberty, patriotism, and humanity, to bear decided testimony against it."

These resolutions were adopted without a dissenting vote, showing no disposition *to retract,* or be "dumb dogs" on the walls of Zion.

Let us here break the thread of historical action, as taken by the General Conference, and return for the consideration of other action, to some instances of which allusion has already been made.

The agent of the Printing Establishment having tendered his resignation to the General Conference in 1835, a Board of Trustees was chosen to manage its affairs.

For about a year and a half, the Star had been advocating the sentiments of abolitionists, and this it still continued to do. One or two members of the Board were dissatisfied, and a meeting was called in December for the express purpose of considering the question.

The Board was known to be divided, but what the decision would be no man could foretell. Some insisted that slavery should be entirely excluded from its columns; some were willing it should speak, if its language was mild and compromising; while others urged the *duty* of boldly and fearlessly exposing the system in all its oppressive features. The meeting was an important one. It was to suppress from the denomination, through its official organ, all light and intelligence on the accursed system of slavery; or it was to increase and make permanent the light then shining with Christian effulgence.

The discussion was continued in the Board through the day; nor did it close with the expiring beams of evening twilight. Through the *live-long night* they considered the question with an interest, equaled only by the consequences that hung upon the decision.

It was not till the radiant beams of morning light were streaming in upon that wakeful, wrestling Board, that a vote was attempted. The question was then submitted: Shall the Star pursue its present anti-slavery course?

Every answer was in the *affirmative*, save *one* dissenting voice. Righteous decision! Glorious news to the millions in bonds.

In June, 1836, the Trustees of the Printing Establishment applied to the N.H. Legislature for an act of incorporation, which was denied them. And why this denial? Let the Reporter of the Legislative proceedings, and the leading journals of the party that controlled the Legislature, answer for themselves. The Dover Gazette, printed in the same town as the Morning Star, assigned the following reason, the very next week after the rejection of the bill. "It was securely progressing through the customary stages, when it was mentioned among the members that this establishment had become the vehicle of abolitionism; this produced an instant inquiry into the truth of the suggestion, and the result was that the bill * * was, on Wednesday, refused a third reading by an overwhelming majority."

The Reporter for the N. H. Patriot, in giving the substance of the speech made by the Chairman of the Committee on Incorporations, used the following language:

"He had heard that it (the Morning Star) was an advocate of abolition, and he felt no disposition that the Legislature should lend its aid to publications, which the Legislatures of our sister States were entreating us to *suppress.*" And to convince the House that he was not mistaken about the Star, he read extracts therefrom, proving, what we joyfully admit, that the Star contended for the abolition of slavery. After speaking of other objections to the Bill, the Reporter says, "The principal objection to its passage, however, was, the fact that the Morning Star, a paper advocating the doctrines of immediate abolition of slavery, was owned by and published under the auspices of the Society proposed to be incorporated; and that the granting of the charter, authorizing and legalizing such a newspaper, would be construed as favoring the designs of the abolitionists."

The Bill was finally rejected by a vote of 188 to 34.

This refusal of a favor, so just and reasonable, affected not the course of the Star. It continued to speak for the oppressed, and soon after had a slavery department, in which the subject was constantly and freely discussed. The Trustees continued to urge their petition for an act of incorporation, annually finding an increase of favor, but were ever rejected. To show that the real ground of opposition to the Bill was never changed, the following proposed amendment is in evidence, viz.: "If the Trustees of said corporation shall publish, or cause to be published, any books, tracts or pamphlets upon the subject of the abolition of slavery, the charter shall be void."

Thus we humbly petitioned for an act of incorporation and thus we were denied, *for ten successive years.* In 1846, an entire change was effected in the politics of the State. The Legislature was strongly Anti-Slavery, and an act of incorporation was then granted us, with as great a majority as it had hitherto been rejected.

In this connection, it may not be inappropriate to show that we were successful laborers in the Anti-Slavery cause, from a paper most violently opposed to agitation. The N. H. Patriot, the leading political paper in the State, in accounting for the recent triumph of anti-slavery principles, paid us the following compliment, in which due allowance will be made for the charge of seeking the overthrow of the Democrats.

We have no unkind feelings towards them or the Whigs; our hostility is against *slavery.* And if, at any time, they, or even nominal Christians, are found with the enemy, they must not expect us to reserve our fire. But to the extract:

"During many years, the Morning Star, at Dover, has labored indefatigably to spread among the Free-will Baptist denomination of Christians the conviction that the Democrats were a pro-slavery party. This has been the tendency of its course. It has held up the evils of slavery, in the darkest features of atrocity, and the Democrats have been, if not by express charge, by implication, denounced as the upholders of these evils. A portion of the clergy of the same denomination have pursued a similar course. In the pulpit, and by the fireside, they have preached abolition, raised sympathy, excited strong feeling, and prepared the minds of a great number of people to believe that they must abandon all other things, to resist the denounced encroachments of the slave power."

In 1837, we petitioned the New Hampshire Legislature for the incorporation of our Home Mission Society, but we petitioned in vain. Different reasons, doubtless, influenced different members to oppose the bill, but the New Hampshire Baptist Register, published at the capital, said the principal objection *urged*, was, that it was probably the design of the Society to send forth missionaries to preach abolitionism. Never discouraged in laboring for righteousness and truth, we pressed our petitions for three successive years, when our prayer was granted.

It matters not what our location may be—Whether in the East, the West, or in central parts of the connexion—we are all inspired by the same love of liberty,—we are all encircled by the same bond of union. When we petitioned the Ohio Legislature for the incorporation of Geauga Seminary, pro-slavery men interested themselves for its defeat. They could not prevent the granting of a charter, but they succeeded in procuring the insertion of a clause that excluded colored persons from the privileges of the school. This charter was indignantly rejected by the friends of the school, and the next year, after *great effort*, a charter was received, unstained by that pro-slavery blot.

Our College in Michigan, the Michigan Central, in its struggles for life and prosperity, among other opposing obstacles, has felt the suppressive influence of Christians and politicians who are in league with slavery. But there are no principles of compromise with slavery taught there, and the Institution shows itself worthy of the denomination under whose patronage it has been established.

We all take a lively interest in the "under-ground railroads," and those at the West, living in their more immediate vicinity, are most of them stockholders, and not a few are either shrewd officers or efficient laborers in the enterprise. By their aid, in common with others, thousands of fugitives are now safe on the Canadian shore, where Victoria's flag in freedom floats. And they still care for both soul and body. Boxes of clothing, and one teacher, at least, have been sent over by our brethren, and many of us have contributed for the support of missionaries among them.

At the commencement of the agitation, two brethren from the eastern part of the State attended the Maine Western Y. M. as Corresponding Messengers, and were kindly received. It was feared by some that the great object of their visit was to unite with their own abolitionists in a general anti-slavery discussion. To prevent this, a resolution was incautiously introduced, virtually declaring that slavery did not come within the range of their deliberations, and would not be entertained by the Y. M. Instead of closing, this opened wide the door for discussion, and for hours, from one adjournment to another, the propriety of adopting such a resolution was warmly contested, and the friends of free discussion, both in and out of the Y. M., were thus favored with an ample opportunity of speaking for the slave.

The result was the rejection of this resolution, the adoption of anti-slavery ones, and the enjoyment of a gracious revival of religion.

In 1837, the Rockingham Q. M. passed a resolution, approving "the principles, measures, and objects of the American Anti-Slavery Society." This brought out the famous "protest," published in the New Hampshire Patriot, a copy of which may not be uninteresting.

"For the N. H. Patriot"

"The following communication was prepared for the Morning Star:

"Whereas the Morning Star, a religious paper, published at Dover, N.H., under the direction of the Free-will Baptist General Conference, is sent abroad in the world as containing the sentiments of the denomination,—and whereas we believe slavery a moral and political evil, and to be very much regretted that it should ever have been countenanced on Columbia's free soil; yet we, as a religious community, can never consent to digress so far from the cause we have espoused, as to lend our influence to any Society that we think has for its ultimate object the dissolution of the Union, or that will create dissension in the moral and religious community.

"Therefore, we the undersigned, professing ourselves to be Free-will Baptists, beg leave, through your columns, to enter this, our protest, on the following subjects which are propagated in your columns, [the Star, of course.—*Sec.*]

"1st. We disapprove of the measures of the Anti-Slavery Society, which is [are?] propagated in the Morning Star, and do not feel ourselves bound to sustain the vote passed in the Rockingham Q. M. in relation to said Society, and also feel and believe the paper may be filled with matter more edifying and interesting to a religious community.

"2. We disapprove of a religious paper descending so far below the object for which it was intended (agreeably to the Prospectus) as to meddle with the political contentions of the day, which has been done by the Morning Star.

"3. We disapprove of the doings of the last General Conference in the encouragement and inducement to preach by note."

This "protest" was signed by *eleven* brethren, leading members of different churches; two of whom were ministers, prominent in the connexion. One of the two has since gone home to rest, and the other is now one of the most ardent friends of the slave.

In 1839, the General Conference assembled at Conneaut, Ohio. Some parts of the session were scenes of the most thrilling interest. The slavery question there came up as it had never before presented itself, and the firmness of our anti-slavery principles was brought to the test.

A communication was received from New Hampshire, signed by *four clergymen*, and as many *clerks*, on behalf of their respective churches, most of them the signers of the above-mentioned "protest." It asked the opinion of Conference on the vote of the Rockingham Q. M., and gave it as their opinion that the Star had descended from a religious to a political course.

This communication was referred, and the committee, not having the particular vote of the Quarterly Meeting before them, reported the two following resolutions, which were adopted:

"*Resolved,* That this Conference, believing the Anti-Slavery cause to be the cause of God, recommend to every Christian and every Christian minister to use all proper means to promote its interest.

"*Resolved,* That this Conference highly approve the decided and straight forward course of the Morning Star on the subject of slavery."

During the summer previous to the Conference in October, a correspondence had been conducted between the Editor of the Star and Dr. Wm. M. Housley, of Kentucky.

This correspondence was published, and consisted principally of inquiries on the part of the Doctor, and answers on the part of the Editor. Dr. Housley attended the Conference, as it was expected he would; and when the delegates arrived, he was already there, and had united with the church at Conneaut. It appeared, from satisfactory testimonials, that he had been a member of the Calvinistic Baptist church, and a licensed preacher; but differing from them in doctrine, he had taken a letter of dismission and commendation. He proposed to receive ordination, if found worthy, and in addressing the Conference, he said, "A large number of the Baptists in the southern country are with you in sentiment, and should you plant a mission in Kentucky, probably you might gather into your connexion, from that State alone, 20,000 members within three years."

It was noticed by some paper in Southern Ohio that Dr. H. was on his way to the General Conference, where he would unite with the Free-will Baptists, and, on his return to Kentucky, would carry with him all those Baptist churches that believed in a free salvation.

A council of five members from the church at Conneaut, and an equal number from the General Conference, was chosen for the examination of Dr. Housley, as to the propriety of his ordination. He related his Christian experience, his doctrinal views, his call to the ministry, &c., all of which were satisfactory. But the most important item elicited in the examination, was the fact that he was a *slaveholder.* He claimed as his property a *mother* and her *three children,* valued at $2000.

The bright visions of a large accession to our denomination, from Kentucky, immediately vanished, as this fact became known.

Among other questions and answers in the examination, were the following:

Question. What do you think of American slavery?

Answer. I think it a great moral evil, a scourge and a curse.

Q. Are you a slaveholder?

A. I am.

Q. Do you think it morally and religiously right for *you* to hold your fellow men in slavery?

A. Circumstances alter cases; if I could believe my slaves would be bettered in their condition by immediate emancipation, I should be as glad to have them liberated as you would; *but* they are ignorant, and *unprepared at present to take care of themselves.*

Q. All circumstances *as they are,* do you think it morally and religiously *right* for you to claim property in your fellow men?

A. It is a difficult question; I choose not to answer it directly.

Q. We will give you satisfactory bonds that your slaves shall have *three years'* good schooling in New England, and other necessary instruction to qualify them for useful life. Will you let us have them on these conditions?

A. No: unless I can have a remuneration for their value.

Q. If you should now see your slaves passing here, towards Canada, what would probably be your course?

A. I should arrest and claim them as my property.

The facts of the Doctor's connection with slavery being publicly known, the excitement was intense, and the decision of the Council was anticipated. Judge M., a man of great influence in Northern Ohio, called on the chairman of the Council, and entreated him not to report against the

Doctor *merely* because he was a slaveholder. Said he, "Do it, and it will be destructive to the Free-will Baptist interests in all *this* country." A prominent man in the ministry said to a member of the Council, "Do you think the denomination will make slaveholding a test of Christian fellowship?" *"I do,"* was the reply. "Then," said he, with *great* emphasis, "I am no longer a Free-will Baptist."

As the Conference opened, the next morning, a crowded house was anxiously waiting for the report of the Council. It was soon presented, and in substance it said, "as Dr. Housley claims property in human beings, we cannot ordain him as a minister, nor fellowship him as a Christian."

The discussion that followed was exceedingly spirited. All the talent of Conference was called into action; and many of our brethren, not members of Conference, several ministers of other denominations, and lawyers, also, asked the privilege, and were permitted, to participate in the debate.

The report was opposed as being in advance of the times— uncharitable—and impolitic.

But it was finally *voted, without opposition,* "that the decision of the Council is highly satisfactory."

The subject of our connection with the slaveholding churches of North and South Carolina, was brought before Conference, and this connection entirely dissolved. The facts relative to the Free-will Baptist churches in Carolina, and the extent of our connection with them are simply these. There were individual Baptists in North Carolina more than a century and a half ago, but their origin is unknown. The first churches gathered there were by Elders Paul Palmer and Joseph Parker, many years after this; and several of the members were the descendants of the General Baptists in England. In 1764, the Philadelphia Baptist Association sent two of their ministers among these churches, and the next year most of them, with their ministers, changed their sentiments, and seceded to the Calvinistic Baptists. Elder Palmer was no more; but Elder Parker and a few others refused to secede. These few churches were regarded as obstinate, heretical, and enjoyed but little prosperity. About the year 1827, they heard of the Free-will Baptists at the North. A correspondence was opened, and the next year they published their records as "The Minutes of the Free-will Baptist Annual Conference of North Carolina;" the simple term *Baptist* having been previously used.

Their ministers never came North, and Elder Elias Hutchins is the only one of our denomination that has visited them. They never formally united with us; but they were with us in sentiment, and strongly attached, down to the time when the Anti-Slavery agitation commenced. Elder Hutchins says, "in conversing with them on the subject of slavery, many would admit it to be a great evil, and that slaveholders would have more to answer for in the final judgment, on account of their treatment to their slaves, than for anything else; but they generally justified themselves by saying that the evil was entailed upon them and could not be removed." The winter after the insurrection in Virginia, he sometimes said to them, "You extol to the skies the unhappy Poles and Greeks for their courageous and patriotic efforts to obtain their freedom, but when your slaves, as in the case of the late insurrection, rise against oppression, infinitely worse than that endured by the Poles and Greeks, you are full of rage, and shoot them as you would if they were so many tigers." After the agitation commenced, Elder Hutchins wrote to the most influential minister among them, proposing a private discussion of the slavery question. He declined the proposition, stating that such were the feelings of the people, he dared not discuss it. Nothing could be done; they discontinued the Star, they made no returns of their number or prosperity, and we voted to count them no longer with us. Their number then was 2 Q. M., 45 churches, 36 ministers, and 3,000 members. Most of them have since joined the Campbellites.

The wrong of retaining *such Christians(!)* in our communion, or that of any other evangelical body, will be seen by the following statements made by Elder Hutchins before the General Conference. "During one of my visits to these churches, a member, who, in everything save slavery, was among the most mild, humane, and hospitable men, and devoted Christians I have ever seen, told me that he once pursued a runaway slave—an outlaw—and, on his refusing to stop, fired at him as he was getting over the fence. And said he, 'I tracked him for some distance by his blood, but he was never seen afterwards,' intimating that he died of the wound."

"Another man, who was among the most zealous members of the North Carolina Free-will Baptist churches, told me that he wanted no better sport, than to take his horse, dogs, and gun, and pursue a runaway slave whenever one came near him; and that it was no more harm to shoot such a slave, than to shoot a deer."

Such *were* Free-will Baptist slaveholding Christians (!) and we believe them equally as good as any other denomination's slaveholding Christians (!) of the present day.

From the time that we sundered the cable of Christian fellowship, that bound to our free bark the old scow of oppression, we have ever and anon been in conflict with the privateers of slavery. Their excursions against us were planned and executed for the pleasure of slaveholders; and, in the eyes of some, they have deprived us of a reputable standing with other denominations—they have denied us for years, of incorporated privileges—threatened our ministers with lean salaries, if they opened their mouth for the dumb—and kept the office seekers in our churches, in constant alarm. But "having obtained help of God, we continue unto this day, witnessing both to small and great," that neither hope nor fear, flatteries nor frowns, worldly favor nor public scorn, shall divert us from our pledged opposition to slavery. Others may veer with the changing winds of popular opinion, and box the compass with the *"great expounder,"* but like the needle to the pole, *our* fidelity to liberty and liberty's God shall be steadfast and persevering.

Believing that slavery is a system of robbery against both God and man, and knowing that the Lord "hates robbery for burnt-offering," our Foreign Mission Society early voted to exclude the contributions of slaveholders from its treasury, and slaveholders themselves from membership. In 1841 the Executive Board agreed that it could not ask aid of Societies, in furnishing our missionaries with books for distribution, that are managed in part by slaveholders, and whose treasury is filled with the price of blood. Thus, while Christianizing the heathen of other lands, we have not failed to rebuke the system of heathenizing Christians in our own land. We may have lost donations from some sources by this action, but we have secured them from others. Gentlemen from other denominations have given us liberally, and a lady of Campton, N.H., willed her property, estimated at $4,000, to the Baptist Mission Society, but, learning that it would pass through our Treasury uncontaminated with the avails of slavery, she altered her will and gave it to us.

Our Home Mission Society is no less free from pro-slavery influence. It neither plants nor aids churches that are non-committal on the slavery question.

Our Education Society is equally adverse to slavery.—The Biblical school teaches the strongest anti-slavery principles, and all its advantages are freely offered to young men contemplating the ministry, irrespectively of color.

In 1842, a denominational Anti-Slavery Society was formed. This Society has no funds at its command, nor agents in the field. The great object of the organization is to have an Anti-Slavery anniversary, in connection with the Anniversaries of our other benevolent Societies, that the fires of freedom may be kept burning on every Free-will Baptist altar.

Half a day is thus annually devoted to the emancipation cause, and no meeting usually exceeds it in interest.

During Anniversary week in Boston, 1848, an Anti-Slavery Convention was there held, in accordance with the arrangements made at the previous General Conference. It was one of interest.

The General Conference at Topsham, Maine, in 1841, took a few steps in advance of any former position. There are times when calm, gentle efforts are perfectly ineffectual in contending with a gigantic foe. And in such contests, when the crisis comes, if we can come down upon the hosts of darkness like a thundering avalanche, we strike a blow that tells for the cause. This was the state of things in '41. The friends of liberty had been so successful in their assaults upon the dark prison-house of slavery, that the enraged keepers began to curse the whole North. To calm their anger, and to prove *themselves* free from the taint of abolitionism, Northern doctors of Divinity, Professors of colleges and of Theological Seminaries, came to the rescue of their *beloved slaveholding brethren.* They transferred to the Bible this hellish institution, all drenched in the blood of its victims, and vocal with their groans. They clothed its defenders with patriarchal authority, and then charged abolitionists with fighting against God. Individuals of other denominations had loudly complained, but it was for the Free-will Baptist denomination, in General Conference assembled, to rebuke this insult upon the Bible and the religion it teaches. It was there

"*Resolved,* That we look upon the attempt to impute Slavery to the Scriptures as moral treason against *God's Holy Word*; tending directly to the overthrow of all confidence in the Bible, and the God of the Bible, and to make infidels of the rising generation."

More truthful sentiments were never penned by uninspired man. So *abhorrent* is American slavery that, when convinced that the God of the *Bible* approves it, men discard *such* a God, and claim to trust in the God of nature. It was said in the United States Senate, by Henry Clay, that "That is property which the law declares to be property; and two hundred years of legislation have sanctioned and sanctified negro slaves as property." But that Conference believed there was no power in the *Universe* that could sanction and sanctify the right of property in man as claimed by slavery; therefore they

"*Resolved,* That if the Bible upheld slavery, it would uphold a system of the most atrocious wickedness, and could not be confided in as a holy book."

The report of the Committee on Foreign Correspondence contains the following strong language, quoted from Rev. J. G. Pike, a noted English author, which report was accepted and entered upon the journal of the Conference. "But of all its (slavery's) wicked supporters, none are more wicked than those who profess to be Christians, and yet uphold it or palliate its enormities, and would even brand Christianity with the eternal disgrace of sanctioning their wickedness. Christians, indeed! What! oppressors, Christians? Robbers, Christians? for every slaveholder is a robber;—he robs the negro of his rights and the produce of his labor.

Christians, indeed! Come, then, ye swearers, ye drunkards, ye adulterers, ye murderers, come all, and be acknowledged as Christians.

Come, Satan and thine angels, we will welcome you into the goodly band! Why should you not be acknowledged as Christians, as well as those who do your will, and work with your machinery."

Here it will be seen that we scaled the highest ramparts of slavery— its Biblical and Christian fortifications—and fearlessly measured swords with the vile monster of oppression. No honied words were used to effect a compromise; but, after the example of our Savior to the Scribes and Pharisees, unequivocal rebuke was faithfully administered. Years ago, we proclaimed to the world that we would neither exchange pulpits nor commune with slaveholders. Higher ground we could not well take; and from this high position we have never descended. Every General Conference since has re-affirmed its abhorrence of slavery, and openly committed itself on every new issue between freedom and oppression.

Seven years ago, the denomination

"Resolved, That we believe it to be the duty of all Christian voters to act upon anti-slavery principles at the ballot-box."

There is but one opinion among us as to the necessity of human government. We believe in its importance, but we take no extreme ground. On the one hand, we do not exalt it above the throne of God, deify the officers, and approve as sacred all their enactments. On the other hand, we do not regard it as undeserving the Christian's notice and attention. Governments, like the individuals composing them, are imperfect and liable to err. God, alone, is infallible. As the *church* is not, much less can a *government* be, especially not if any of its members are slaveholders, infidels, licentious or intemperate. Good rulers and equitable laws are among the greatest blessings vouchsafed by God. But wicked rulers and unjust laws are among the most intolerable evils endured by man. This was the view taken by the Pilgrims in leaving their fatherland, and by their descendants in the days of the Revolution. And is it nothing to you, Christian friends, under what government you live? Then go to

England, and be taxed exorbitantly for the support of a religion in which you have no faith. Then go to France, where the government selects the Sabbath for every election and public demonstration. Go to Spain, where the constituted authorities suppress the reading of the Bible and the conscientious worship of God. Go to Rome, and every month be compelled to confess your sins to a priest, and empty your purse for their pardon. Go to Russia, and become a mere tool in the hands of the autocrat for executing wicked designs of a despotic government. Or *stay at home,* and catch slaves for your lordly masters at the South.

The Christian will not, he dare not, say that he has no interest in the character of the government under which he lives. But is it wise to leave the affairs of government in the hands of the irreligious? If it is desirable to have good rulers, should not the Christian aid in their election? If it is desirable to have good laws, should not the Christian aid in procuring them? If the great object of government is to protect man in the peaceful enjoyment of his rights, who has, or *ought* to have, a greater interest in seeing that it subserves this important end, than the Christian? When great moral questions are to be decided by the election of particular men, it may be as much the Christian's duty to *vote* as it is to *pray.*

And has the *minister* no part to act in preserving from infamy and despotism a government established by the toil, blood and treasures of our sacrificing ancestors? A political babbler he should *never* be; but an active citizen—ever interested in whatever affects the morals or happiness of the people—he should *always* be. But we are told that he always compromises his dignity and prostitutes his calling by going to the ballot-box. That depends altogether upon the spirit with which he goes. If he has religion enough to there "do as he would be done by," and to "have always a conscience void of offense toward God and toward men," he is not only justified in voting, but it may be one of his most imperative duties. Is it not mockery to pray for an object, and all the while refuse to *act* in securing it? And think you there are no such prayers for good rulers and good laws?

But who are the men thus tender of our clerical reputation? Most of them we know to be men that are well pleased with the prompt payment of our taxes, and an occasional sermon on the duty of blind submission to the laws of the land, especially if they are "painfully repugnant" to the moral sense of the people; and they would be no less pleased with our votes, *provided they could control them.* Other men may accommodate themselves to the pleasure of politicians as they please, but the opportunity of exercising our elective franchise we ask not as a *favor,* we claim it as a *right.* We were *men,* with the civil rights and privileges of other men, *before* we were *ministers,* and we have yet to learn how a person ceases to be a man by becoming a minister.

These remarks on government, and the duty of the Christian citizen, seemed called for, not merely as an exposition of our views, but in justification of our anti-slavery action in politics. We are a voting people, and early remembered the slave at the ballot-box. One of our clergymen was on the Committee that brought out the first Liberty ticket before the American people. We praise God for liberty, and vote for men that would extend it. We deplore the existence of slavery, and vote for men that would prevent its extension.

Such being our views and practice on the slavery question in general, our position on the Fugitive Slave Law will be anticipated. The last Congress was a scene of the most exciting interest between the champions of freedom and slavery. For more than nine months, slavery claimed equal protection with liberty, and, in rampant fury, threatened the flow of blood if thwarted in its purpose. And during these nine months, a Spartan band, to freedom pledged, stood unmoved, while their colleagues quailed before the storm. But might prevailed against right. The North, through her treacherous servants, was compelled to bow the supple knee to the Moloch of slavery, and become bloodhounds for the South in hunting the panting fugitive. This, with two or three kindred measures, was "the salvation of our country"! "the quietus of the Agitation."

In just fourteen days from the passage of the Fugitive Slave Bill, our General Conference assembled at Providence, R. I. No religious body had then expressed an opinion of the law, so disgraceful to the nation, so aggravating to the North and so insulting to God. The subject was introduced by one of our brethren, a minister of Him who was sent "to preach deliverance to the captives." He asked advice, for he was himself a fugitive, liable every hour to be torn from his home, his family, and the flock of his charge. Sympathy for this distressed fugitive swelled every bosom. Christian indignation towards the law glowed in every countenance. And determined opposition to its requirements was frankly avowed.

The scene may be imagined, but never described. Suffice it to say that, after discussing the subject for an hour or two, it was referred to the Committee on Slavery, and a day assigned for the consideration of their report. When the day arrived, the capacious church was filled to overflowing. The report specified the particular nature and requirements of the Law, and closed with the following resolutions:

"*Resolved,* That we deliberately and calmly, yet earnestly and decidedly, deny any and all obligation on our part to submit to the unrighteous enactments of the aforesaid Fugitive Slave Law. Also, that, regardless of unjust human enactments, fines and imprisonment, we will do all we can, consistently with the claims of the Bible, to prevent the recapture of the fugitive, and to aid him in his efforts to escape from his rapacious claimants.

"*Resolved,* That, as 'we ought to obey God rather than men,' (Acts 5:20,) in disobeying a cruel and wicked human law, and patiently submitting to its unrighteous penalties for such disobedience, we are 'subject unto the higher powers—the powers that be,' (Rom. 13:1,) in the highest and holiest sense of that command; that is, in the same sense in which the apostles, primitive Christians, and subsequent Christian martyrs obeyed it, when they disobeyed the Jewish, Heathen and Popish laws.

"*Resolved,* That we do most deeply sympathize with those who, after having escaped from human bondage, are now in great fear, anxiety, and distress, on account of the passage of the Fugitive Slave Bill. We also recommend them to use all the means to preserve their liberty, that religion, conscience and reason will justify, under their harassing and distressing circumstances."

The report was discussed for nearly four hours by gentlemen from eight or ten different States, and unanimously adopted.

The crowded audience that had, at times, hung in breathless anxiety upon the lips of the speakers, and then again breathed the indignant sigh, as the revolting features of the law were presented, was called upon for an expression of opinion. With scarcely an exception, that immense throng approved the report. Since then, each of our twenty-six Y. M.'s has been convened, and not the first word of complaint has been whispered against the above action of the General Conference. Indeed, most of them have passed resolutions equally strong and decisive.

Because of our action on the Fugitive Slave Law, we are denounced by the pro-slavery press and demagogues, as a denomination of disorganizers. We deny and repel the charge. We again declare our faith in human governments, though we abhor some of their *inhuman* acts. We acknowledge our obligation to submit, even to unjust laws, ordinarily, till we can procure their repeal. But when the unjust laws are such as to contravene the laws of God, and offer us the choice of obeying their requirements, or suffering their penalties, the government has no right to complain if we obey God, and, without resistance, suffer the penalty it threatens to inflict. If "the powers that be are ordained of God," then are they clothed with no authority to require that at our hands which God himself has forbidden. When the government says, *"Thou SHALT deliver unto his master the servant which is escaped from his master unto thee,"* it transcends the object for which it was established, and disobedience is then a virtue. Governments not only may, but *must*, do that which individuals are not allowed to do. But when an act is wrong in itself, no legislation can make it right.

It was intrinsically wrong to say that no one "shall ask a petition of any God or man for thirty days," save of the king of Babylon. And when "all the presidents of the kingdom, the governors and the princes, the counselors and the captains, established a royal statute and made a firm decree" to that effect, and procured the signature of king Darius, thus clothing it with all the legislative authority of the realm, it was no more right than before; and both heaven and earth will forever honor the prophet Daniel for his love of prayer.

It was wrong in itself to aid the blood-thirsty enemies of our Savior, in their efforts to seek him for crucifixion. And when "both the chief priests and Pharisees had given a commandment that if any knew where he were, they should show it, that they might take him," (John 11:57,) Judas was under no more obligation to betray him than before; and *hell alone* will honor him as the only law-abiding citizen among the twelve apostles.

And so the Fugitive Slave Law, being intrinsically wrong, cannot be made *right* by the legal enactment of the United States Senate and House of Representatives, with the signature of Millard Fillmore, duly countersigned by his — — Secretary. Regarding God as our Supreme Ruler, in the language of the Kennebec Y. M., "we say to this government and to all the world, that the only obedience we will render to said Fugitive Slave Law, shall be to *suffer its penalties."*

In surveying our past action and present position, a few truths press themselves upon the mind and demand an utterance. We cannot refrain from acknowledging the manifold blessings that the Lord has bestowed upon us in our labors of love for the poor slave. He has enabled us to speak and to prosper, though our foes have been many and mighty. Our denomination has been continually enlarging its borders, increasing its moral strength, and, during the ten years of warmest conflict—from 1834 to 1844—it nearly doubled its number of members. The number of subscribers for the Morning Star has increased since 1832, from 1700 to more than 9000. We have sustained no great loss from secessions, but our abolitionism is one of our strong bonds of union. There is now scarcely an efficient man in the ministry, who is not an abolitionist—a talking, praying, and (if he votes at all) a voting abolitionist. In the laity, a large majority are of the same class. There are many, however, that have held some trivial office, or *hope* to, and so keep in league with party leaders. These men have a few that look to them for direction, and thus there are too many of our numbers that are pro-slavery in their influence.

Those ministers and churches that took decided anti-slavery ground are almost invariably among the number that have enjoyed the greatest prosperity. While the few ministers and churches whose "religion," *they say*, "had nothing to do with *niggers*," have accomplished but little. And those members of churches that are abolitionists, are generally among the most efficient ones; while those who complain whenever allusion is made to slavery, have usually shown themselves as having the spirit of the world quite as much as the spirit of Christ. In the most powerful revivals that have been enjoyed in any of our churches within the last fifteen years, the duty of "remembering them that are in bonds as bound with them," has been urged upon converts as a part of the religion they were professing before the world. And, instead of grieving the Holy Spirit and checking the revival interest, it has evidently promoted both spiritual and practical religion.

Having thus imperfectly traced the rise and progress of the Anti-Slavery enterprise in the denomination, it will be seen that our position is a prominent one among the hosts of freedom. But there is nothing of which we can boast. It may seem to some of us that we have done what we could; but were *our* parents, children and friends to day smarting under the lash, who would be satisfied with his efforts? But our fellow beings are there. Our Savior himself is there—brutally insulted in the person of his little ones. And shall we be weary in well doing? Never. No: never. They have heard that there were friends at the North who pitied their condition, and on every balmy breeze come their plaintive cries for help. From the depth of their anguish they look up to nature's God, and the hope of deliverance at times flashes upon them. Days, months and years pass slowly away, and in the agony of despair they exclaim, "How long, O Lord," how long!

Slavery never wore aspects more appalling than at the present hour. New Mexico and Utah are left exposed to its blasting mildew. California may yet be divided, to give it a foothold upon the Pacific. The proclaimed annexation of Cuba, and the recent movements in the South, are all ominous of evil.

The greatest heroes of the age, who have braved famine, bloodhounds, and death itself, to obtain their freedom, find no repose beneath the stars and stripes of our national flag. What ruin to our beloved country slavery may yet work, God alone can tell. One thing is certain, it is bad enough for *anything;* and, being hell's great ventilator, its sulfurous stench may, for a time, suffocate the breath of freedom. But we will not fear; for "the Lord God omnipotent reigneth." Let it fill up the cup of its iniquity in hot haste; the day of vengeance draweth nigh.

We have reason to "tremble for our country, when we recollect that God is just, and that his justice cannot sleep forever." The bands of oppression must break. If *truth* and *mercy* break them not, *judgment will.* And if nothing else will suffice, *let it come.* Our bodies may rest with the dead before that eventful day, but our spirits, being with God, we shall join in the rapturous song,

"Jehovah has triumphed—his people are free."

I. D. STEWART, *Cor. Sec.*

Meredith Bridge, N.H., Oct. 1, 1851

Appendix C

FIDELITY HONORED

EULOGY

ON THE

LIFE AND CHARACTER

OF THE LATE

WILLIAM BURR:
DELIVERED BY REQUEST

OF THE

CORPORATORS OF THE FREEWILL BAPTIST PRINTING ESTABLISHMENT,

BEFORE THE

FREEWILL BAPTIST ANNIVERSARY CONVENTION,

AT DOVER, N.H., OCTOBER 8, 1867.

BY

REV. GEORGE T. DAY.

Great and good men are the richest fruit which any civilization bears, and the choicest gifts which God sends to any land or people. All the lower products serve us chiefly when they contribute to this result. The first chapter of Genesis would be a riddle and a mystery if it did not close with the story of Adam coming forward to interpret the creative process and take his place as lord over a world that still lacked an obvious purpose and end. History is prosy and uninstructive till it has hung picture galleries with the portraits of heroes and thinkers and saints, and dramatized the life of the past as it went on in castle and cottage, in the scholar's brain and the ruler's cabinet; after that every leaf we turn introduces us to men that seem no longer among the dead, and each successive paragraph has a lesson that fits, in part at least, the life we are living to-day. Biography, when it is real and adequate, is the very pith and juice of history. We cannot understand the planting of a colony, or read intelligently the story of a campaign, till we know the men who seemed to go into exile but who really went out and founded a state, or who animated every private soldier's arm and gave momentum to his blow. Till one has comprehended Cromwell and the first Charles, the terrible protest of England against royalty in the XVII. century remains an unsolved enigma. When one has mastered Plutarch's Lives, it is no longer difficult to separate the fact from the fable in the many and wondrous stories which the stream of time has borne down to us from the days when Greece and Rome were not mere names to conjure with, but great powers making themselves felt in the daily life of three continents. Scripture itself teaches largely through human examples. Abraham incarnates faith; the story of Joseph is chiefly the emphatic assertion of God's care for a trustful integrity; David is a standing proclamation that only purity is power; and the apostle John is the abiding proof that Love has an insight deeper than the penetration of Logic; while Pharaoh's overthrow, and Ahab's suicidal vices, and Belshazzar's ruin which trod upon the heels of his sacrilege, and the terrible fate of Judas, which was all his thirty pieces of silver would buy for him,—are the Divine methods of warning against tyranny, of proving how moral recklessness is sure to beat itself in pieces against omnipotent law, of helping us feel the sanctity of what God has hallowed, and of making us stand evermore aghast at the crime of being a traitor. Indeed, the gospel itself, coming as Heaven's gift of salvation, appears in the form of a simple biography of Jesus of Nazareth, written by men who only partially saw the majesty and glory which they were developing, and whose wonder and reverence and love chastened the narrative into a transparent luminousness beyond the reach of all art, and gave it such a majestic and brief simplicity as compels the quarreling skeptic to feel it to be true, and more than half divine.

It is not unfitting, therefore, that we sit down for a little time at the end of our work in setting a memorial stone at the grave of our departed fellow-laborer, study his character, and draw out, if we may, the moral lessons of his life. Being dead he yet speaketh, and we shall long continue to hear his voice. His relations to us were such that we shall often be reminded of him. The memory of him will frequently come back from the bygone years. What he did and said will every now and then recur to us as we are busy with the same sort of tasks as those which he has finally laid down. The thought of him will surely be so frequent that it must needs impress and influence us. An impulse of some kind will come from these recollections to our hearts, and modify our own plans and purposes and deeds. It is, therefore, not simply just but needful that we endeavor to understand him, for only as we perceive him as he was shall we get the full and healthful impression of his qualities and his life, and receive the prompting which the abiding influence of his character and service waits to give. *He* deserves such a study, and *we* need it.

It would have seemed very proper if this task of portraying him had been assigned to some one whose relations to him had been more intimate than mine, whose acquaintance had been close, constant, and personal. Many little traits and incidents come out to the view of one so situated which suggest much and elucidate still more. There are such men among us who have known the more secret passages in the inward and outward life of Mr. Burr, who have therefore had ample opportunity for the study of his character in detail, and who have not lacked interest in the study. I have not had such opportunities. My Personal intercourse with him was limited and unfrequent. I have seen him mostly at a distance and in his official relations. He has been beheld generally in his position as editor, financial and managing agent, and denominational representative. The simple, individual manhood which underlay all this official position and service had to be largely inferred. And in becoming in some sense his official successor, the tendency to think of him as editor and agent is probably somewhat strengthened beyond its original force. I may add, perhaps, that a man's successor in office is not usually supposed to be in the best position to judge fairly of the qualities that used to sit in the chair which he now occupies. The incoming man is not regarded as having any excessive tendency to glorify the outgoing man, even though the going out is an answer to the unmistakable beckoning of Providence, and the movement keeps time to the death-march and is only arrested at the grave.

But I do not stop to say this in the tone of complaint or deprecation or apology. You have asked me to speak to you of him whom we all in common loved and esteemed as a friend and fellow-laborer, and whom we in common mourn with the sense of bereavement still keen; and I yield without stopping to disparage either your judgment or my own ability. There may, possibly, be some advantages as well as some disadvantages in selecting such a calm and comparatively distant observer. The intimate and sympathizing friend may perchance be too close for a fair view. His sympathy and identification with the man may color his estimate of the character, and prove an unseen weight in the scale of his judgment.

Personal attachment may sway the mind and obscure the vision; or if one were able to keep his judicial fairness and restrain his impulse to tell more than the exact truth, every warm word of commendation might be suspected of hyperbole and estimated at a discount. I speak to those who knew him long and well; to those who have been closely identified with him in plans and efforts, in anxieties and triumphs, during more than half his life-time; to those who have lived with him in the community since they were children, and seen his daily walk in all the vicissitudes of a long experience; to those indeed who have sat with him amid the deepest and most sacred confidences of home, sharing his thoughtful interest which never abated, and the love of his heart which bereavements only intensified and which years could not chill. To such I speak; and you will prize his higher qualities all the more if you find them perceived and appreciated by a remoter observer, and you can readily correct the faults which may appear in the portrait which an imperfectly instructed painter comes forward to execute. I shall speak of Mr. Burr as he appeared to me, rather than embody the impressions which he may have made upon the minds of others; and I shall occupy myself chiefly with the qualities of his character, instead of stopping to dwell at length on the incidents that merely go to make up his outward history. In being asked to deliver a eulogy I take it for granted that nobody expected or wished me to treat you to an hour of indiscriminate and fulsome panegyric; and in accepting the service I gave no spoken or implied pledge that I would utter myself only in a strain of high-wrought compliment. In asking for eulogy you meant a fair portraiture, and I meant the same thing when I promised to try and furnish one. You honestly believed that to paint the man justly would be to praise him unmistakably; and I honestly believed so too. We alike believed his merits to be real and substantial, though we never thought of ascribing perfection to him. What follows will perhaps help to answer the question, whether our conviction was well founded, and whether our estimate of him had few or many things in common.

Mr. Burr was a good specimen of what may be called the self-reliant and persistent type of character which is everywhere recognized as eminently American and peculiarly Yankee. The New England characteristics and training clearly and early appeared in him. He grew up where and when the necessity, the duty and the dignity of work were generally believed in; and he accepted the ancestral and surrounding faith, in this particular, without a dissent or a mental reservation. He was the seventh in a family of ten children, and the daily bread which supplied their wants came in perfect accordance with the old decree that promised it only to him who earned it in the sweat of his face. He learned the meaning of toil in his father's fields wielding the implements of husbandry, and found the first strong stimulants to thought in the problems which were wrought out at the district school and by the hearth-stone on which glowed the winter evening fire. He was born to no other inheritance than a good physical constitution, a wholesome example of industry, and an opportunity to test his capacities for achievement where real merit was not likely to go unrecognized nor true service wait vainly for its just reward. And he accepted his lot with a cheerful courage. He believed that there was no need of his making only a failure and getting a defeat out of life. He did not lean weakly on his father's arm, nor stand timid and shivering on the brink of his venture into the world of competition, waiting for some good genius or good fortune to give him a successful and promising start. He had faith, resolution and pluck. Leaving home at fifteen to work his own way in the world, he looks for honest work,—hard he expects it will be, but he is used to that,—and when his search becomes prolonged and wearisome, he is not diverted nor discouraged, nor does he cast about to see if life may not go on without work. To earn his living by paying for it a fair equivalent in toil is what he takes for granted must be done,—is indeed what he believes he can and what he determines he will do. And so a new application follows every successive refusal, for he never distrusts himself nor distrusts that law of God's providence which brings supplies to willing and patient and manly industry. And so it was the natural outcoming of his spirit and his ideas when, finding that an employer persisted in being exacting and unjust, he calmly and confidently went away and took the risk of another trial. The spirit of the man spoke out in clear tones and without disguise when a Boston employer endeavored to compel his submission to injustice in his labor by threatening to prevent his obtaining work at any other office in the city. *"Boston is not the only place in the world,"* promptly replied the young man of nineteen, with that air of half-modesty and half-defiance which some of us have witnessed more than once; and three days afterward he went out of the city as Abraham went out of his native country, not knowing whither he went; but confident as ever that his manly persistence would find a field somewhere and win according to its worth.

And this quality, thus early exercised and strengthened by the taxation laid on it, tarried with him to the end. It was the first element appearing in all his active life, and it was one of the large factors whose product appears in his success. Every one of our foremost men has it, and but for this would not be foremost. To timid and self-distrustful natures this thorough self-reliance appears as egotism or presumption, or both, and so indeed it sometimes is; but it is a part of every man's success who really wins it. It was quiet in Mr. Burr; but though it never blustered it was always there. It was not an impatience of other men's opinions or suggestions or counsel; instead, it prompted him to listen to other men that he might learn; to study their methods that he might discover their merits; to consult other men's preferences that he might judge whether to expect co-operation or opposition; but, after all, he must have and work out his own ideas; he could not sink his own individuality through excess of deference to others. He felt himself to be a real, responsible man, representing an integer in the sum of life; and so he could not and would not try to sink himself to be a mere parrot, or copyist, or echo, or negative quality, or cipher. One could never mistake him for another person, and he was never accused I think of being the mere mouthpiece of any other man, or of any clique or faction or party. He could yield when fairly beaten, but his dissent usually accompanied his submission. It never frightened him to be found in the minority; confident that he was right, he could not only stand alone without dismay, but would, if the emergency seemed to require it, set himself to reverse a deliberate popular verdict against which his own solitary voice had been recently raised in dissent. Such self-reliant natures do sometimes assert themselves in a disagreeable way, though he was very rarely offensive in the time or the manner of asserting his individuality; but it must also be said that they chiefly furnish material out of which all the nobler leaders of society are fashioned. And firmness is itself sometimes thoroughly heroic, and obstinacy now and then rises till it is truly sublime. No man becomes a power or does any very significant work who lacks this primary quality; and so I have put it in the foreground of this mental picture.

It was another of Mr. Burr's mental traits that he was thoroughly practical in his views and methods of life. He may possibly have had his dreams of sudden opulence while he was a young man, as most young men do have; and he may have had his ambition kindled to realize by a venture the results which properly flow from laborious years, for that is rather the rule than the exception. But whether he reached his practical conclusions by the road of earlier reasoning or of later experience, he had manifestly come to rest his confidence, in his maturity of mind, only upon what appeared a solid and substantial basis. He was no mere theorist.

Indeed, the imagination was rather weak in him than otherwise, and he rarely attempted much in the way of philosophic generalization. He wanted something tangible before he felt wholly secure. A brilliant but untried project, so far from captivating him, was very likely to excite his decided distrust partly because it was brilliant and untried. He asked after facts that he might lean on them, and he was constantly taking an appeal from prophecy to experience. He settled a few plain and obvious principles which he had often seen tested, and clung steadily and strongly to these. He walked in the light which the past offered him, not liking to venture beyond reach of the traveled highway for the sake of finding a directer and shorter road across untrodden soil. He believed in careful, steady and even plodding work; he did *not* believe in hazardous ventures as either humanly politic or morally allowable. His idea and his method were to keep right on the safe way of fair doing. He was regular and constant in service, not spasmodic and driving. No single day or deed stood out in his case, distinct and prominent by its transcendent significance, from the general average. He built up the results of his life by quiet, steady, regular additions, not by now and then a strained and magnificent effort, separated by long intervals of heedless indolence. He had more faith in the service of coral insects that work on through centuries to build a barrier against the sea, than in waiting for a submarine volcano to fling one up at just the right point from the depths of central fires. His only, or at least his chief, system of arranging his labor so as to economize and make it most effective, was just to take hold of the first task that came along, perform it promptly, and so be ready for the next as soon as possible. And, hence, he liked the good old ways to which he had been accustomed,—flaming novelties and startling experiments were looked upon with both distrust and aversion. He never worshipped sudden, ostentatious and unearned success. He doubted its genuineness, its permanency and its value, and he had little veneration for it even when it stayed. He believed profoundly in having men earn what they had and claimed, and thought of those who failed to do so as little less than enriched by fraud. They were in his eyes either gamblers deserving the curses of the victims whom they had spoiled, or beacons set up by Providence to warn others against their folly and their fate.

And so, of course, his tendencies were naturally conservative. He deprecated rashness, he was jealous of hot and impatient blood, he would not enter into responsible fellowship with restless and daring spirits; and the crusaders whose work was only one of demolishing, hardly gained his patience or his pity. He was not naturally a pioneer of thought or action.

He would have steadily refused to take passage with Columbus if he had lived in Spain when the three little vessels set out to find an unknown world, and one may be sure that he held no stock in the first Company that undertook the laying of the cable across the Atlantic. As a result, he was sometimes found coming both reluctantly and late into sympathy with the new measures which were essential to progress, and which flowed as a logical necessity from the principles that he had already accepted and the policy that he was pursuing; though one could be always certain that when he refused to go forward and take a venture, it was not will but conviction that restrained him. And when this practical and conservative tendency of his mind is considered, it reflects the more credit upon him as a true, earnest and faithful adherent of the great progressive national ideas which were vainly fought by public opinion and wealth and power and private violence for thirty years, and then as vainly fought by armed traitors and foreign sympathy for five years more, till their vitality was established and their supremacy conceded by the world. A man who would persist in being a Christian Abolitionist in New Hampshire from 1830 to 1860, has thereby proved that his conservatism was something better than a blind and stubborn clinging to what is prudent and popular in a worldly sense, and that he is not hindered from joining in any work of true progress through lack of either courage or conscience. If he is constitutionally practical, and inclined to put his trust in experience, it is plain enough that no clear principle of right will be put in jeopardy with his consent, even though the chief priests and money changers have given it over to crucifixion with solemn formalities, and the populace have ratified the act with threatening clamor and passionate shouting. Such conservatives may indeed sometimes be behind the front rank in the Lord's army, but they are not likely to be found enrolled among the soldiers that belong to any hostile camp.

Of his integrity as a man of business there is need of but few words. In all his years of trust and responsibility I do not know that a suspicious word was ever uttered, or a suspicious thought indulged by any candid and well informed man, respecting the rectitude of his business transactions. Straightforwardness and a transparent sincerity always distinguished him. He carried a conscience into the whole details of business. He was ever asking what was just and right. He believed the golden rule found a proper theatre on the exchange, and he took care that the entries in his Day-Book and Ledger should not reproach him with hints of unfairness when they recalled his dealings. If he made no rapid gains by doubtful and desperate ventures, and if he was sometimes over-cautious in the judgment of other men, it was plain that he felt the claims of prudence, and that he looked upon the mania for speculation as to the outer circle of a destroying whirlpool. Business seemed to him as fully under the law which requires a fair payment for what is received as any other department of industry. He abominated gambling, however it was christened,—it was the evil thing at which he was ever looking, and not merely the pleasant name by which men had agreed to call it. The lottery of stocks was in his eye not less a moral offense than the lottery whose prizes were simply money, and Opera Houses and suburban villas,—grand pianos and famous pictures. And especially when the funds of others were entrusted to his care and management, did he feel bound to guard them from peril and account for them with the greatest conscientiousness. In thorough uprightness, and with a steady and wasteful interest, did he deal with the larger and smaller sums which were ever passing through his hands as Agent of the Printing Establishment and Treasurer of several Benevolent Societies; and from first to last probably not one of all the thousands who trusted their money to his hands or his judgment, ever seriously believed that he had mismanaged a single trust through lack of care or conscience;—much less did they suspect that a single penny of another man's money had stuck to his fingers or hid itself in his pocket. That is a strong statement, but I think not stronger than the truth; it is a somewhat rare eminence upon which his integrity is thus put, but I think it is entitled to the position; it is a virtue that warrants much commendation, but a plain, square fact like that needs nobody to push it into special notice, or interpret its meaning, or trumpet its praise. It carries its own meaning and lesson on its face, and settles itself quietly like a crown upon the head of its possessor.

It was also a noticeable trait of Mr. Burr's character that he kept his mental freshness and teachableness quite to the end of his life. At sixty years of age no one could possibly think of him as having really commenced to grow old in spirit, even if the loss of some of his physical elasticity compelled him to lay off some outward burdens. He was indeed in, some sense, to us who were younger, a representative of an earlier generation; but he was still emphatically a man of the present. He remembered the objects of his early veneration with moistened eyes, and spoke of them in tones charged and tremulous with feeling; the halo around their heads seemed to him peculiarly bright and mellowed; and though, like many others of use, he may never have seemed to find in later

life any other men whose spiritual stature quite equaled that of the heroes
of his youth, yet he never fell into cynicism or despair of the world as its
course lay steadily downward. He had nothing antiquated about his tastes
or style of thought. He recognized with gratitude the evidences of
progress which met him on every hand, and looked for a brighter future to
dawn upon the world. He did something more and better than to repeat the
maxims and plead the methods of a by-gone period, as though they
embodied the final wisdom of the world; instead, he was ever a learner,
frankly and openly correcting to-day the misapprehension and the error of
yesterday; always desiring the better thing, and not less ready to recognize
and welcome it because it was new. He did not let the world outgrow him,
nor in the grand march of humanity was he ever willing to be driven along
with resisting steps by a rear-guard of the host. The latest truth was as
fully the voice of God to him as the earliest Scripture;—Moses's "Let
there be light!" and Lincoln's "Let there be liberty!" were to him
evidences alike that God's purpose to regenerate the earth and beautify
life with brightness is positive and eternal. He kept his mental activity and
his social zest all through his career; filling a day of the last earthly
Summer which he knew with his friends with almost a boy's sportiveness;
and he settled down to die on that last evening of his life with words of
Christian joyfulness and of pleading affection still trembling upon the lips
that had just borne their testimony for God and his life-giving truth.
Brother Burr was the designation given him by the general voice of his
denomination;—and it was expressive both of the genuine and familiar
affection which he had awakened and kept, and of the common life-level
which he and they occupied. The youngest and most vivacious could
hardly think of him as having either the age or the venerableness which
would suggest the appellation of *Father*.

He had a good degree of what is known as public spirit. Strong in his
personal friendships,—an intense lover of home,—with no personal
ambition for place or notoriety,—appreciating quietude, and very fully
identifying himself with the special circle of interests within which he
daily moved, yet he never forgot or felt indifferent toward the general
welfare of the community or the necessities of mankind. He was much
less and much more than a professional reformer,—less, in that his tastes
and convictions forbade him to spend his time and strength in merely
searching out and laying bare the excrescences and defects, the sins of
omission and of commission, which attached to general society and the
race of mankind;—and more, in that he kept himself busy in living out the

Christian faith and the sacred precepts which he had found in the gospel, and thus commended to all who knew him the only effectual remedy for man's sin and the only source whence his necessities could draw a supply. But he was no narrow religionist nor careless spectator of social life and miseries. He saw that human welfare depended not a little upon wholesome laws wisely administered, upon the restraint which society puts upon the passions of evil men, upon a right and strong public sentiment, upon a general and true education of the young, upon prevalent habits of industry, upon such a care for the suffering classes as will prevent them from becoming armed with evil purposes and embittered by prejudice, and so be transformed into dangerous classes;—and, seeing all this, he interested himself in whatever could be made subservient to these ends. It was not enough that his own private affairs prospered; he wished to see public affairs in a healthy condition as well. It was both an evidence of his interest in the welfare of the people, and a fitting testimony to his capacity, that he was chosen a municipal officer in his own city, and sent to represent his fellow-citizens in the Legislature of the State. He had a true patriot's love for his country,—saddened by every disaster which befell Justice, mourning as if a friend had been smitten whenever Liberty was wounded in the house of her friends, hailing the successful framing of equity into a national statute with a grateful enthusiasm, and reading of the Russian Czar's edict which gave manhood and citizenship to his serfs through the mist of youthful tears. Because our Great Rebellion was a desperate attempt to dehumnize a wronged race, and burden the masses of the people with the weight of a huge and remorseless oligarchy, he put down his strong aversion to strife, and demanded that it be fought into its grave at any cost and risk; he writhed when the first shot was fired at Sumter as though a Minie ball were cutting his own flesh, and he swelled the national pean with his full strength when that often-baffled but never-yielding army of the Potomac crashed through the defenses of Richmond and occupied the citadel of the confederacy. Always counting himself one of the people, whatever helped or harmed them was sure to wake his sympathy and touch his heart. Ever properly mindful of his own interests and rights and duties, he never forgot to care for his neighbor; giving special regard to what claimed his attention near at hand, he fairly weighed the claims of the most distant interests, and his noblest sympathies had arms that could clasp the globe.

He made no pretension to thorough scholarship, to deep critical acumen, to literary polish, or to fine aesthetical tastes. What he might have acquired and become in these respects, had he shared the advantages of early and generous culture, it is not easy to decide. That he possessed mental capacity enough to win something more than a respectable position in any legitimate field of effort to which he steadily devoted himself, is plain enough; but whether his mind had not in early life too positive and practical a tendency for a thoroughly successful literary career, may be properly doubted. God does not make every man for books and scholarship; and when he has fashioned a nature for the world of action, we are likely to make somewhat sorry work if we attempt to chain it down to the sphere of ideas. We are very fond of telling what great achievements might have been wrought in and for a man of practical sagacity and efficient common sense by ten years in Seminary and College. The ten years might perhaps have elevated the plane and multiplied the efficiency of his service; but they might also have switched him off upon the wrong track, given him chiefly an experience of baffled effort, and sent him to the garner of God with a harvest of chaff. Greek and Latin, Rhetoric and Belles Lettres, crammed into a youth do not always reappear afterward in the form and substance of greatness; instead, they sometimes strut on the stilts of pretension, provoking impatience and ridicule, and sometimes they worry their possessor into exhaustion and discouragement in his vain attempt to fit them to his hands and his sphere. When Heaven sends us a ready actor in the field of beneficent work, no matter whether he be inventor, organizer, artisan or tiller of the soil, we are only making his life a punishment to himself and cheating the world of a real boon when we set the man to devour libraries which he cannot digest and keep him manipulating ideas which only tumble into chaos as often as he attempts to reduce them to order.

And so it is not certain that early opportunities would have made an eminent and finished scholar of Mr. Burr, or added so very largely to the value of his life.

It is true that he had never attempted the thorough mastery of any one of the great departments of thought which keep strong minds busy for a life-time, and he was too active and busy and responsible among material interests to allow him to follow the pursuits or exhibit the air of a student.

But still, notwithstanding he joined the army of labor so young, and kept his place most creditably in the ranks to the very end of his life, he so faithfully and so well used his ability to observe, acquire and reflect, as to be recognized in all circles as an intelligent citizen, a clear thinker, an able reasoner, and a man of excellent judgment, ready tact, quick apprehension and real force of mind. If he felt out of his sphere in the company of eminent literary men, and if he took up his pen rarely and reluctantly to write for a reading public, he was generally recognized as the possessor of more than the average mental ability, and his long editorial service was strongly commended by scores of voices where it was adversely criticized by one.

The religious elements of Mr. Burr's character were the most marked characteristics of the man. They stood out clearly, they were strong and positive. Perhaps it would be still nearer the truth if I were to say that the religious spirit was with him a permeating influence that settled into every part of his mind, diffused itself through the whole spiritual being, lent a force to each faculty and found expression throughout the whole domain of action. It is difficult to think of him in any department of life or form of effort without taking into account the religious element which manifestly helped to make him what he was. It was in part his religion that made him so steadily industrious, that rendered him accurate and painstaking in the details of business, that solidified his integrity, that rendered him firm and persistent in contending for a principle, that prompted to economy and caution, that forbade rash ventures and speculations, that kept his interest alive in the public welfare, that made him resolute to render his life serviceable, that imparted the thoughtful seriousness to his manner, that often filled his heart with mellow sunshine and rippled out in his most genial smiles, that made his friendship so strong and tender and significant and sacred, that so often brought out his tenderness in his tears, that filled his home with an atmosphere of sympathy and crowded every day with little offices of love, that made him now and then walk solemnly and softly as in the presence of great moral mysteries which he could not solve and that kindled the great hopes in his face and eye as he sometimes beheld the benedictions of prophecy descending from God upon the weary and smitten world, as Jacob saw the angels coming down the ladder from heaven in his dream at Bethel. His religion was not a foreign quality superadded to his qualities as a man, but an enobling influence that saturated his entire manhood; not a something borrowed from afar and worn more or less as an outward ornament, but a vital force working perpetually from the very centre of his being, and coming often to the surface in purposes that rose to new heights, in plans that broadened into beneficence, in deeds that gave the right interpretation to the word Duty, in daily aspirations that spread a broad wing and went trooping up to the bosom of God.

Of course his religion,—as religion usually does where there is enough of it to make a mark and be seen and studied,—his religion exhibited both personal peculiarities and a family likeness. His religious experience was largely determined by what he was in his own mental tendencies, and by the peculiar type of spiritual life and theological teaching with which he was so early and vitally brought in contact. The men who taught him effectually his need of God and a regeneration by the power of his Spirit, were men from his own rank in life, not displaying much human lore, but earnest, zealous, devoted men, who had faith in the promises of God, to whom man's sin and depravity were terrible realities, who preached repentance with an unction that reminds one of John the Baptist, whose faith in Jesus as the soul's Justifier and Hope had something of a Pauline grasp and fervor, to whom the new birth was the grandest of all realities, and who filled day and night with their repetition of the cry—"Behold now is the accepted time!" In his early manhood Mr. Burr met these men, heard their words, sat with them in counsel, listened to their plans, looked into their eager and resolute souls, inspected their daily lives; and his judgment testified,—"these men are servants of the most high God which show unto us the way of salvation." It was not in his heart to fight long against such a conviction. He wept while he listened, prayed while he wept, and yielded while he prayed; and no one of us who has done likewise needs to be told the rest. Peace succeeded the inward battle; the laboring soul was restful in its trust, humble beneath the sense of its long straying and the burden of its great gratitude, resolute and heroic at last in the waking of a purpose worthy of life. Under such influences did Mr. Burr's religious character receive its first impress, and during almost its entire formative period it was being trained with his own glad and joyful consent in the same spiritual school. Not many pupils have had more single-hearted and appreciative teachers; not many teachers have had a more reverent, sympathetic and docile scholar. What followed can be easily inferred.

He had a tender and exacting conscience. A right life was in his eyes the only trustworthy proof of a regenerated heart. A lofty profession weighed very little with him, against lax conduct. However he may have exalted faith he firmly demanded works. However charitable he may have been he had little patience with a double-dealer; he was ready to endorse the strongest of those denunciations which Christ flung at the heads of the Pharisees and hypocrites, and he believed them as applicable to the grievous sinners of the nineteenth century as to those of the first.

But his demand for rectitude did not at all measure his idea of the Christian life. He profoundly believed in Christian piety no less than in Christian morality. Religion with him meant heart force as the first and chiefest thing of all. Unless it were vital inward experience it was very little to him. Till the soul realized God, nothing would content him. He must feel Christ's nearness, know the quickening of the Spirit in the heart, carry the sense of unworthiness and gratitude to his closet and come back lifted to hope and consecration as by an unseen but omnipotent arm, look out upon the world with something of the yearning with which Jesus wept over Jerusalem, and be lifted out from the depression born of outward griefs into an atmosphere of submission and peace and comfort by the blessed visions of the Hereafter,—he must have all these things before his ideal of religion had become actualized in himself, and he must see evidences of their presence in others before he was satisfied with their credentials.

And so, though disliking all ostentatious shows of sanctity, and having not a little questioning at times over his own faith, he was devout, meditative, prayerful, even fervid and sometimes melting. He was not ashamed of his tears when the view of his own defects, or his perception of others' peril and unfaithfulness, or his apprehension of Christ's sympathy, sent the blinding moisture to his eyes. He was thoroughly content with so much of the evangelical theology as he had apprehended, rejected at once and decidedly all opinions and inferences that would let the blood of atonement out of his creed as sure to bring death, was disposed to hold fast to the form of words in which he had first heard the message of salvation, and was jealous of whatever really modified the methods of Christian effort upon which his newly-opened eyes saw the seal of God's approval so manifestly set. He loved the prayer meeting and the hour of religious conference with a love that years only strengthened; he wanted the preacher should always touch his heart and give him the freshness of a believer's feeling, more perhaps than he desired to have some rare and royal mind in the pulpit open to him the sublimity and wealth of Christian thought. He loved the organized church as Christ's own appointed school for the training of souls, and as the divinely organized band of workers through whose blended toil and prayer the kingdom of God was to be made visible and supreme among men. Her interests were daily carried on his heart, his soul was kindled while she worshipped with hymn and prayer, and her ordinances yielded him a solemn joy, such as thrives on the border-land which joins this life to the other. Day after day and year after year he went on in the way which he chose in the little printing office at Limerick when he knelt among his types and manuscripts on that Saturday evening in February, 1828, and which he openly avowed to be his chosen way on the next Sabbath evening in the prayer meeting held in the private dwelling of a family whose hearts and house the Lord had opened that he might make a sanctuary of both. So he went on, if sometimes faint yet ever pursuing, never faltering in his good purpose, always preserving his interest, growing stronger in faith, wiser in counsel, more abundant in labors, and more commanding in Christian influence to the very end. And that end came to find him in the full vigor of his strength, standing at his post of duty, happy in the sphere and the service which he so much loved; and it hallowed forever the faithful testimony which he had just ended in this very room by the sacred silence that settled at once upon his lips—that deep, sudden eloquent silence which we shall wait in vain to have broken on earth.

Of his work for us as a Christian denomination it would be easy and pleasant for us to speak freely; but it may be too soon to estimate that properly, and a few words will be better than many. That work was a needed and peculiar one, and it was large, important, interested, laborious,—a work prompted and sustained by love and distinguished by fidelity. He felt both the privilege and responsibility of his position and his service. He had many cares, anxieties and trials in connection with his service, as every real, useful, responsible worker must have. He came to us when we were weak and unorganized; he helped us into strength and unity. He came to fill a sphere for which we had no fitted occupant; he filled and then enlarged it, growing himself as the functions increased their proportions; managing an institution which began in debt to the amount of half its value, and providing for a steady prosperity which has made it a growing bond of union, a medium for the effective exercise of our power, and a scatterer of benefactions which have fallen in abundant blessing from the valley of the Mississippi to the shore of the Ganges. Few men would have brought to his task among us so true a heart and so free a service as he laid down through so many years at our feet; and few could have done for us so ample and fitting a work, even if they had possessed his rare and unselfish devotion. He was identified with us as a people scarcely less closely than with his own family; and next to his love for them was his abounding affection for us. He was a good and discreet manager;—a balance-wheel that kept our ecclesiastical machinery steady in its movement without taxing our motive power;—successful in harmonizing conflicting interests and opinions;—blending firmness and conciliation;—knowing when to resist innovation, and yet yielding without bitterness and after-complaint to what was a decisive verdict;— not daringly and audaciously attempting to lead the body on the one hand, nor reluctantly dragged onward by its providential momentum on the other, he generally marched abreast with its best sentiment as did Mr. Lincoln with the nation; giving it his sympathy, keeping its confidence, growing in its esteem, and himself lifted into higher hope and nobler moral stature by the reciprocal blessing which the denomination poured back into the spirit of its benefactor.

He lived through a most significant period in our history, as it was a most significant period in the history of the world. He witnessed and aided in the establishment of most of the various Institutions of the denomination. He printed the first number of the *Morning Star* and planned and superintended most of its successive enlargements and improvements, and so made the way easier for the incoming of a denominational literature. He saw our first graduate at college and helped to shield him from suspicion and keep the way open for his success; he saw the rise of Parsonsfield Seminary and the Biblical School, the parents of two vigorous, young Colleges and many noble Academies that are flourishing to-day; he witnessed the ordination of our first foreign missionary; he was an interested observer when our various Benevolent Societies, whose anniversaries we have come to celebrate, were born; he was in the fight when that question was so earnestly debated, whether the Freewill Baptists should be dumb over the sin of oppression for the sake of quiet and the show of prosperity, or speak for justice and liberty when speech cost a reputation and was sure to purchase opposition and peril; and he helped in that long contest of ours which followed, never faltering when the tempest of public sentiment rose to fury, and never doubting the final issue even when the higher law was howled at from the pulpits that were set to proclaim it, and petitions for the security of national honor were flung out of the Legislative Assembly chosen to frame equity into statutes. He was a faithful co-worker and an influential leader through all these many years of our history, whom no hour found false, and whose aid true men rarely sought in vain. He may sometimes have found it hard to realize that a change in our circumstances and in society required a change in our plans and methods, and so may have been sometimes a little jealous and fearful lest we should forget the real mission of the denomination,—lost our spirituality in our ambition,—get above our true work in our aspiration for a broader field, fail to lean on God when we had become humanly strong through culture and a good reputation—and cease to carry the message of salvation to the masses of the people in the power of the Holy Ghost as our fathers had carried it to him. He may possibly have been needlessly anxious over these points, but even if we think he was it is fitting to remember that it was a real jealousy for what is vital in religion always and everywhere,—that he could not help prizing and loving the spirit of the fathers as they were when the life they were living came upon him as spring airs come upon the barren fields and leafless forests to cover them with greenness and blossoms,—that we cannot be too often nor too strongly reminded that soul-force is the chief force in the sphere of religion,—and that we shall be palsied and powerless the very moment we cut loose from God.

We owe Mr. Burr a large debt for his long and faithful service; it is fitting to acknowledge it by working with an equal devotion to carry forward the work which he leaves to our hands; we have reared a monument to his memory; it will be well if we build our lives into one as noble and enduring as that which thousands of grateful men and women are carrying in their hearts to his memory. His sudden departure in the midst of his strength and service may seem at first thought a peculiar calamity; but there is a sort of blessing even in this unheralded blow which so startled and shocked us. Dying at his post as he did, he leaves upon our minds the abiding recollection,—not of a man feeble, jaded, tottering, his strength wasted, the light of his eye quenched, and the stalwart intellect, sympathizing with a worn-out frame, stumbling in its thought like the steps of a child;—no, not this, but the recollection of a man of sturdy spirit, of unabated energy, of clear vision, of warm heart, of high purpose, of steady and strong activity, and beneficent service. Is it not well that such a picture as this should hang perpetually before us as often as we recall him of whom we shall frequently think, symbolizing the thoroughly manly character and service which have passed from us and stirring us as often as we look upon it to a life and service not less manly and noble?

The one common and impressive lesson taught us by this life is one which lies on the very surface of the story, and which it is not easy to overlook. Mr. Burr's character and career show us how ordinary abilities and opportunities may work out high and grateful results, when the leadings of God's providential hand are cordially accepted, and when the true work of life is entered on in a submissive and resolute spirit, without repining, or complaint, or the indulgence of a mischievous ambition, and wrought out in patience and fidelity. Look at the picture. Here was a man without brilliance of parts, without unusual opportunities or marked abilities, inheriting no fortune, helped by no influential friends, having at least his full share of hardship and discouragement, sharing nothing of what men call good luck, amid unpromising surroundings, lifted to no eminent station, gaining nothing save what he honestly earns by persistent and taxing industry, taking every ascending step up the hill of difficulty, and living by his labor, whose common implements he never lays down to the end of his life. He is a fair example of our common lot and life; he springs from the people and is eminently one of the people; he shares their common hardships and carries their common burdens; he has only the helps and resources which are their usual inheritance, and no grander career is opened before him by Providence than is opened to them. He starts from only the average level of American citizenship, and he is supplied with simply the usual stimulants. And in what he became and in what he did—in his industry, his economy, his integrity, his acquired ability and skill, his study and growth in knowledge, his Christian virtues, his official positions, the growing confidence which he inspired, the increasing influence which he wielded in a whole denomination, the strong friendships which he won, the prayers that were daily offered for him in a thousand homes, the eagerness with which men sought his counsel, the deference paid to his opinions, the grief and tears which burst forth when he fell, the spontaneous standing still of business with uncovered head, when his body went by on its way to the grave, the crystallization of religious esteem into a shaft of marble which you have just left standing above his dust to speak your thought of him to the future, this gathering here to-night that you may lay your tribute on the altar that guards his memory,—in all these things we have but so many indications of what a common lot and life may be when the highest duties are honored, and God has put the crown of his waiting favor upon the loyal and loving soul. This greatness is all the more admirable because it may be common, and not rare and exceptional. It is a familiar dignity attainable by the mass of men; not a magnificent, isolated, awful, distant dignity, which can only be vainly coveted or wondered at from afar. For this reason his example is one of peculiar interest and value to us, and especially to all young men whose characters are yet to be fashioned, and whose life-work is still to be wrought out. It is a lesson which comes home to most of us both as a rebuke for what we have failed to attempt to do, and an encouragement to undertake our work with a similar spirit, in the assurance that we shall not fail of success and reward.

In his earlier works, when he was more a philosopher and a seer and less a cynic and an ogre than he is now, Thomas Carlyle was wont to write in the spirit of appreciation and charity. Among his finer passages, which are luminous with original genius and saturated with just sentiment, there is this admirable tribute to the true worker, which has such a bearing upon Mr. Burr's character, and so puts emphasis upon what I have called the main lesson of his life, that I cannot do better than to reproduce it both for the sake of what it tells and of what it suggests.

Carlyle says:

Two men I honor, and no third. First, the toilworn Craftsman that with earth-made Implement laboriously conquers the Earth, and makes her man's. Venerable to me is the hard Hand; crooked, coarse; wherein notwithstanding lies a cunning virtue, indefeasibly royal, as of the Sceptre of this Planet. Venerable too is the rugged face, all weather-tanned, besoiled, with its rude intelligence; for it is the face of a Man living manlike. O, but the more venerable for thy rudeness, and even because we must pity as well as love thee! Hardly-entreated brother! For us was thy back so bent, for us were thy straight limbs and fingers so deformed; thou wert our Conscript, on whom the lot fell, and fighting our battles wert so marred. For in thee too lay a god-created Form, but it was not to be unfolded; encrusted must it stand with the thick adhesions and defacements of Labor; and thy body, like thy soul, was not to know freedom. Yet toil on, toil on: thou art in thy duty, be out of it who may; thou toilest for the altogether indispensable, for daily bread.

A second man I honor, and still more highly: him who is seen toiling for the spiritually indispensable; not daily bread, but the Bread of Life. Is not he too in his duty; endeavoring towards inward Harmony; revealing this by act, or by word, through all his outward endeavors, be they high or low? Highest of all, when his outward and his inward endeavor are one; when we can name him Artist; not earthly Craftsman only, but inspired Thinker, who with heaven-made Implement conquers Heaven for us! If the poor and humble toil that we may have Food, must not the high and glorious toil for him in return, that he may have Light, have Guidance, Freedom, Immortality?—These two, in all their degrees, I honor: all else is chaff and dust, which let the wind blow whither soever it listeth.

Unspeakably touching is it, however, when I find both dignities united; and he that must toil outwardly for the lowest of man's wants, is also toiling inwardly for the highest. Sublimer in this world know I nothing that a Peasant Saint, could such now anywhere be met with. Such a one will take thee back to Nazareth itself; thou wilt see the splendor of heaven spring forth from the humblest depths of earth, like a light shining in great darkness.

In no mean measure does Mr. Burr fill out this truthful and touching portrait of the peasant saint. He too takes us back to Nazareth, for he learned his main life lessons of him who was the son of the carpenter, and he has also followed the Nazarene up to the fountain of that light which streamed upon the world's darkness, where he sits ever learning from the same lips, and waiting for us to join him in the fellowships and service of the immortal sphere. To him, and to the great company of the faithful and victorious, gathered into rest, may we each go joyfully at the great Master's call, bearing a story of like heroism and faith.

Appendix D

FUNERAL SERMON
OF
REV. ELIAS HUTCHINS,

Delivered at Dover, N.H., September 15th, 1859

by

By REV. J. B. DAVIS.

The funeral was attended at 2 o'clock, on Thursday, at the Washington street church, the place of his labors for thirteen years as pastor. Before assembling at the church, a number of ministers called at the house of the deceased, and prayer was offered by Rev. Theodore Stevens, of North Berwick, Me. The remains were then carried to the church, accompanied by Revs. D. P. Cilley, J. Stevens, S. Curtis, L. B. Tasker, J. M. Durgin, O. R. Bacheler, T. Stevens and D. Mott, as bearers. The house was crowded, even the aisles and vestibule, and many who desired were not able to gain admittance. There were about thirty ministers present, and many others would have been there had not the session of one Yearly Meeting and two Quarterly Meetings in the region called them to duty elsewhere. The occasion was one of deep solemnity, and no doubt will contribute to the cause to which the subject devoted his life, the conversion of souls.

The invocation by Rev. L. B. Tasker, of Strafford, opened the service. Rev. D. P Cilley read the 1105th hymn of the Psalmody, which was sung by the choir in a style and spirit befitting the occasion, as were the other hymns. Select scriptures were read by Rev. Silas Curtis of Concord, and prayer offered by Rev. O. R. Bacheler, returned missionary. Rev. J. M. Durgin, of the 1st F. W. B. church in Dover, read the 1122d hymn. The sermon, which was a chaste and appropriate production, was by Rev. J. B. Davis of Lowell, Mass. This was according to an arrangement made by the departed. The text was well chosen: Ps. 37:37, "Mark the perfect man, and behold the upright; for the end of that man is peace." After the sermon, brief remarks were made by Rev. D. M. Graham, of New York, O. R Bacheler, S. Curtis, and D. P. Cilley. Prayer was again offered by Rev. S. Curtis, and benediction pronounced by Rev. J. M. Durgin.—*Morning Star.*

THE PERFECT MAN

Mark the perfect man, and behold the upright; for the end of that man is peace. Psalms 37:37

The storm has passed, the goodly tree has fallen, the precious fruit is gathered home; and we come to-day to meditate on the useful life of our Brother, and mourn for ourselves.

Long years ago, when I expected to live but a short time, I requested my Brother Hutchins to preach my funeral sermon; he assented and made the same request of me, and a few weeks since renewed that request. I little thought then this painful task would so soon become my duty; yet, our Father has called, and we should meekly submit.

There are some circumstances which make this funeral peculiarly impressive to many of us here.

We are informed by one of the oldest inhabitants of the town, that this is the only death of a minister which has occurred for over eighty years in the city or town of Dover.

Here are a number of our old and intimate brethren in the ministry, who come from the setting up of the monument at Randall's grave, yesterday, to the funeral of our much esteemed Brother Hutchins to-day. One the founder, and the other a most faithful laborer in our denomination.

Again, we are just on the eve of our eighteenth General Conference; and may we not consider this baptism of sorrow and tears is given to prepare us for the great work at that important gathering.

Brother Hutchins was a native of Maine. At his death, he was fifty-eight years of age. Converted quite young, he commenced preaching when about the age of eighteen, and has been in the ministry some forty years. He has served in all our important benevolent societies, with honor and fidelity; he has been a long time the Corresponding Secretary of our

Foreign Mission Society; he was at this post at his death. Within the last thirteen years, he has attended the funerals of eight hundred persons—more than could gain access to hear *his* funeral sermon.

But his life and history are known to most present, and will be written, we hope, for others who may wish to know, and follow the life of a good man, as a pattern of piety and usefulness.

Men are so constituted, they can only appreciate and describe things and characters as they have attained to a knowledge, or understanding of them; hence it is very difficult to describe the character mentioned in the text, because so imperfectly understood.

It is also more than probable, that every thing and every being, in and of this world, approximate nearer to their perfection than man. Absolute perfection is not to be found among men. Each, and all men, find some faults, flaws, failings, or sins, which should bring them to repentance and a confession of the need of the perfection of Christ's redemption to save them.

There is a *relative, comparative,* or *intentional* perfection in and for man; but not entire in this progressive state. The wisest and best of all ages have felt and realized this want in man, and cried out "unclean, unprofitable servants, not unto us, not unto us, but unto thee." And at the last day the perfected ones are represented to say, "When saw we thee, in need, sick, or in prison, &c., &c.—showing the same sense of man's lack in himself of perfection.

Indeed, a part of man's perfection, consists in understanding, confessing, and overcoming his imperfections through the atonement of Christ.

The text speaks of a comparative perfection, or the good man in contrast with the wicked man. See verses 35, 36. "I have seen the wicked in great power and spreading himself like a green baytree. Yet he passed away, and lo, he was not." There is nothing to the wicked man worth any one remembering. See Prov. 10:7, "The name of the wicked shall rot" "But the memory of the just is blessed." "Mark the perfect man, and behold the upright."

I. We shall notice this relative or comparative perfection in man.

1. The perfect man is like the sun. View him from what point or place you may, under what circumstances, or in what condition you will, in prosperity or adversity, in public or private, at home or abroad, in sickness or health, living or dead, he always shines. There is a lustre in him the wicked cannot attain to, or understand, and also that which good men and angels love to look and dwell upon. The light of the perfect man

is not the fitful glare of the falling meteor, blazing comets or the flashing flame; but the daily sunbeams, and moral electrical currents which thrill in atoms and flush in every ripening ear. It is the light of Jesus shining through the good man, and making this dark world better and brighter. I will mention an anecdote here which has been related to me since Brother Hutchins's death.

While but a boy, at work with the lumbermen of Maine, the workmen became inflamed with ardent spirits and bad passions; profanity, quarreling and fighting followed. In the midst of the altercation, the . . . boy came forward and fell on his knees among the strong men, and with his soft tones and childlike prayer, cried for mercy, on the hardened transgressors. The tumult ceased, order was restored, and a large number of those hardened men were converted and submitted to Christ and became worthy members of the church. Thus his work commenced. From that day, to the day of his death, what a glorious light has illuminated his whole course; he has lived, walked and shone in the light of divine truth— a whole life of light.

2. The *patience* and *forbearance* of the perfect man may be compared to the springs of living water ever gushing; the soft rains distilling; or the gentle dews of evening, that come not to rob, but to enrich all the land. "Niagara with all its thunder, brings no fertility; but the Nile, with noiseless fatness overflows; and from under the retiring flood Egypt looks up again, a garner of golden corn." "Patience is power." The world may be the better for moral cataracts, and its spiritual sons of thunder; but the influences which do the world's great work, which freshen and fertilize it, maturing its harvests for beauty and glory in heaven's garner, are not the proud and haughty spirits, but the patient and persevering sons and daughters of the church of Christ, toiling on in humility whole lives, without presuming to ask or demand a passing notice. What modest retirement! what self-mortifications, fasting, watching, and prayers! lest they should injure a fellow creature, or offend Divine Goodness. Self denying to a fault, temperate to the injury of physical health, struggling against adversity, laboring day and night with the smallest possible compensation, forbearing until forbearance ceases to be a virtue, and continually praying for the worst of enemies, *"Father, forgive them, they know not what they do."* Thus the perfect ones of earth "go forth weeping, bearing precious seed," over hill and dale, through all lands, with dewy richness watering all the garden of Christ, until flowers bloom, fruits mature, and a great harvest of ripened souls are gathered home to God.

What a greeting in heaven shall the perfect man have from those who have preceded him.

3. One thing more deserves especial notice in this wonderful character. It is benevolence. The first and great command is, *"Thou shalt love the Lord thy God with all thy soul."* The second is like unto it. *"Thou shalt love thy neighbor as thyself."* These two commands embrace the whole duty of man. They enter into the heart and soul, become the very life of the perfect man; yet the two emotions are very different. It is with adoring complacency that he loves God; desiring *His will* should be the mind of the intelligent universe, and His honor creation's glory. It is with affectionate good will that he loves his fellow creatures, desiring they should be happy in obeying God. One love is worship: the other is simply out-going. The one is filial devotion: the other is fraternal fondness.

When the buds form, if the soil is soft, and the sky genial, it is not long before they burst; for the richness and beauty within, haste spontaneously to appear in blooming brightness, and spread delicious fragrance on the air. *"And Christian charity is just piety,"* with its petals fully spread, developing itself, and making this a more lovely, because a better world.

The perfection which fancies that it loves God, and turns the poor empty away, is not piety, but a poor mildewed theology, a dogma, dead flowers with worms in them. Benevolence is blessedness. It is more blessed in giving, than receiving; it receives sparingly and thankfully, but gives freely and bountifully. Benevolence is God in the soul of the good man, who can only be happy in making others so. *"Mark the perfect man:"* the heart of the *"perfect man"* ever burning like the fire on sacred altars, or in the bush, yet not consumed. How vividly every suffering object of humanity is painted on such a mind; how he pants with every flying fugitive; how he would snap every fetter, and break every bond, and let the oppressed of every nation go free.

He would build churches, and support ministers and missionaries in every part of the world; his bank stock and real estate are in schools, hospitals, mission societies, and all the safes of charity. His will to his living and bereaved relatives, is one no litigation will ever disturb—it is God's will, to be done with all he leaves, and all the faithful are his executors; for while he lived he cultivated the highest and broadest benevolence so that it might be said, he not only had a covenant of his redeemed relation, but the beasts of the field, and the very stones were in league with him, as Wordsworth has it.

"In the silence of his face I read
His overflowing spirit. Birds and beasts,
And the mute fish that glances in the stream,
And harmless reptile coiling in the sun,
And gorgeous insect moving in the air,
The fowl, domestic, and the household dog,
In his sympathetic mind, he loved them ALL.
He was rich in love.
And sweet humanity, he was himself,
To that degree, he was beloved"—in heaven.

II. We come to contemplate the end, for "the end of that man is peace." This embraces three things, viz: 1. The object for which he labored. 2. The closing of life on earth. 3. The final resting place of the holy.

1. We notice the object for which the perfect man lives and labors. It is peace. It is not the false conception, that all are safe, and no danger of the loss of the soul. No, no. The good man knows the flash of burning lust; he hears the thunder of the human passions, and he sees the ashes, cinders and corruption, which flow out from the depraved human heart; he understands the ills and evils of society, in the individual, the family, town, city, or nation. He knows the pride, errors, and lukewarmness of selfish churches, and hypocritical membership. The blackness of darkness of sin, is all before the good man's mind. He knows the justice of God, and "the terrors of the Lord, therefore he persuades men to be reconciled to God," that they may have peace. It is not the peace of carnal security, sought in false doctrines, wealth, repose, the song and the dance, nor is it the peace of change, the pleasing journey, bracing air of mountain summits, or the spray from the ocean's rocking billows. These may strengthen exhausted physical frames, but never can wash out the stains of sin, cure the turbulence of ill humor, the cravings of covetousness or give rest and peace to a sin-cursed mind. Nor shall this peace be found in flattery and a compromise with sin, or in the use of the deadening stupor of intoxicating narcotics.

"Attempt how vain, with things of earthly sort, with aught but God,
With aught but moral excellence, truth and love.
To cleanse and satisfy the human soul."

It is that peace, that is like a river, the peace obtained by Godly sorrow, in true repentance, and forgiveness in the Lord Jesus Christ; a love to God, and man, in the great laws of justice and truth to all. This is the peace the good man seeks to establish; for this he labors at all times and places; this is his object and aim. Whatsoever things are true, honest, just, pure and lovely, of good report—those things he would have all the world do, that the peace of God which passeth all understanding, might fill the world as the waters cover the mighty deep.

This is the prayer, the teaching, dealing, conversation and life of the good man. No wonder David, the sweet singer of Israel, should exclaim, "Mark the perfect man, and behold the upright,"—the object, end, of that man is peace.

2. We come to the closing labors of such an one as mentioned in our text.

Life's work finished, toils, trials, pleasures, cares, are all closing in the sad evening of decline. Weakness, trembling, no appetite or relish for anything earthly! Gloomy foreboding and fearful apprehensions. In this condition Kings and Queens tremble; statesmen and mighty warriors shudder. All things human fail, here honors, princely crowns, gold, reputation, and friends, all, all that make human life agreeable, or dear to thousands and millions, cease here. Each one enters that state of untried realities empty and alone. Yet, "Mark the perfect man!" with what composure, courage, and even joy, he is enabled to pass away: for the "end of such a man is peace"—peace in himself, at peace with men, angels and God.

We will note for a moment, some of the last testimonials of those who have known the joys of Christ.

King David said, "Though I pass through the valley and shadow of death I will fear no evil."

Paul: "I am now ready to be offered, the time of my departure is at hand. I have fought a good fight, I have finished my course, I have kept the faith. Henceforth, there is laid up for me a crown of righteousness with the Lord, the righteous judge, shall give."

Simeon: "Now lettest thou, thy servant depart in peace."

The poet says:

"Jesus can make a dying bed
Feel soft as downy pillows are;
While on his breast I lean my head,
And breathe my life out sweetly there."

Father Wilson, who preached what was called the "golden lectures," so many years in London, one evening said to his daughter, "I have long dreaded dying in my sleep; I have nightly prayed it might not be so; but this night I have withdrawn that petition, and will leave this and all my matters in God's hands."

That night he slept in Jesus. "O, how sweet, from which no one wakes to weep."

Father Faber, one of the reformers, said, "I am now an hundred years old, nothing remains, but that I go back to God; for I perceive He calls me." Thereupon, the old man saying, "I want rest," bade the company a cheerful good night, and retired. The friends thought him sleeping, and so he was, to awake no more on earth.

The late Horace Mann, when told he was dying, brightened up and uttered precious words for two long hours as he was passing away. Time would fail us to mention the numerous testimonies of thousands, all going to show that the religion of Christ takes away all the tormenting fear of death.

And to the numerous host, we can truly add some of the excellent words of our much esteemed and long beloved Brother. "Now that the silver cord is loosed, the golden bowl broken," the patient and faithful one gone from labors to rewards; now shall his words, prayers and sermons fall with double weight on all our minds; for "being dead he yet sleepeth." O! how his deep toned prayers, and soothing sermons, sound around our family altars, and from all our pulpits where he has labored for a long number of years. Like the beloved disciple he leaned on the breast of Jesus, not only at supper time, but at all times; a man of prayer and of God. The labor and anxiety which filled his heart, and absorbed all his time and property while in health, was the burden of his thoughts, and prayers in his last sickness.

Some of his precious words were treasured. He said at one time, "It does seem to me it would be for the glory of God to raise me up. Could I live to see Brother Bacheler sent out to India, and Brother James Phillips in the field, and our ministers awake to their duty in the cause of missions, I could say, "Lord, now lettest thou, thy servant depart in peace."

And may I not ask, "Who shall occupy his important place, and take the burden of our Mission work?" O Lord cast a perfect lot!

Again, while meditating on the state of the churches, he said, "If it would please God to raise me up to labor and suffer more for his cause, I should rejoice; but, He is not dependent on men, or any of his creatures for means to carry forward his work."

As he approached the iron gate, he seemed conscious of all the waste and decay going on; he was exceedingly emaciated, and as his attention was attracted to the rapidity with which his flesh was passing away, his spirit triumphed, and he exclaimed, "My flesh and my heart faileth, but God is the strength of my heart, and my portion forever." Then raising his wasting arms, he said, "There is enough of this 'vile body,' for God to fashion a glorious body. It doth not yet appear what we shall be, but we know that when He shall appear, we shall be like Him." A little while after he said, "I want no other gospel, the truths which I have preached to others are a sure and unfailing support, as I am passing through the valley and shadow of death. All is bright beyond the grave, and blessed by God, I am not afraid to die."

As he was closing up his labors earthly on last Sabbath evening about 10 o'clock—how fit a time—when far out in the cold river, he pointed upward, and looking back and trying to comfort the weeping ones, to his beloved wife, daughter, and brother, he said—accompanied with the last grasp of the cold hand, and that look peculiar to the dying saint, when feelings are too deep, to sacred to be uttered, with their true force by any but dying lips steeped in the love of God, "I shall not live through this night; but there is a glorious day ahead. My home is above." Then as the cold spray was hiding him from earth, and just as the shining ones with glittering noiseless oars and white life-boat were lifting him aboard, he whispered, "TRUST—TRUST." These were the last words of the dying Hutchins. Let them always be remembered; for they are applicable in all our trying positions and moments. And may the mantle of that peaceful spirit fall on many a young man, who shall be raised up to fill the ranks of our fast thinning Zion.

We must now notice, for a few moments, what God says of the "perfect man." "Precious in the sight of the Lord, is the death of his saints." Again: "Blessed are the dead who die in the Lord, yea saith the spirit from henceforth, for they rest from their labors and their works do follow them." And again; "I will give to them a crown of life, I will be to them a God, and they shall be my people." And how much more our Father has promised. The new name—the tree and river of life—paths of victory—the Jasper city—harps of gold; and the great company of harpers, saints, and angels with garments of light. And then, there is the fullness of God, the Creator, Preserver, Redeemer, all-holy, all-glorious, the infinite EXCELLENCE. The river of pleasure, which makes glad the city, is just so much of His goodness as He is pleased to reward, but the fountain full and complete is in Jehovah himself; an ocean which Gabriel's line cannot fathom, and athwart which the Archangel's wing cannot traverse—an abyss of brightness to which immensity alone is the margin, and of which holy intelligences are but sparkling drops.

Then, there the "perfect man," rests. Behold, "the end of the upright,—it IS PEACE."

Time will allow but a word to those dear, deeply afflicted relatives and mourners. All are mourners to-day. To the beloved wife, daughter, and near relatives, words cannot express your loss; and sorrow bursting forth cannot express your loss; and sorrow bursting forth cannot relieve your burdened souls. Too deep, too heavy is your grief to be measured or weighed. Yet, you would not, you could not call him back to suffer again. O! no, no, never! But you will remember his words, "Trust, trust," and prepare to follow him.

To this large company of ministers, stricken and sorrowful as we are, what shall I, what can I say? We have lost a brother, some of us a father, and all of us, a most amiable and worthy example in all the Christian graces.

In all our great gatherings, meetings, and councils, how those soothing tones, mollifying words, excellent sentiments, and peaceful spirit, will be missed! When we meet hereafter, it will be said, "Brother Hutchins will come no more to mingle with us on earth." But words will not express our loss, a loss in the family, the church, the ministry, and the world. But our loss is his gain.

Permit me to say a word to the church and townsmen of Dover; for our Brother was not a sectarian, he loved all Christians, as is shown by his reply to the Congregational minister who called to see him just before he died, and when he said to him, "You are going, Brother, where there are no differences." "There are none between Christians and myself here," said Brother Hutchins. No, he loved all Christians in all Churches. And the closing of your places of business, the attendance of ministers of other denominations, and crowding numbers who could not obtain admittance, all show your high esteem for one of the best husbands, most worthy citizen, and devoted minister, who has fallen in your midst. The life and death of Rev. Elias Hutchins are identified with the history of his denomination, and your city. What a fact to record, that in a city or town with a population of thousands, and so many churches, there has not been the death of a minister in eighty or ninety years; over two generations have passed away since a watchman of Christ has fallen here.

In conclusion, let us pray that this death may be sanctified to the good of all, and we follow his most worthy example and die his peaceful death, and meet him in the glorious resurrection where there is no death, sorrow or mourning, forever and ever—Amen.

Appendix E

The Dover Enquirer
May 4, 1882

DESTRUCTIVE FIRE

The Washington Street Church Destroyed

Other Losses, Aggregating $30,000

The Burned Property But Lightly Insured

Tuesday morning at 7:40 o'clock, fire broke out in the brush factory operated by Alderman Lewis B. Laskey, situated on Washington street. The factory sat about fifty feet back from the street and was quite surrounded by frame buildings, ranging from one to two and a half stories in height, and in the rear of the Washington Street Freewill Baptist Church, of which the Rev. Mr. Chase is pastor. A breeze was at the time blowing with sufficient force to waft the flames in the direction of Fayette street, and in such close proximity to the church and the two-story dwelling in the rear, that in less time than it takes to write it both the latter structures had caught, and for a while the wholesale destruction of the surrounding buildings seemed imminent. The barn in the rear of the factory and church, and situated between the latter and the dwelling house occupied by Mrs. Chase on Fayette street, had caught and was rapidly burning.

At this same moment flames were discovered issuing from under the eaves of the church, and soon had spread to its roof, a large portion of which was almost instantly ablaze. The whole upper story of the structure, including the tower, was one unbroken sheet of flame. The fire in the church continued steadily to burn and increase in magnitude, the tower being completely enveloped in flames, which were now burning with increased fury, while above their roar and crackling was heard the crash and boom of the upper floor as it descended to the one beneath with a terrific report. The fuel thus added caused the flames to shoot high in the air, the tower began to show the effects of the suddenly increased heat and swayed perceptibly. The boards began dropping from its sides until the bare frame of the tower and steeple were all that could be seen, and this gradually weakened and finally tottered over into the flames which filled the interior of the church where it fell with a heavy crash.

The church which is partially destroyed, was built in 1870 at a cost of $23,000, the last installment on the church debt having been paid within the past fortnight. The building was insured for six thousand dollars, half of which was placed with the Royal, of which Geo. B. Prescott is agent, and the balance with the Fire Insurance Co. of Philadelphia, H. A. Redfield, agent. The insurance was apportioned as follows: church $5,000, organ $500, furniture and fixtures $500, but it is thought the total loss will be $12,000

The brush factory was owned by John B. Stevens, Sr., is valued at about $600, on which there was an insurance of $300. This building, with the stock and fixtures owned by Lewis B. Laskey, was totally destroyed. The stock was valued at $1500, insured for $800, in agency of Daniel H. Wendall. The cause of the fire remains a mystery. Various theories are afloat, but to none of them is given more than a passing notice, unless it be to that stereotyped one of "spontaneous combustion," which in many cases silences discussion. In this instance, however, it strikes us as very reasonable.

The fire broke out in the attic and was first discovered by one of the operatives at work on the first floor. Brushes which hung up about the room began to drop from their places, and this drew attention to the cause, which proved to be the fire upstairs, which by this time had gotten under good headway.

Mr. Laskey is at a loss to account for the fire, and is quite confident that no combustible material in any form had been communicated to the locality in which the fire was discovered. If this is so, and we do not doubt the gentleman's integrity, then the mystery deepens, and the greater the importance of having the matter thoroughly investigated, and, if possible, ascertaining the actual or probable cause.

While the fire was burning its brightest some of the burning brands sailed off in the direction of Second street and dropped on the top of Dr. Pike's stable and roof of the house occupied by Clark, the teamster.

At one time the residences of Mr. J. W. Welch, Mrs. John Stackpole, John W. Fogg, John C. Varney, John B. Stevens and Dr. Hill were in great danger of catching from the burning shingles and sparks which were flown from the church roof and steeple.

The Portsmouth Journal
May 6, 1882

Fire and Sad Accident at Dover

A fire broke out in L. B. Laskey's brush factory in Dover Tuesday morning and spread to the Washington Street Baptist Church, which was destroyed. Laskey's loss on stock $1550; Insurance $800. Loss on the church $25,000; Insured $6000. General Holt's barn was also burnt. Loss $300. Numerous houses in the vicinity were considerably damaged by fire and water. After the fire was extinguished, the ruins were visited by a large number of people. About 4 o'clock that afternoon while several persons were in and about the ruins a portion of the church floor fell, burying five persons beneath the ruins. Judge John R. Varney, who was among the number, was instantly killed by the falling timbers.

An alarm was at once given, and hundreds of citizens rushed to the aid of the sufferers. Four persons were taken from the debris in a badly mangled condition, but not dead. Their names were Mrs. Whitneys, Mrs. Steward Clifford, J. H. Burleigh and a lad named Peters. When found, they were with difficulty distinguished from the ruins beneath which they fell, and from which they were with great difficulty extricated. The accident was caused by the falling of one of the chimneys and the gable end of the church. These with their great weight and violence bore down the hanging portion of the second or church audience room floor to the chapel room on the ground floor, where the victims were at the time standing and gazing at the ruins made by the morning fire.

The lad who was found among the ruins was the means of furnishing a clue to the whereabouts and identity of Judge Varney, who had been missing from his home since noon time. Upon the lad's representation and his full description of Mr. Varney, Mayor Murphy ordered a strict search to be made by the police, who in about an hour came upon the body of the unfortunate man at the entrance of the small vestry. The body was lying upon its face, which was mangled beyond recognition, and was with great difficulty removed from between two timbers. The remains were at once taken to the City Hall and deposited in the court room, and his wife and two daughters, who were at home anxiously awaiting his return, were also notified of his terrible death. Their grief was heartrending in the extreme. Few men in the county were more widely known or more highly esteemed than the deceased. During life he had held many places of trust, and had won the confidence and esteem of the community in which he has always resided. He was 63 years old, and at the time of his death was Police Justice, Register of Probate for Strafford County and one of the editors and proprietors of the Dover Inquirer, a weekly, and the Daily Republican. He received his education at the public schools in Boston, fitted for college at Franklin Academy, and was graduated at Dartmouth in the class of '43, taught Franklin Academy two years, followed the profession of civil engineer ten years, was Clerk of the Court of Strafford County four years, was Professor of Mathematics in Dartmouth College three years, was admitted to the Bar in 1863 and became a partner of Hon. John P. Hale. He was postmaster of Dover for four years. In 1868, he became a partner in the newspaper named above. The sufferers who were taken from the ruins are still alive and faint hopes are entertained of their recovery.

The Dover Enquirer,
May 4, 1882

Terrible Accident!

The Walls of the Washington Street Church Fall In.

Instant Death of Hon. John R. Varney, one Of the Victims.

Several Other Persons Terribly Injured

The high wind of Tuesday afternoon blew over the gable end and both the chimneys of the Washington street church, which had been left standing after the serious fire of that morning, falling with such force as to crush down a part of the floor of the audience room.

There were several persons in the vestries looking at the ruins, some of whom were severely injured, and one of them, HON. JOHN R. VARNEY, senior editor of this paper, was instantly killed.

Among the severely injured were Mrs. Stuart Clifford, residing on Washington street, who had a leg broken, and was badly injured otherwise.

Mrs. Jed Whitney, who had a leg broken and also one arm, and was otherwise jammed, cut and bruised.

Job. H. Burleigh, blacksmith, on Locust street, who was badly jammed, but had no bones broken.

A Dominique lad, employed by G. W. Tash, was injured on the head and leg, but was able to walk away. The injured were with difficulty got out from under the debris, and removed to their homes, where the best of treatment was provided, and this morning seemed better, although some of them are not out of danger.

At first no one supposed Mr. Varney to be in the building at the time of the crash, and no efforts were made to find him. As he did not go home to tea at the usual hour, his daughter came down town to learn the cause. The door of his office was locked, but he could not be found. Upon this being known inquiries were raised, and it was soon learned that he had been seen in the church about the time of the crash. The Dominique lad was interviewed, and he described Mr. Varney so accurately, although not knowing his name, that search among the ruins was at once instituted, under the direction of Mayor Murphy. Many willing hands, some unused to such work, volunteered to help remove the blackened timbers and rubbish, and at 11 o'clock the body was found prostrated upon the face, with a large stick of timber lengthwise upon it, and above this several feet of rubbish. He was taken up and carried to the court room, and delivered to the care of John A. Glidden, who prepared the remains to be taken to his late residence, which was done this morning. Coroner Pray was called, but deemed an inquest unnecessary. From the position in which he was found, and other circumstances, it is evident he must have died instantly.

Appendix F

Foster's Daily Democrat, Feb. 13, 1896

BURNING OF MORTGAGE.

Washington Street Baptist Church Now Free From Debt.

Great Rejoicing By the Congregation at that Edifice Last Evening.

A Delightful Event Which Was a Complete Success From Beginning to End.

Great rejoicing!

Out of debt!

The mortgage burned!

Thus could be briefly told in the event at the Washington street church last night. But such a report will not suffice. Time was taken to wipe out that mortgage and get it into condition so that the event of last evening might be realized, and it is but due to all that we give it space in our columns today.

Rev. R. E. Gilkey when he came here found a debt of $3,000, and in less than four years he has, by the assistance of the congregation, a $1000 bequest from Robert Christie and $500 from Mrs. Abra Caverly, been able to pay up the mortgage and make the church free from debt.

It was then proposed to celebrate the event by burning the mortgage. A committee consisting of Rev. R. E. Gilkey, C. A. Rand, Orin Clark, F.

E. Meserve and C. E. Ames, were appointed to carry out the details, and last night's affair was the happy culmination of the event.

The church was thrown open early in the evening, and there was an informal reception in the vestry until 8 o'clock when the Rev. Mr. Gilkey and Rev. Mr. Chase were congratulated upon the result they had brought about. At 8 o'clock the auditorium was filled, and the exercises of the evening began.

There was an organ voluntary by Mrs. Florence V. Steeves.

Anthem, "O, come let us sing," by a choir of twelve voices.

Reading of the 103d Psalm and prayer by the pastor Rev. R. E. Gilkey.

Rev. Mr. Gilkey made a short address of welcome to those present, hoping that all strangers who might be present would rejoice with them on this occasion. He stated that invitations had been sent to all members and former pastors.

James Y. Demeritt then read letters from John W. Hutchins of Malden, Mass. and Rev. Geo. C. Waterman of St. Johnsbury, Vt., regretting that they were unable to be present. The letters congratulated the society upon the event of being able to burn up the mortgage.

HISTORICAL ADDRESS

Miss Vienna Hill then read an historical address as follows:

On Feb. 4, 1840, thirteen persons met and organized what is now known as the Washington street F. B. church. Meetings and Sunday school were held in a small room on central avenue. Rev. J. B. Davis was called to be its first pastor in the following November. During his pastorate 27 members were added to the church. As the congregation so increased, the meetings were held in the Belknap school house then on Church street, and afterwards in the Court house. One year later A. K. Moulton was settled as pastor. During his stay J. C. Dow was elected and ordained as a missionary to India.

Some years later as Rev. A. K. Moulton, who then resided at Cleveland, was returning from a Sunday school festival on a dark evening, he fell from a high bridge and death was the result.

At one of the business meetings it was voted to introduce a bass-viol at the morning service. In the years that had gone by, the people felt a great need of a religious paper, and at the suggestion of two men who consulted the quarterly meeting, nine men were found ready to assume the publication of a paper. They commenced with capital of $800. William Burr, one of the chief organizers of our church and its first deacon, was then a young man of 20 years, employed in the Traveler office at Boston, and he was engaged as printer for this paper. The type for the first issue was mostly set up with his own hands, and May 11, 1826, was issued the first number of the Morning Star. It was published at Limerick, Me. About seven years later it was removed to Dover.

In connection with this office for the Morning Star publication, the first house of worship was built and dedicated Sept. 21, 1843. Rev. R. Dunn became its pastor with a salary of $400. The membership numbered 150 and the church changed its name from Central street to Washington street. The vestry partly underground was finished and occupied for 20 years, and then abandoned as it was damp and unhealthful. In 1845 Elias Hutchins was called from the church at Newmarket, there receiving a salary of $400, to this church for one of $300. He remained as pastor of this church 13 years, and in that time attended 800 funerals. He performed the duties of a city missionary, visiting the sick and attending the funerals of a class that frequented no religious meetings, and for whose souls no man seemed to care. He remained a true, loyal friend to the church until his death.

Rev. C. E. Blake was called to fill the vacancy, who remained but one year, and was followed by W. Vary, who continued for five years. One bright, sunshiny Sabbath morning a good old Free Will Baptist deacon slowly, sedately walked down the aisle with his hat in his hand and his gloves on his head.

The Rockingham Quarterly Meeting met with this church for the first time in January, 1860. May 17, 1867, Rev. I. D. Stewart was installed as pastor. It had been the custom of holding two preaching services on the Sabbath, but on Aug. 30, '67 it was voted to dispense with [the] afternoon service, also to grant the Sunday school one Sabbath evening in each quarter for a concert. The house of worship had already been enlarged twice, and in 1868 sold its interests to the printing establishment, which needed larger accommodations. For two months worship was held with the First Congregational church, afterwards in the City Hall until the vestries were completed. During this time a large brick edifice was being erected on the corner of Washington and Fayette streets at a cost of $24,000. The church was completed and dedicated Oct. 28, 1869, the sermon being preached by the pastor Rev. I. D. Stewart. The society adopted the plan of systematic giving for missionary needs, the funds to be divided between home and foreign missions and for educational work.

It is often true that a mind becomes so absorbed in its plans and the carrying out of the same, that it does not grasp the immediate wants or even a pressing engagement. And it is a fact that a pastor of the

Washington Street church was so deep in thought that he forgot to attend to the matter of making two people one, until the summons came a second time, plus a hack. While another instance comes to mind that a free will pastor will travel over a thousand miles to perform a like ceremony.

The resignation of Rev. I. D. Stewart was accepted in September, 1873. The following year Rev. G. C. Waterman became its pastor.

A Young People's Union was formed at this time which brought the young people together for social, literary and benevolent purposes, and it proved to be of efficient service.

In the resolution of the accepted resignation of Rev. G. C. Waterman, it was acknowledged that the pastor's wife had lessened the church debt by $1000. The last Sabbath in October, 1879, Rev. F. K. Chase began his labors with the church, and was installed soon after.

April 3d, 1882 the hearts of the people were made glad with the announcement that the debt was all paid and the church free.

On Tuesday the 2d of May, the church caught fire from a brush factory, an adjoining building. The flames leaped from rafter to rafter, threw their cruel arms far into the air, defiantly laughed at the helpless firemen, and swallowed up the efforts of love, answered prayers and rewards of faithful labors, all out of sight. In less than one hour the church was a mass of smoldering ruins. In the afternoon a terrific wind sprang up and blew the northern gable and part of the standing wall over upon the audience floor, crushing it like an egg shell, and burying beneath it five human beings. For a moment no one stirred to their rescue until our brave true-hearted janitor cried, "For God's sake come and help me get them out." With willing hearts and hands they tore away the debris, saving four lives from a terrible death. The fifth was not missed until late at night when a midnight search was made and he was found crushed and lifeless beneath the ruins of mortar, brick and broken timbers.

It seemed that the very heart and life of its then present pastor had gone with the house of worship but the following incident, some days later, will show that his thought was to be up and doing:

"Mary, where do you suppose I saw our pastor today?"

"I don't know, where did you?"

"Down in the ruins cleaning mortar from off the bricks."

I said to him, "Pastor, that is no place for you."

Said he "I don't know, some one must do it, and I might as well help."

Very soon after the loss the heart of the pastor was greatly encouraged by receiving a silver dollar, all that a child of 12 years possessed, enclosed in an encouraging letter, looking towards the building of a new church home.

Sympathy was kindly offered on every hand, nearly every church in the city was placed at their disposal for church services. As the Belknap Church was then without a pastor and not holding any services it was thought best to worship there.

It was voted to rebuild the church and architect Chas. E. Joy presented a plan which was accepted. Beede and Shaw contracted to build and pushed the work forward with dispatch and on Dec. 24 services were held in the large vestry. the audience room in which we are gathered this evening was opened to the public and dedicated March 21, 1883.

The church was steadily growing, gaining a firmer foothold, untiring in its efforts to lift the burden so suddenly thrust upon them. Harmony and good will existed between pastor and people. On a certain Sabbath morning, while the choir was pleased and amused to witness the appearance of our pastor clad in a brand new coat from the market place, still bearing the vendor's souvenir in the form of a sale tag, we were forcibly impressed that he more earnestly desired to be clad in robes of righteousness and to so teach his flock, than to spend the morning hour in admiring his new worsted garment.

In 1890 the younger members of the church organized a society of Advocates of Christian Fidelity; four years later it was changed to an A. F. C. E. It has been a strong band and proved an efficient helper of the church. It now has a membership of 92 and is steadily pushing forward, endeavoring to be meet for the Master's use and a help to the world. In connection with this there is a junior C. E. society.

A cloud arose on the horizon of our church Feb. 21, 1892, in the form of a resignation of one who had been our leader for 13 years. It was accepted with a "not our will but Thine be done" and his labors closed with this church the last Sunday in March.

Please to note that an ex-pastor, who now resides at the capital of the old Granite State, has such an extensive territory to traverse and whose work is so varied in all lines of Christian calling, that he has employed the help of "an assistant pastor, Molly," by the way, former citizen of Dover. Our present pastor, Rev. R. E. Gilkey began his pastorate with us May 10, 1892, and installed June 2nd.

The 53rd anniversary of the church organization was held Feb. 3, 1893. Nearly 100 responded to the calling of roll, letters were received from many out of the city. Three of the charter members were present at the time.

Since then one has passed from earthly cares to her heavenly home. We are grateful that the lives of the remaining two are spared to cheer us with their presence on this evening of our jubilee, Mr. E. B. Chamberlain and Mr. Asa Littlefield.

The Hills Home and Missionary Society was formed in January of 1895, independent of the Ladies Mission Society. Occasionally our hearts have been made to rejoice when the hearts of men have been prompted to lend for the service of the Lord of their substance.

A short time since one of our friends remembered the needs of our Woman's Mission Society to the extent of donating the proceeds of the snug sum of $40,000 for the education of the colored people; also $1000 to this church, the interest of which is to be used in assisting the poor of the church. While dead he yet speaketh and his work goes on.

Mrs. Abra Caverly kindly gave the society $300 as a memorial of her first love, having been a member of the church in early life. She has recently gone to her reward and her flight removed a cloud from over our church edifice, "Blessed be the memory of those who die in the Lord."

Ten pastors have presided over the interests of the church during its existence of 56 years. Of this number four are left to break the "bread of life" and point out the way to an eternal home, Revs. R. Dunn, G. C. Waterman, F. K. Church [Chase] and R. E. Gilkey.

Our church has a membership of 135, and the S. S. numbers 278.

One other important item we would not omit from our church history is that of the festival which occurs on the 25th of December of each year. It has been and is the custom for pastor, people and children to gather at an early hour for a social informal round of healthful merriment. After which the hearts of all are made glad by exchanging gifts.

Once in a while even the church leader will receive from the Christmas tree what he absolutely refuses previously, though it be a black and white rat he will cherish and tenderly care for it and think it "very lambrequin." We refer you to higher church authority for the definition.

At 12 m. Dec. 31, 1895, the seats of the Washington street church issued an "emancipation proclamation" and extend a cordial welcome to one and all, who are without a spiritual home, to our Father's House and worship the Lord, and feel that they are at home.

Well may our hearts feel glad and jubilant when we, good old Freewill Baptists think that on Jan. 20, 1896, a new life began. Now we worship [with] free seats, in a free church, on free soil, free from debt, with none to molest or make afraid.

Singing, "Through the Lane of God, Our Savior" by a male quartette.

An original poem by Mrs. V. G. Ramsey, was read by Miss Hattie Roberts which showed the feeling of thanks giving that the debt had been paid.

REMINISCENCES.

A paper entitled "Reminiscences" written by Mrs. M. M. H. Hills was read by Miss Ethel Brown which was a very fine thing, and we are sorry that space does not allow us to publish it. It covered some points that is given in the above history, but was in the main about the people who had been connected with the church in the past.

Duet, "Rose of Sharon", by Miss Florence V. Steeves and Miss Carrie Simes.

Address by Rev. Frank K. Chase of Concord, who was for thirteen years pastor of this church. It was the intention of the reporter to have taken part of this address but he was called out to go to Rollinsford to the fire and only got back as it closed. Those who heard it refer to it as a masterly piece of work. He was glad the church was out of debt and congratulated them over and over again. He closed with prayer.

Singing, "Come Said Jesus, Sacred Voice", by a quartette.

BURNING THE MORTGAGE

At this point Mrs. Florence V. Steeves stepped forward and laying the mortgage upon a large waiter said:

Mortgage, Oh Mortgage, we have nothing but bonds of kindness and love for you tonight. What a blessing you have been these many years. You are an instrument of high repute and have been of great value to us. On your authority, at your command money has come to us to make it possible to complete this beautiful edifice which we can now call our own church, our Sunday home. How bravely you have stood the test of time never for a moment faltering, never flinching, but ever and always you have stood at your post.

But mortgage, our kind Father has given us the money to pay the indebtedness for which you have so long stood, in short we have no further use of your service. We appreciate the mission you have filled, and lest you should fall into the hands of someone who would deal harshly with you to me has been committed the task of consigning you to the flames. Your ashes will be carefully preserved and let us hope that unborn generations will rise and call you blessed.

As the paper burned to ashes the congregation sang "Bless[ed] be the tie that binds."

After which Rev. F. K. Chase pronounced the benediction and all went away delighted that the church was free from debt.

Dover Daily Republican, Feb. 13, 1896

BURNED THE MORTGAGE.

THE WASHINGTON STREET SOCIETY IS FREE FROM DEBT.

THIS POINT IN ITS HISTORY APPROPRIATELY MARKED.

[NOTE: The Republican ran an abbreviated version of the historical sketch printed in the foregoing item, but ran more complete reports of the reminiscences and Pastor Chase's sermon, which are excerpted below.]

. . .

Some reminiscences of the Washington street church during the pastorate of Rev. E. Hutchins contributed by Mrs. M. M. H. Hills were then read by Miss Ethel Brown from which we make a few extracts.

When I came to live in Dover near the close of the year 1846 the Washington street church had its home in a very humble building set on the summit of the Free Baptist Printing Establishment now owned by the Odd Fellows. Entrance was gained by a long flight of outside stairs. The audience room was severely plain but neat. At a little later date the wall directly back of the pulpit was adorned by a beautiful fresco painting of a large open Bible and a dove hovering over it. I do not know as a judge of paintings would have called this a picture of much merit but I can say as Mrs. Stowe said of the European galleries "If I am not a judge of paintings, I know what gives me pleasure." So to me this wall painting with its beautiful suggestions, as for years I faced it on the successive Sabbaths, was a source of delight. A small vestry underneath the Printing Establishment furnished the place for prayer meetings. The outlay for this addition, $300, was given by brother Jacob Ford, and the seats were furnished by brother Wm. Burr. At the time referred to Rev. Elias Hutchins, rich in faith and poor in this world's goods, worth according to his highest estimate only $500, was then in the second year of his pastorate. For several years he had been pastor of the Free Baptist Newmarket church on a salary of $400 a year. Though rich in the confidence and love of his people and against their most earnest protestations, his sympathy and interest for this struggling church had led him to accept its call with a pledged salary of $300. A little later this was raised to $350. In 1851 the salary was $400 and his last four years of service the salary was $500. He was content with its meagerness if he could only develop in the minds of members the spirit and practice of Christian liberal giving. At this time Mr. Hutchins was editing gratuitously a small missionary paper entitled "The Gospel Rill" and was also serving gratuitously the Foreign Missionary society as its Corresponding Secretary. About the fourth year of his Dover pastorate he gladly welcomed as his guest, Rev. Dr. Jabez Barnes of London, Eng., a prominent leader in the missionary work of the England General Baptists whose mission field in India joined the Free Baptist field. His soul was aflame with zeal and plans for sending heralds of the gospel to these fields. He considered weekly pledges the best means of securing funds for this purpose. Personal solicitation was begun and very few refusals were met with. One year the sum total pledged and paid amounted to $235 and for several years the Dover Washington street church was the banner Free Baptist Mission church of New Hampshire. The church did also a great deal towards preparing the outfits of seven of the first missionaries who were sent to our own India field. In those days the preparation of a missionary's outfit for a voyage of from four to six months in a sailing vessel around the Cape of Good Hope to Calcutta, together with the needed supplies that could not there be obtained except at very exorbitant prices was no trifling matter. Now the opening of the Suez Canal and the swift steam ships have changed all this. The Sabbath school was a faithful auxiliary in the work.

Hon. Wm. Burr, founder of the church, was a tower of strength from the time of its organization to the day of this death, and his memory is blessed. So wise was he in counsel and prudent in action that his sudden removal seemed too great a calamity to be borne.

The church early enlisted in the temperance war and was among the first to substitute unfermented wine in the place of alcoholic wine at communion service. Only a few that were then members are now living and we are old and well stricken in years. May the Lord help us, with the new generation, to stand as firmly for the right and truth or even more so, than did those who have passed away.

. . .

Rev. F. K. Chase of Concord, formerly pastor of the church in substance spoke as follows:

Rev. F. K. Chase was introduced by Mr. Gilkey in a very appropriate manner for one who is an ex-pastor. Mr. Chase commenced his address by humorous suggestions, hinting that he could talk all night if necessary. He said he was glad to be present on this occasion though they could, no doubt, have had their celebration just as well without him. He had been intensely interested in the addresses which had been made, and what seemed to cover about all the ground.

He then told the story of his experience at the burning of the church, May 2d, 1882, and the rebuilding of it. They had but just got out of debt when the new debt and burden was imposed on them. He described, in graphic language, the scene at the burning of the church how the flames crept along the eaves and up the tall spire, higher and higher, to the very pinnacle; then the beautiful structure, weakened at the base, wavered and fell northward and with one tremendous crash broke down the burning roof below. He said he was never more grief stricken and thoroughly discouraged than on that day. When all was over he went home and wept in almost despair.

Very soon, however, he received kind and encouraging messages from friends offering help. The first of these to cheer him was a letter from Florence VanTassel, then seven years old, who sent him a letter and a silver dollar, all the money she had in the world, and asked him to accept it as the beginning of a fund to rebuild the church. Mr. Chase read the letter and then called for the parish clerk to come forward and take it and deposit it with the records of the church to be forever kept as a memento of that sad day.

Mr. Chase then retold the story of the falling of the north wall and the death of Judge John R. Varney. He had started for home about 9 o'clock that night but on his way was so strongly impressed that he ought to go back and make further search that he turned about and went to the City Hall where he learned that Judge Varney had not returned to his home at his usual hour and that his family had become anxious about him; and a young man said he had seen the Judge walking about the building just before the wall fell. On the strength of this a large crew of men was set to work to dig over the ruins. Mr. Chase pictured the scene; John W. Place was the first to find the missing man. As Mr. Chase told these stories he was overcome with grief and could not refrain from tears, and many in the audience had moistened eyes.

Mr. Chase told the story of the rebuilding of the church. He helped build the first pier in the north end of the cellar for the new church and helped put in place the first beam on the foundations. He labored incessantly till all was completed, even to making the cushions for the pews with his own hands and putting them in place. He said he had often thought that if he should die suddenly he would ask for no greater privilege than that his body might be buried somewhere under the church, for which he had labored so much, and which he loves so dearly.

Mr. Chase explained how it happened that the debt was incurred which they had recently finished paying. They started out with the idea for the original pew owners to give up their rights in the pews in the burned church or subscribe a certain sum with the right to select pews in the new church. After the church had been rebuilt Judge Jeremiah Smith rendered a decision that this plan of procedure could not be pursued, without risk of an injunction from the court should any of the old pew owners object; so that plan had to be given up and the church had to assume the whole debt.

Mr. Chase congratulated them on the completion of the payments of debt, but he cautioned them not to think they can get along now without work, and hard work. He said the tendency is to think that there is not much to do now that the debt is paid. Such ought not to be the case. They have simply gained a vantage ground for doing greater and better work than they could when burdened with debt. He congratulated them on the fact that the church is not only free from debt, but also that the pews are free to all. It is a free church as well as a Free Baptist church; everyone has a right to go in and sit where they please without imposing or intruding on the rights of any one. Of course all who go there are expected to contribute according to their means for the support of the cause of the gospel, but no one is shut out because he can pay but little.

Mr. Chase said this society had always been a strong denominational church; they were Free Baptists all over, and through and through, but they had always treated other denominations generously and liberally without compromising any of their principles of religions belief. He hoped they would always continue thus, firm and steadfast in the Free Baptist belief, with malice towards none.

. . .

Appendix G

SERMON:

DELIVERED IN THE

BELKNAP CHURCH,

SUNDAY MORNING, MAY 7, 1882,

BY

REV. F. K. CHASE,

PASTOR OF THE WASHINGTON STREET CHURCH

TEXT I KINGS, 19.

A Student of Biblical characters cannot fail to perceive how much of real human nature they all possessed. It is a strange, but perfectly apparent fact, that even the strongest natures sometimes contradict themselves. Again and again we find men doing the very last things we should have expected them to do. We find them failing us in the very points where we expected them to be the strongest. Just so with many of those of whom we learn in the Bible. John, the tender, loving man who leaned upon the bosom of our Lord, was one of those who wished his Master to burn the Samaritan village with a whirlwind of flames. Peter, the strong, impetuous defender of Jesus, when challenged by a little maid, denied with oaths that he ever knew such a man. So with Elijah, a man by whose faith the heavens were shut up and opened again, a man who had faced Ahab and all his idolatrous hosts with the most burning words of condemnation, who had caused the slaughter of a great number of the priests of Baal. The same man when threatened by an angry woman fled like a frightened boy, and throwing himself under a bush asked for himself that he might die.

But as he lay and slept, the angels came and fed him. And then taking up his journey once more, he went away to the mountain where the Jewish laws had been given amid the thunderings and the tempests. He entered a cave of the mountain and, feeling himself secure from the power of his enemies, he lodged there. But the great Jehovah spoke to him, "What doest thou here, Elijah?" And he said, "Go forth, and stand upon the mount before the Lord. And behold, the Lord passed by, and a great and strong wind rent the mountains, and brake in pieces the rocks before the Lord; but the Lord was not in the wind: and after the wind an earthquake; but the Lord was not in the earthquake: and after the earthquake a fire; but the Lord was not in the fire: and after the fire a still, small voice." And Elijah rose up and girded himself like a man and went forth again strong and brave because God had spoken to him.

I think there never was a time we could so fully sympathize with the great prophet in his very remarkable experience, as at the present. Such a week I never saw. I never wish to see another such.

The hard work and successes of the past two years are too well known to you all to need that I should dwell at length upon the subject; with what thankful hearts we have thought of these things, during the past two weeks, you also know. Again and again as I have passed our beautiful church home in the evening, I have stood and looked upward to the tall spire lifting its summit gracefully toward the shining stars, and my own heart has been thrilled with tender emotions, and tears of thankfulness have come all unbidden to my eyes. We had assured ourselves that now, after a long struggle, we had reached a place where, unhindered by any financial embarrassments, we could engage more earnestly in that work which lies so near all our hearts,— the gathering in and saving of those about us, and we were glad. There was a song of joy and thanksgiving in our hearts and upon our lips. How little we knew what was before us. The last Sunday we spoke of the cross each one of us should bear after the Master, but we knew nothing of the heavy cross which would soon rest upon us all. In our Sunday-school, we studied of the spiritual worship which God requires, but we did not dream that never again under that sacred roof should we study together.

In the evening we sang and prayed together, and spoke of our Savior's tender care for his disciples in times of trouble. How little we thought of the dark clouds even then gathering all unseen about us. Monday came and went, bright and beautiful. Tuesday morning dawned and still our beautiful spire pointed heavenward.

Then, while we were busy about our work, an alarm was heard, and soon from lip to lip the intelligence flew through the whole city, that our church was threatened with ruin. We rushed to the rescue. We fought with the utmost desperation, but we were doomed to utter defeat. I am not here to-day, nor have I any desire, to speak unkindly of any one, but we know and this whole city knows that our beautiful church *might* have been saved, *ought* to have been saved from such dreadful ruin. I will say no more than this; but with all our modern appliances, it seems to me a fearful thing that this whole city should be left at the mercy of the fire demon.

Who shall describe our feelings when we saw our church enwrapped in living flames? saw the cruel, remorseless fire running in mad glee over the roof and leaping up the graceful spire?

We saved all we could, and then we stood looking on with heavy hearts and tearful eyes. It was not so much the loss in dollars and cents that hurt us (although that loss was heavy enough, Heaven knows), but that dear old church was a sacred place. It represented prayer and toil and sacrifice. Within its walls you have gathered with those whose voices have long been silent in death; there together we have sat around the Communion table of our divine Master; there our hearts have been lifted up and stirred within us as we have listened to the gospel messages of God's servants; there together we have wrestled in prayer for human souls dear unto us and unto our Lord; there some of you, yes, many of you, first started in the Christian life and publicly consecrated yourselves to the Master's service. There Sunday after Sunday we gathered in our Sabbath-school, and learned like little children, all of us, the dear, sweet lessons of Jesus' life and teachings.

Before that altar, now broken and in ruins, loving hearts have come, while the organ pealed forth its joyful notes, and there they have been made husband and wife; to that altar, while the organ breathed forth its saddened tones, we have brought our dear dead, have spoken our last tender words of love, and there have sought for comfort from the Infinite One.

I said that church was a sacred place, and so it was; hallowed memories clustered thickly about it. It was dear to many hearts. Aged men and women, strong young men and women, the dear little children who have learned to love their home,—all of us were grieved beyond expression. But the flaming, raging fire passed on and left to us only a mass of smoking and blackened ruins.

And all day long, like a solemn funeral procession, people came and entered and looked, and went away, and we thought our cup was full. But only the fire passed. Even then dreadful blackening clouds of the tempest were rising upon us. In those vestries stood a little group talking in subdued tones of the sad ruin. Over the city the blackened clouds gathered. Out of the cloud the whirlwinds leaped; and before the tempests, that fated wall went down burying, crushing the massive floors like an eggshell. And the whole city held its breath as the fearful word passed here and there, that men and women were buried beneath those dreadful ruins. We rushed to the building. We heard the cries and groans of those human victims. We worked with eager hearts. From beneath the fragments we drew them forth. With tender hands we bore them, broken and bruised, to their homes. We did all we could to alleviate their sufferings, and then when the evening shades gathered thick about us we sat down in grief and silence.

Probably this city never saw such a day and night as that. But the end was not yet. When most of you were sleeping, it became known to a few of us that one of Dover's strongest men was missing. Our thoughts turned instinctively to the ruined church; and when it became certain that he had been seen to enter it, just a little before that awful crash, we knew only too well where we should find him.

And Oh, friends, that solemn midnight search for the dead! How shall I describe it? I pray God I may never be called to witness such another scene. A score of men, rich and poor, high and low, pure and sinful, with all distinctions forgotten, moved by one common feeling of humanity, searched, with hushed voices and pained hearts. And the old walls, which had been for a protection, now rose threateningly over our heads, and the pale moon sent its rays through all those dreadful crevices, lighting up the scene, making it weird-like. And the silent, pitying stars looked down upon us, and the winds blew in heavy gusts, filling all the place with its sad moaning. But still we worked on; and at length the word passed from one to another, "We have found him." And there he lay—In our room of prayer, on our night of prayer, on the very spot where some of us have bowed in prayer—there he lay, himself a man of prayer. And when at length we raised the great, noble form, still now in the silence of death, raised him and bore him forth, is it any wonder that strong men looked upon that pale, death-stricken face, and wept like children? It was a sight to melt a heart of stone; and as they bore him away, bore him to that darkened home, bore him to that stricken wife, and those orphaned daughters, our hearts offered up an earnest prayer that the Lord would comfort and sustain, and "put underneath his everlasting arms;" and the midnight bell rang out its solemn tones ere we sought a sleepless couch.

And thus the fire and the tempest have passed. They have left us blackened ruins; they have left us broken limbs and bruised bodies; they have left a vacant place in our city, and in one of the churches, that will not soon be filled. They have left in one home a vacant place that can never be filled; they have left sorrowing hearts that only the tender Father of all mercies can comfort. If there were nothing more for us to say, we might well sit down in sorrow and darkness.

But as the prophet stood on the mountain top, after the tempest and the fire and the earthquake had passed there was a still, small voice; and the voice said, "What doest thou here, Elijah?" Over us also the fire and the tempest have passed; but, if we will but listen, is there not speaking unto us a still, small voice; and unto us, feeling perhaps almost like hiding ourselves where none will see our grief, and where we may be free from the heavy burdens resting upon us, this voice is saying, "What doest thou here, O my people?"

Will you bear with me while I seek to interpret to you what this voice would say to us? And I remark,

1st. 'The voice declared to the prophet that he must go away from the wilderness back to the kingdom of the Jews. There was still a work for him to do. Not yet could he lay his armor down. So, it seems to me, the Lord is saying to us as a people. Of course under the pressure of such a terrible burden, falling upon us in an utterly unexpected manner, the first feeling was naturally one of discouragement. I presume that we may be pardoned if at times we have felt like hiding under some juniper tree, as Elijah did, when Jezebel threatened his life; but the still, small voice is speaking to us, has been speaking to us, and the Lord God of our fathers, our God, is bidding us to go forth, for there is still a work for us to do. Never before perhaps have we realized how great is that work, as, during the past few weeks, we have looked out and around us, and we have seen that hundreds of immortal souls are looking to us for religious instruction. Not even by this disaster will their numbers be diminished. I am inclined to think that, if we are wise, they may be largely increased. There are other hundreds that we may reach. Our efforts to draw in the young people and children must not slacken.

There is a work for us to do in the direction of repairing our beautiful church. It means toil; it means sacrifice on the part of all, but it can, it will, be done. I consider it a marvelous thing—but I have not met with one single man or woman who has expressed an accent of doubt in regard to that, and as I look into your faces, saddened, it is true, by the memories of the past, I read there only one sentiment; and that is that each and all of us are ready to work and sacrifice as we never have before, if need be, that once again we may have a church home of our own. And with the blessing of God not many months shall pass before that church shall rise remodeled, improved, a beautiful house for a glad-hearted and thankful people.

There is a work for us to do to illustrate to those about us a true Christian heroism.

The darkness of night brings out the shining stars; the dark storm brings forth from their hiding places the beautiful spring-tide flowers; the fire of the crucible tests the precious metals, and from it they come forth purified.

Just so with a true Christian heroism. It does not seek danger and trial, nor yet does it shrink from them when they are in the path of duty. The next few months will test our strength as a church, the strength of our Christian courage, as they were never tested before. By the grace of God, who is our strength, we shall not fail; and this Christian community shall see that our heroism is of that kind which bears the banner aloft even amid the thickest of the fight, a courage which knows no such word as "defeat."

Again; we have a work to do to still defend the great moral principles, and to still advocate great reforms. From that pulpit where I stood one week ago, which is to-day, alas, only a mass of crushed and broken ruins, on all these great questions, no uncertain sound has gone forth.

Your pastors have had the courage to speak our Christian truth, and you, my people, thoughtless of popularity, fearless of criticism thoughtful only of the truth of the living God, have stood by your pastors and sustained them in their position.

A man said to me one day, "We all know where the Washington St. church and their pastors stand in regard to any question of moral reform." I tell you, friends, it is an honorable, even if a dangerous, position to occupy. In the very front ranks of the advancing army, we stand, and we do not propose to give it up.

Nor fire, nor tempest shall drive us. Where the still small voice shall bid us go, there we shall be found. I remark,

2. It seems to me that this voice bids us to be encouraged and thankful for many things. Our circumstances might have been far worse. Had this come when we were carrying a debt the burden would have been far more heavy. Had our house been destroyed by any carelessness on our own part, we should not, as now, have had the sympathy of the whole city. All know that it was by no fault of our own that this loss has come, and I believe that very many are ready to take hold with us and help us to repair our loss. We have reason for thankfulness that such a spirit of union and love prevails among our people. It is by no mere figure of speech that we may say we are all brothers and sisters, and even the dear children are

anxious to do all they can. Again, we have reason for thankfulness that we have the advice and counsel and financial assistance of the noble men who have been your pastors. They will pardon me for the personal allusion, but I want to say before you all that I am profoundly grateful to God that these two brethren are with us now.

We have reason to be thankful that our services need not be seriously interrupted. These kind Christian people have thrown open their doors, and with full hearts bidden us to enter, and be welcome. And may the Lord bless them for their kindness. And so I might mention very many things for which we have great reason to be thankful. Think of them yourselves, dear friends, and do not fail to thank our Heavenly Father for all his mercies. But I remark,

3. This voice which is speaking to us bids us to learn from the sad events of the past week the entire uncertainty, the utter instability, of all things earthly.

Who can say what shall be on the morrow? We walk amid the shadows of coming events, but what they portend we cannot tell. Is it sorrow? Is it Joy? Is it light? Is it darkness? Is it life? Is it death? Only the Infinite knows. A veil is before our eyes. Only as the events of our future life shall come, can we know what they shall be. There is no oracle unto which we can seek. Who could have foreseen what has already come?

When we looked out on Tuesday morning and saw our church spire pointing heavenward, who could have thought that in one or two short hours it would fall in ruins? When our friends left their homes on Tuesday afternoon, who would have thought that so soon some of them would be brought back crushed and broken? When our judge left his office and passed with swinging step and strong up our streets, how little he thought what was before him! Well for us, my friends, that we cannot foresee. Surely,

"He kindly veils our eyes."

The future lies all unknown before us, like the vast, unbroken expanse of the ocean. We see the undulating, restless waves, we hear the voices of the sea; here and there we catch a gleam of a snowy sail, but where our path shall lie we cannot tell. Well for us if we have Him on board who has

"known in storms to sail."

Well for us if

"Above the raging of the gale,

We hear our Lord."

Well for us if day by day we have the assurance that by-and-by we shall cast anchor in the fair haven of rest.

Out of the ruins of our fallen church this voice speaks to us: "If riches increase set not your heart upon them." "Lay not up for yourselves treasures on earth, but lay them up in heaven." It bids us to seek for that "building of God, that house not made with hands, eternal and in the heavens." O happy we, if out of this shall come a deeper spirituality, if our souls swept by this sorrow, shall be more fully opened to the influences of the divine Spirit. O happy, if with chastened hearts we draw nearer unto him who has said, "Not by might nor by power but by my Spirit."

If there shall now be a more earnest seeking unto God, if now more earnest praying, if the dear precious souls for whom we have long prayed shall only be consecrated to the Master's service, we will even praise God that he has permitted this to fall upon us. My dear people, for whom I have worked and thought and prayed, dearer now than ever before, as we go forth to-day let us go with a calm, unswerving faith in the living God.—go with an unconquerable determination to do as this voice of God shall direct.

Like true Christian heroes let us stand by our work, and "God shall bless us and cause his face to shine upon us." Let us hold ourselves in readiness, men and women and little children, all of us, to do the work which our Master bids us to do. "Watch ye, stand fast in the faith, quit ye like men, be strong." "Underneath are the everlasting arms," and we will not fear.

"Keep me, my God! my boat so frail
Can scarce withstand the rising gale;
Thy ocean spreads so deep and wide,
So swiftly sweeps the surging tide,
Such perils 'neath its surface sleep,
I die, unless Thy hand shall keep!

"Keep me, My God! Thy ocean sweeps
My barque o'er vast unmeasured deeps;
Uphold! and guide by that strong hand
Which reared the mountains old and grand,
Secure from all the gales that rise,
To peaceful port 'neath stormless skies!"

Appendix H

Items appearing in Dover's anti-*Morning Star* Newspaper

Dover Gazette and Strafford Advertiser
July 5, 1836

The Legislature vs The Morning Star.—
The last Morning Star contains an article of about three columns in length of "words, words, words," *professedly* on the subject of the refusal of the Legislature to incorporate the trustees of the Freewill Baptist Printing Establishment and Book Concern, but, (with the exception of a few of the first paragraphs,) no more relating to that subject, or to any thing else connected therewith than is the first chapter of the first Book of Chronicles.

So very destitute is the whole article of argument or of ought else requiring a reply, that we should have passed it without notice had it not, after quoting from our paper of a few weeks since, unqualifiedly asserted that there is no "connection between *Abolitionism* and *Federalism*," and directly charged with falsehood all *political papers* which "promulgate that idea." Now we never thought, said, or intimated that *all abolitionists* were connected directly with the federal party, but we do believe that many of the abolition movements warrant the idea that there is a certain understanding between their "wire movers" and the federal leaders, equivalent in fact to a treaty of alliance offensive and defensive between the two parties. Of the understanding the writer for the Star (who by the way is its editor No. 5) is probably ignorant. He is one whose honesty of intention would prevent him from joining knowingly in any attempt to effect party politics by the "holier objects" he professes to have in view, but at the same time he is so enthusiastic and over heated in the pursuit of his *holier objects* as to be easily rendered a very pliable tool in the hands of an artful party leader.

That Abolitionism is used as a political engine in attempting to break down and destroy the party now conducting the affairs of the General Government needs no other proof than a bare reference to the movements and conduct of the opposition leaders in the two Houses of Congress whenever any question connected with the subject of Slavery has been there agitated.

"Wide as the poles asunder" as are their views upon the subject itself, yet upon every question in the House of Representatives having the least allusion to slavery, Adams of Mass., Everett of Vermont, and their adherents, have been invariably found voting with Wise of Virginia and all the slave holding leaders of South Carolina Nullification. If conduct such as this does not show a *coalition formed* between the Abolitionists and the different factions of the opposition it at least shows that these factions are more than ready to unite with abolitionists for the purpose of effecting their own *unholy objects*; and as the abolitionists have never yet seen fit to disavow their concurrence in such attempts at union, but have equally applauded the speeches of Adams and the votes of Wise we hope that the editor of the Star will not consider us treating him disrespectfully if we retort the charge of *falsehood* and "throw it him in his teeth."

Dover Gazette and Strafford Advertiser
April 24, 1838

Messrs. Editors:—I well recollect, that soon after the annual election last year, the Morning Star, a religious paper published in the town, the conductors of which claim to be strict temperance men, came out and accused the Van Buren party of putting men into office, who drank and vended Ardent Spirits, the truth of which I do not deny, and I supposed at the time, that they in making that statement, were doing what a sense of duty compelled them to do. They probably came to the conclusion, that the cause of temperance was retarded by such proceedings, and that the Philanthropists of the day, ought to speak in decided terms against a party that should be guilty of such intemperate conduct. My opinion at the time was, that they were sincere in their pretensions, and it would have remained unaltered, had I not witnessed the manner in which the federal party in this town conducted, in order to carry the election in favor of their candidates, by causing a certain Bar to be made free for their party, and others whose political opinions might be changed by partaking of the intoxicating contents: and that these same temperance loving conductors of the Star, have not uttered one word against it since. Where is all their boasted love of temperance? Why not come out in the same way they did last year, and expose the evils of intemperance, and hold up to public gaze such base conduct? Where is the Rev. Mr. Mack, who is an Editor of a temperance paper, that we do not hear from him upon the subject? He cannot be ignorant of the facts, for he with the rest of the Clergy who voted at the last election, made this once pretended *"Temperance House"* their place of resort during the day, and must have witnessed the great flow of "liquid poison," and the many cases of worse than beastly intoxication, in and about that House. "O consistency thou jewel."

N.

Dover Gazette and Strafford Advertiser
May 8, 1838

The Morning Star accuses us of manifesting a desire for the last two or three months to have a quarrel with it. We disclaim all such unchristian intentions. We have no wish to quarrel with any one if they will be consistent and mind their own business. It severely galls the feelings of this would-be-thought conservator of the public morals, because we have adverted to the subject of the federalists in the last election making use of Rum and electioneering Priests to aid their cause. The Star, or a dirty sheet, the spawn of the Star, began upon us a long time ago, by abusing and slandering us for opening our advertising columns to merchants; abused some of our townsmen who were guilty of being Democrats and town officers for keeping Rum to sell, and broadly hinted that the health, virtue, morals and prosperity of the town could not be secured until all the office holders and all the inhabitants ceased to use or deal in the article of Rum. His invectives and anathemas last spring and summer were long and loud upon this topic. All of this might have been very well, but where is now the voice of this astute man of the Star? What to us appears astonishing is that all his zeal in that good cause, all his fears in that respect about this town, since the March election, seems to have departed from him; not a word is said respecting the crime of office holders selling or giving away Rum. He seems to have put upon his eyes a pair of spectacles through which the signs of the times and the affairs of men appear very different now the several offices in town, *little and big,* are held by Federalists, and which to say the least, sell, give away and drink as much of the article as the Democratic officers of the town last year. Verily if we may judge by his silence upon the subject, he thinks he has brought about the great reform which so exclusively occupied his voice and pen, or his eyes are blinded by the God of this world. Truly his organs of vision must have been strangely perverted or he would have seen from his situation at the head quarters of the Priests of the "holy order" at the "in-Temperance House," the torrents of "liquid poison" that ran down the throats of his brother federal voters, on the day of election, or perceived the effluvia thereof, which must have been any thing but savory to his refined olfactory nerves, or they have become much less sensitive than they were last summer. Why did not he and his temperance brethren step out upon the balcony, ornamented with "Wilson and Reform" and with stentorian voice "hold forth" against the destroying monster? Where are now the columns of those papers issuing from the Star office, ere while so rife with federalism and temperance, now so chap-fallen and silent? Has his faith grown cold? or is the lash of the federal office holders suspended over his back? or has his compunctious feelings prompted him to return to his professed duty of disseminating the peaceful principles of the Gospel, and warning his fellow-men of the "wrath to come," and make up for time mis-spent upon baser and more ignoble objects and unconnected with his ostensible occupation as a "minister of Christ" and editor of a religious paper? These questions he can best answer himself, and to assist him in his illustrations we would cite him a story that comes to our recollection, in a book which he has probably read, respecting a certain Farmer and Lawyer about an unlucky bull.

Dover Gazette and Strafford Advertiser
May 15, 1838

In good time we believe the "Star" will be of the opinion that we are gifted in some measure with a spirit of prediction. Sometime ago we kindly advised it to stick to the business for which the order to which it belongs at first designed it—a *Gospel paper*. But this paper has in many instances made a wide departure from the "faith once delivered to the saints" and intermingled with Politics, Abolitionism, and the Lord knows what, until some of the most respectable members, Elders and others of their own persuasion, have become disgusted with the paper and the puerile course it has taken for the year past, and prepared a communication for its columns, disapprobatory of the course pursued by said paper, but which communication was refused by the Morning Star and ultimately was published by the Patriot; which publication we subjoin:

The following "Morning Star" a religious paper published at Dover, N.H. under the direction of the Freewill Baptist General Conference, is sent abroad in the world as containing the sentiments of the denomination, and where as we believe slavery a moral and political evil, and to be very much regretted that it should ever have been countenanced on Columbia's free soil yet we as a religious community can never consent to digress so far from the cause we have espoused, as to lend our influence to any society that we think has for its ultimate object the dissolution of the Union, or that will create dissension in the moral and religious community.

Therefore, we the undersigned, professing ourselves to be Freewill Baptists, beg leave through your columns to enter this our protest, on the following subjects which are propagated in your columns.

1st. We disapprove of the measures of the American Anti Slavery Society, which is propagated in the "Morning Star," and do not feel ourselves bound to sustain the vote passed in the Rockingham Quarterly Meeting in relation to said society, and also feel and believe the paper may be filled with matter more edifying and interesting to a religious community.

2nd. We disapprove of a religious paper descending so far below the object for which it was intended (agreeably to the prospectus) as to meddle with the political contentions of the day which has been done by the "Morning Star."

3d. We disapprove of the doings of the last General Conference in the encouragement and inducement to preach by note.

SAMUEL B. DYER,
JOHN KIMBALL,
DANIEL HAINES,
JOHN JAMES,
DANIEL LADD,
SAMUEL COLCORD,
JOHN H. HOIT,
EDMUND RAND,
JOHN DEARBORN,
EDMUND BATCHELDER,
NATH'L DEARBORN, JR.
April 14, 1838

Footnote Sources and Abbreviations

A Fast Sermon on Slavery. Delivered April 2, 1835, to the Congregational church and society in Dover, N.H., Root, the Enquirer Office, Dover, N.H.1835. (Dover Public Library.)

A Historical Sketch of the Methodist Episcopal Church in the City of Dover. (Dover Public Library.)

A History of the Baptists, Torbet, third edition, Judson Press, Valley Forge, Va., 14th printing, 1993. (Author's collection.)

Bennett: A Farmer Boy Becomes a Doctor of Medicine : Memoirs of Roland J. Bennett, Dover, N.H., Unpublished. (In private hands.)

Burr: *Fidelity and Usefulness: Life of William Burr*, Brewster, Freewill Baptist Printing Establishment, Dover, NH, 1871. (Author's collection.)

CABC: Central Avenue Baptist Church Record Book. (Dover Baptist Church archives.)

CRFB: *The Centennial Record of Freewill Baptists 1780-1880*, Freewill Baptist Printing Establishment, Dover, NH, 1881. (Dover Baptist Church archives.)

DBC: Dover Baptist Church Record Books. (Dover Baptist Church archives.)

DDR: *Dover Daily Republican.* (Microfilm, Dover Public Library.)

Discourse on the Freedom of the Will, Dunn, Freewill Baptist Printing Establishment, Dover, NH, 1850. (Author's collection).

Dover Baptist Church : History and Rededication, Dover, N.H., 1983. (Author's collection.)

FBC: *Free Baptist Cyclopædia, Historical and Biographical*, Burgess and Ward, Free Baptist Cyclopædia Co., Chicago, 1889. (Author's collection.)

FFBC: First Freewill Baptist Church Record Books. (New Hampshire Historical Society Library, Concord, NH.)

Foster's: *Foster's Daily Democrat.* (Microfilm, Dover Public Library).

Gazette: *Dover Gazette and Strafford Advertiser.* (Microfilm, Dover Public Library.)

Handbook of Denominations in the United States, 10th Edition, Mead, Abingdon Press, Nashville, Tenn., 1995. (In private hands.)

History of Baltimore City and County, Scharf, Philadelphia, L. H. Everts, 1887. (Page copies from Baltimore Public Library.)

William Lloyd Garrison: The story of his life as told by his children, Garrison, Century Co., New York, NY, 1885. (University of New Hampshire Dimond Library)
Littlefield: Church history manuscript notes left by Deacon Willis E. Littlefield, Unpublished. (Archives, Woodman Institute, Dover, N.H.)
Manual of Washington Street Freewill Baptist Church, 1885. (Dover Baptist Church archives.)
McArthur Public Library archives, Biddeford, Me.
Not all is Changed : A Life History of Hingham, Hart, Hingham Historical Commission, 1993. (Author's collection.)
Place: *Journals of Enoch Hayes Place,* Wentworth, New England Historic Genealogical Society and New Hampshire Society of Genealogists, Boston, 1998. (Author's collection.)
Star: The Morning Star.(Microfilm, Dover Public Library.)
Strafford Third Baptist Church Record Bk. 2. (Archives of the church.)
The Boston Herald. (Item clipped from paper).
The Genealogical Record, Journal of the Strafford County Genealogical Society, Dover, N.H. (Author's collection.)
The History, Articles of Faith and Government of the Franklin St. Baptist Church. (Dover Public Library)
The New Hampshire Churches, Comprising Histories of the Congregational and Presbyterian Churches in the State, with notices of other Denominations, Lawrence, Claremont Mfg. Co., Claremont, N.H., 1856. (Author's collection.)
WFBS: Washington Street Freewill Baptist Society Record Books. (Dover Baptist Church archives.)

Index

Joseph Bennett Davis   Albanus K. Moulton   Ransom Dunn

Charles E. Blake   Elias Hutchins   Willet Vary

Isaac D. Stewart   Granville C. Waterman   Frank K. Chase

Ransom E. Gilkey

Amos E. Wilson

Albert E. Kenyon

Arthur L. Snell

Lester C. Holmes

Buell W. Maxfield

William Burr

Enoch H. Place

Cyrus L. Jenness

First Washington Street church building, at left with 3 windows and peaked roof. Dedicated in 1843, the Freewill Baptist Printing Establishment was on the first floor, with second-floor church facilities accessible from the sidewalk. The only building shown here still in existence in 2008, is the four-story building to the right of the church, separated only by what then was Myrtle Street.

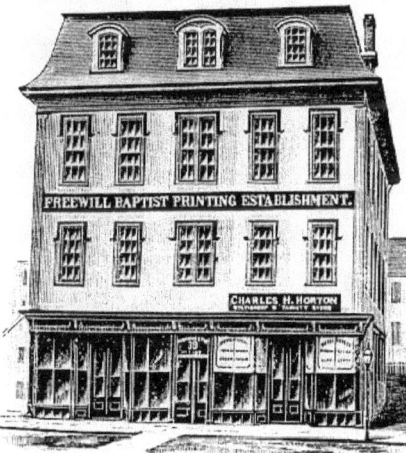

With sale of the church's interest in the original building, the printing establishment renovated the structure, added two floors (left in drawing), but kept the outside access to the top floors, shown by the central door opening onto the sidewalk. At right, photograph shows the enlarged building with the new church, built in 1868, two blocks west on Washington Street. The four-story building to the right, mentioned above, remains there in 2008.

The original church building at the corner of Washington and Fayette streets had a central spire, as shown here in a stereoptical view from Atkinson Street. A large central door 22 feet high, with large stained-glass windows to the side and above, were features of the front of the building. Note that the streets are unpaved. The octagonal shape of the spire was an unusual feature. Across the street, to the left here, was a four-story brick apartment and commercial building.

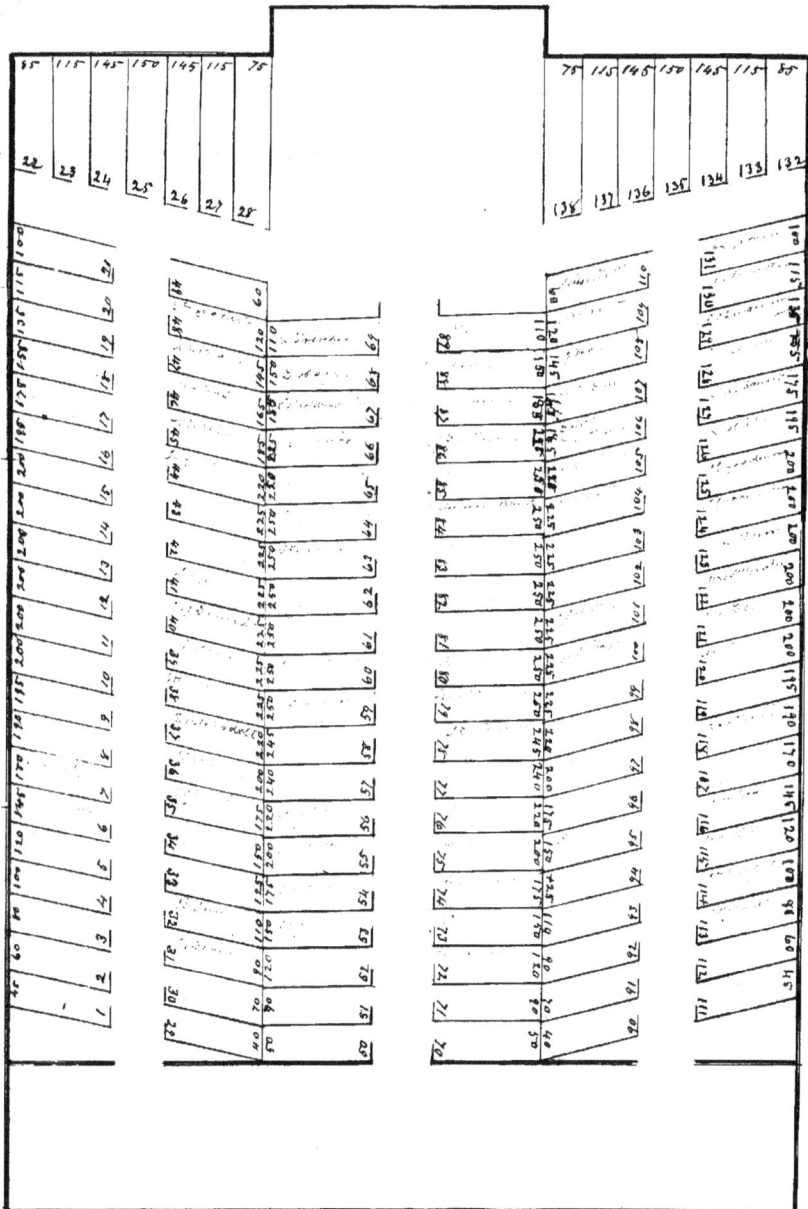

1869 - AUDIENCE ROOM

Map of the numbered pews in the auditorium of the original church at the present location. A second number on the pew is the price subscribers paid.

Washington Street Freewill Baptist Church, above, after the devastating fire of May 2, 1882. At right is a sketch of the re-built church, showing areas in which the original building design was retained on the outside (outlined here). Charred remnants from the fire still cling to the inside of the tower just above what was the curved top of the original second-floor window (above), which was bricked in (see photos opposite) to create the present tower design. Note the brickwork above the door retains the design above the original window before the fire, the door having replaced the window.

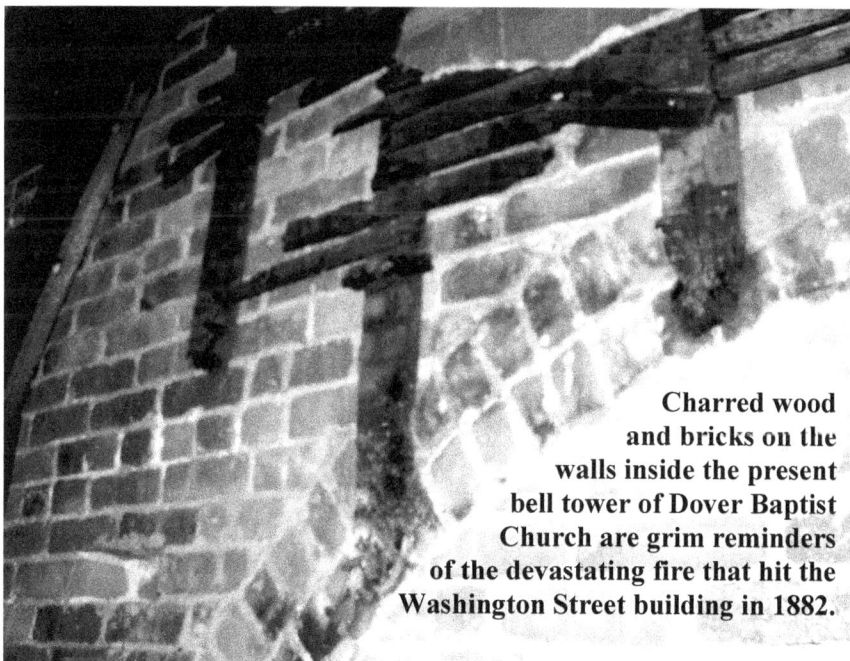

Charred wood
and bricks on the
walls inside the present
bell tower of Dover Baptist
Church are grim reminders
of the devastating fire that hit the
Washington Street building in 1882.

The rebuilt church has an auditorium much different from the original. A central section has high wooden gothic arches, each resting on columns seen here on the side of the main section. Between those columns are additional arches opening into lower sections of additional seating. The pews shown here still were in use at the end of the 20th century, but the only other original furniture or decoration remaining in the auditorium is the leaf and grape fresco along the edge of the high arch in front of the platform. After consolidating with the Central Avenue Baptists in 1918, the platform chairs and lectern, shown here, were donated to the Third Baptist Church of Strafford, N.H., where they still were in use in 2008.

Central Avenue Baptist Church, which in 1918 united with the Washington Street Freewill Baptist Church to become today's Dover Baptist Church.

Home built by William Burr on the corner of what now is Belknap and Washington streets in Dover, just a block from the present church building. This is where he died in 1866 after suffering a stroke during church services.

Bell in the tower at Dover Baptist Church

Bell
cast
in
1884

The bell, obtained from Biddeford, Maine, was cast in Baltimore, Md., in 1884 for the Pavilion Society of Biddeford, a Congregational Church organization. It was cast by J. Regester & Sons, owners of the Baltimore Bell Foundry, to be used in the Pavilion Congregational Church of Biddeford, now the McArthur Public Library. The size of the bell and the close quarters in the Dover church tower prohibit a picture of the entire bell.

Photos courtesy of Keith Tabor

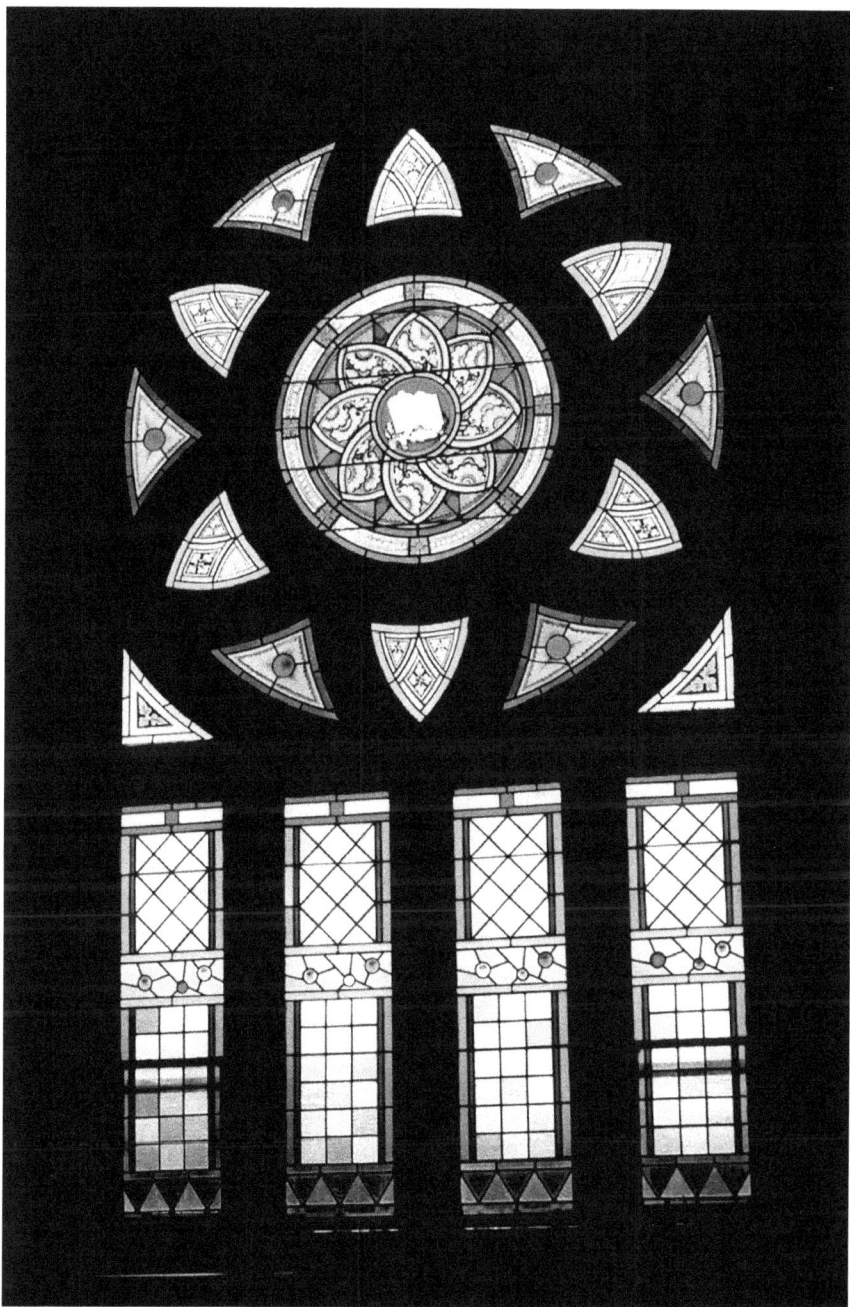

Large Stained-glass rose window facing Washington Street.

Trio of identical windows, west stairway. Similar windows are located in bell tower directly above windows in East stairway, shown below.

Trio of windows, east Stairway

Twelve stained-glass windows adorn the east side of the church, in six pairs as shown above. The west side has four pair. Below the rose window are four similar windows, at right, in what is now the church library.

Pine Hill Cemetery, Dover

Rev. Elias Hutchins, born June 5, 1801, Ordained Feb. 1, 1824, Cor. Sec. of the F. W. Baptist For. Miss. Soc. 19 years. Pastor of the Washington Street Church in this city, 13 years. Died Sept. 11, 1859, aged 58.

Devout and genial in his (unreadable), earnest and tender in his ministrations, intelligent and sincere in his philanthropy. He died in the faith and peace of a Christian rich in the love and honor of unnumbered hearts.

Stone commemorating Marilla Marks Hutchins Hills, widow of Rev. Elias Hutchins and long-time leader of the church's extensive missions program.

.

www.ingramcontent.com/pod-product-compliance
Lightning Source LLC
Chambersburg PA
CBHW060918040426

42445CB00011B/684